The Book of Job,
on Unconscious Responsibility

The Book of Job,
on Unconscious Responsibility

Job's Tale in Four Acts

JOSÉ ANTONIO ÁLVAREZ CAPEROCHIPI

RESOURCE *Publications* · Eugene, Oregon

THE BOOK OF JOB, ON UNCONSCIOUS RESPONSIBILITY
Job's Tale in Four Acts

Copyright © 2025 José Antonio Álvarez Caperochipi. All rights reserved. Except for brief quotations in critical publications or reviews, no part of this book may be reproduced in any manner without prior written permission from the publisher. Write: Permissions, Wipf and Stock Publishers, 199 W. 8th Ave., Suite 3, Eugene, OR 97401.

Resource Publications
An Imprint of Wipf and Stock Publishers
199 W. 8th Ave., Suite 3
Eugene, OR 97401

www.wipfandstock.com

PAPERBACK ISBN: 979-8-3852-6150-5
HARDCOVER ISBN: 979-8-3852-6151-2
EBOOK ISBN: 979-8-3852-6152-9

11/12/25

Unless otherwise stated, Scripture quotations are the author's translation.

Contents

Preface | ix

I. Introduction to the Book of Job | 1
    1.1 Job's Request for an Explanation | 1
    1.2. Dawn of Systematic Religious Thought | 4

II. The Storyteller Presents Job | 8
    2.1 Flawed Prosperity of Job | 8
    2.2 Job's Abuse of Prosperity | 10
    2.3 Job's Abuse of Divinity | 12

III. Job's Trial in Heaven | 14
    3.1 Portrait of Satan in Religious History | 14
    3.2 Illusory Court of Heaven | 18

IV. The Abuse of Prosperity | 23
    4.1 Divine Etiquette and Accusatory Questions | 23
    4.2 Satan's Reply, Job's Collective Guilt | 25

V. The Abuse of Serfdom | 28
    5.1 Incoherence of Submission to Divinity | 28
    5.2 Satan's Reply, the Defective Creation | 31

VI. The Punishment of Job | 34
    6.1 Supposed Institution of Satan | 34
    6.2 Job's Confession | 36

VII. Satan's Second Hearing | 40
    7.1 Hypostasis of Serfdom | 40
    7.2 Satan's Reply | 42
    7.3 Rejected Institutionalization of Submission | 45

VIII. The Foundation of a Separated Social Order | 48
    8.1 Awakening from a Dream | 48
    8.2 Role of Job's Wife in Job's Awakening | 50
    8.3 Job's Response to His Wife | 53

IX. The Dogmatic of Authority | 56
    9.1 Three Friends' Authority | 56
    9.2 Collective Sin as Justification of an Organization | 59
    9.3 Three Friends' Arrival at the Council of Heaven | 62
    9.4 Job's Affirmed Innocence as a Collective Accusation | 64

FIRST ACT. THE DEBATE WITH THE THREE FRIENDS

X. Job Curses His Day | 69
    10.1 Job Laments Divine Hedge | 69
    10.2 Historicity of Job's Laments | 71

XI. Job Confronts His Violent Past | 74
    11.1 Moral Dilemma of the Debate | 74
    11.2 Debate on Supposed Divine Inspiration | 76
    11.3 Divine Duty to Base Creation on Individual Justice | 78
    11.4 Divine Wisdom as Publicity of Individual Justice | 81

XII. Servitude Confronts Social Identity | 84
    12.1 Second Cycle: The Abuse of Authority | 84
    12.2 Supposed Social Identity of Evil | 86
    12.3 Third Cycle, Divine Identity of Collective Realm | 89

XIII. Job's Messianism | 93
    13.1 Job Reiterates Collective Damnation | 93
    13.2 Job Denies Responsibility for Collective Disorder | 96

SECOND ACT. COLLECTIVE GUILT

XIV. Dogmatic Traditions on Elihu | 101
    14.1 Debate on the origin of collective guilt | 101
    14.2 Duality of State and Religion | 104

XV. The Double Presentation of Elihu | 111
    15.1 Narrative Presents Elihu | 111
    15.2 Elihu Presents Himself | 113

XVI. The Supposed Inspiration at Night | 117
    16.1 Inspired Collective Guilt | 117
    16.2 Denial of Free Will | 119
    16.3 Defective Creation | 122

XVII. Providence's Dictatorship | 126
    17.1 Punishment of the Righteous | 126
    17.2 Anger of Vengeful Providence | 128

THIRD ACT. JOB'S MORAL RIDDLE

XVIII. The Apotheosis of Idealism | 133
    18.1 Dogmatic of Authority and Organization | 133
    18.2 Evil's Lack of Content | 138
    18.3 Revelation as Systematic Thought | 142

XIX. Revelation in the Storm | 148
    19.1 Deus ex Machina | 148
    19.2 Unconscious Guilt and Collective Responsibility | 152

XX. Allegories of Exile | 156
    20.1 Institution of Authority in the Desert | 156
    20.2 Institution of Social Order in an Animal Farm | 159

XXI. Job's Answer to the First Theophany | 163
    21.1 Job's Interpellation | 163
    21.2 Job's Responses to the First Theophany | 165

XXII. Second Theophany in the Storm | 168
    22.1 Personal Responsibility | 168
    22.2 Alternative to Inspiration | 170
    22.3 Interpretations of Behemoth and Leviathan | 172
    22.4 Animal Representation of the Second Theophany | 175
    22.5 Dogmatic of Collective Guilt | 179

XXIII. Job's Answer to the Second Theophany | 182
    23.1 Job Reiterates His Protests against Divine Justice | 182
    23.2 Job Eludes Personal Responsibility | 184

FOURTH ACT. GUILT AND RESPONSIBILITY

XXIV. Job's Righteousness | 189
    24.1 Final Reproach to Eliphaz | 189
    24.2 Debate on Job's Virtue | 192
    24.3 Double Praise of the Servant Job | 195
    24.4 Meaning of the Epilogue | 197

XXV. Establishing a Social Realm | 200
    25.1 Incoherent Prosperity of Job | 200
    25.2 Job's Social Development | 202
    25.3 Rationalization of Exile | 205

XXVI. Job's New Prosperity | 208
    26.1 Job's Blessing | 208
    26.2 Daughter's Name | 210
    26.3 Inheritance of the Daughters | 212

XXVII. Job's Death | 215
    27.1 Job's Life | 215
    27.2 Virtual Dimension of Job's Death | 217

    Bibliography | 221
    Subject Index | 225

Preface

I wrote my first essay on the book of Job in 2010 and have been fascinated by the subject ever since. In 2017, I published a draft about Job in Spanish.[1] Since then, I have developed and shared several drafts online.

    I aim to interpret the book of Job as a coherent theory of guilt and responsibility—one that develops the concept of unconscious and collective guilt as a form of personal guilt, and offers a critique of the doctrine of collective guilt as a foundation for social order. A language has a soul that cannot be translated without betraying its meaning. In this new version, I have attempted to rewrite the text from the ground up, thinking and writing directly in English. In this English text, I have set aside the doctrinal framework present in the original version.

---

1. Álvarez Caperochipi, *Libro de Job*.

I.

Introduction to the Book of Job

1.1 JOB'S REQUEST FOR AN EXPLANATION

a) Confrontation Between Divinity and Its Creation

In an allegorical and somewhat naïve style, the book of Job stages a (supposed) confrontation between divinity and its creation, seemingly corrupted by greed and pride. Persecuted by divinity, Job protests against his unjust suffering, rebels against the dogmatic institution of religion in the doctrine of collective guilt, and seeks, based on (personal) merit and guilt, a coherent foundation for social ethics.

Many religious cultures explore the dilemma of a man confronting a seemingly unjust divinity and affronting the inconsistencies of religious dogma. The book of Job is often interpreted as a critique of Persian Manichaeism following Alexander the Great's conquest of the Achaemenid Empire. However, I find it compelling to situate the book of Job within a broader framework as a justification of Jewish religion amid the symbolic funeral of the Greek deities, seeking to overcome the direct critique of wordiness that Socrates and Plato directed at Greek religion.

b) Historicity of the Characters

The trial of Job in heaven debates the history of religion, presented as a critique of Satan—the accuser of mankind—who embodies the multifaceted, intertwined forms of collective guilt. Satan represents humanity's confrontation with divinity and functions as a cornerstone of the coherence and critique of former religious thought in the book of Job.

The narrator presents Satan as misfortune (ויהי) in the context of a dual punishment: *It happened that day* (1:6). The book of Job does not concern itself with idol worship or its destruction, as in the Pentateuch or historical books, nor does it warn of the dangers of foreign women, as in the reconstruction of the Second Temple. Satan appears only in the prologue, as a mythical element within Job's historical messianic vision of religion. The book aims to challenge the justification of violence or submission based on supposed divine inspiration.

Satan's symbolic function enriches the allegorical development of Israel's religious history. Job's unjust suffering challenges the priestly and prophetic narratives of religion, both labeled as sacrificial dogmas. The dual character of Satan institutionalizes serfdom by exalting organization over free will, blaming individuals for collective disorder. Satan's accusations must be read as allegories and critiques of Israel's dogmatic past—whether through divine order imposed by violence (First Temple) or through submission (Second Temple).

Each character in the book of Job personifies an allegory of Israel's religious history, presenting Job's history (exile) as a reflection of his internal doctrine (dogma). The book, with a dreamlike tone, unfolds a series of responses to Job's demand for explanation. The three friends represent a sacrificial dogma that constructs authority (Behemoth), while Elihu embodies a dogma of submission aimed at legitimizing institutional order (Leviathan). Both tendencies envision a divinity who redeems humanity through collective accusation, employing unjust means—violence without (personal) guilt, deceit, or untimely delay—and failing to protect the innocent.

Job denounces a seemingly arbitrary divinity who creates a flawed world, institutes evil, induces temptation, or passively waits for the destruction of foreign kings and peoples—parts of his creation: *Are his days like the days of a mortal, or are his years like the days of a man, that he should seek out my iniquity and search for my sin?* (10:5–6).

The prologue casts Job as the embodiment of all characters in their historicity, leading toward a rationalization (of the folly) of sacrifice as an abuse of authority (in the dialogues with the friends) and awareness (of the absurdity) of submissive patience as abuse of institutional order (in Elihu's monologue).[1]

c) Personal Origin of Unconscious and Collective Guilt

The book of Job employs the structural framework of Greek drama, divided into four acts and a concluding epilogue. It uses a dialogical style popularized by Socrates and Plato. The friends serve as a chorus, and Elihu plays the role of coryphaeus. The voice in the storm corresponds to deus ex machina, a technique frequently used, for example, in Euripides.

The divine presence in the storm establishes a philosophy of history and law, as divinity transcends time and space. The two theophanies dismantle the notion of religion as the (supposed) direct divine inspiration of collective guilt. Divinity resolves Job's moral dilemma not through might or authority but through the coherence of argument. Evil is neither tolerated nor concealed by divinity and cannot be institutionalized. Evil exists only as an ideal testimony—the duty to unveil and repair—the defective earth (as damage or restitution) due to guilt or responsibility for (actual or former) conduct or omission that unjustly benefits the heirs and impoverishes the foreigner.

The theophanies resolve Job's moral conflict: the servant Job speaks rightly (42:7–8) because, by demanding an explanation, he challenges two successive disguises of false divinity and its incoherent ethics. The theophanies reveal the personal origin of unconscious and collective responsibility, refuting the (collective) rationalizations of guilt offered by the three friends and Elihu (the doctrine of an unjust divinity). The first theophany identifies two distinct forms of personal guilt—abuse of prosperity and the perversion of servitude—as the sources of unconscious and collective guilt. The second theophany affirms that only individual,

---

1. The book of Job has been variously attributed to Moses—as a paradigm of inspired or revealed religion—to priestly circles during the final period of the First Temple, to theological developments during the Babylonian exile, to the institutional reform of the Second Temple, to the crisis of Judaism following its second destruction, and even to a revolutionary movement opposing the priestly and prophetic traditions at the dawn of rabbinic Judaism. The Talmud debates both the historical period in which Job lived and whether he was of Jewish origin—a subject of endless discussion. The prophet Ezekiel refers to Job as one of three righteous men of antiquity, alongside Noah and Daniel, whose personal merit spared them from disaster (Ezek 14:14–20). While the early Tannaim regarded Job as Jewish, later rabbinic tradition discredited this view, instead portraying him as one of seven non-Israelite prophets sent to the nations—along with Balaam, Beor, Eliphaz, Bildad, Zophar, and Elihu.

not collective, merit and guilt can explain a creation that is compatible with divine justice.

The book of Job presents Job's doctrine of divinity as judgments of Job about himself. The violent Job invents a violent divinity (the three friends' violent sacrifice), and the dogmatic of patient suffering (Elihu's patient submission) reveals a false Job. The central moral problem of the book lies in defining the scope of Job's responsibility for social and collective disorder. Violence ultimately destroys the prosperity gained by violence; that which is conquered through submission will be ruined by its sterility. Sacrifice and submission deny divine justice and turn the land to ashes; violence and alienation produce a flawed social order cursed by its defective foundations.

1.2. DAWN OF SYSTEMATIC RELIGIOUS THOUGHT

a) Meaning of the Narrator

Despite his seemingly shocking arrogance, the prologue establishes the narrator as a faithful scribe—one who scrutinizes the souls of men and passes moral judgment on the characters. He affirms that Job was peaceful, upright, feared the Lord, and turned away from evil (1:1), and divinity appears to ratify the narrator's words almost verbatim, thereby approving the text as written by the narrator (1:8; 2:3).

The narrator introduces each character by name and title, signaling the moral roles they will play in the dialogue. These introductions define the ethical parameters of the debate, and the book of Job becomes intelligible through the narrator's explicit and implicit judgments. He identifies the three friends and directs their conversations with Job. Eliphaz of Teman, Bildad of Shuah, and Zophar of Naamah are lords of their respective lands (authoritarian figures) who reproach Job for his servitude. The narrator conspicuously omits any introduction of Elihu in the prologue, subtly emphasizing a character who lacks roots and the fictitious nature of his intervention. Satan, the main character of the prologue, does not reappear in the main text or the epilogue; Elihu, a nuclear character of the plot, does not appear in the prologue.

Without a doubt, the narrative identifies and presents divinity, weighing his anger and judgments. The deity presented lends coherence to a systematic explanation of Job's guilt. This portrayal rationalizes and organizes Job's religious experience, presenting divine authority and institutional order as the result of a systematic doctrine of guilt and responsibility—one that would later be fully developed in the canon of Scripture. The voice of divinity speaks amid turbulent winds, symbolizing Job's existential perplexity. The earth itself, as a witness to justice, temporarily resolves the dogmatic contradictions raised by Satan in the prologue.

But who is the narrator? The narrative guides the tale toward a veiled, critical reevaluation of the earlier Jewish religious doctrine rooted in sacrifice and submission. The book of Job seeks to expose and transcend the doctrine of sacrifice, grounded in collective guilt, as an incoherent ethical foundation of a historical religious worldview. Collective guilt accuses divinity of tolerating evil and using defective means to achieve redemption, denies personal merit and individual guilt, and presupposes a flawed and unjust creation that man must rectify by suffering.

The book of Job hides its revolutionary ideas in literary aesthetics. A direct critique of the doctrine of collective guilt would have been unacceptable at his time to the prevailing religious and secular authorities. As in Greek tragedy, a genuine artist, while respecting traditional forms, subtly subverts their underlying principles.[2]

---

2. The significance of the book of Job lies in its role at the dawn of authoritarian and systematic religious thought grounded in monotheism. It aims to critique sacrificial and submissive dogma as incompatible with monotheism, concealing its subversive conclusions in allegorical and seemingly paradoxical language. The book is often unfairly accused of lacking internal coherence—dismissed as a patchwork text compiled over centuries, with a disjointed prologue that appears unrelated to the central narrative. Critics often point to the contrast between the submissive Job of the prologue (1:21) and the defiant Job in his dialogues (e.g., 9:22), or the reconciled Job who responds to the theophanies. On the contrary, the book of Job is a meticulously crafted work (shaped by centuries of reflection on guilt and responsibility) with influence from and on religious, philosophical, and literary traditions. Its internal coherence, intertextual references to other scriptural texts, and original theological vision suggest that it seeks to renew Israel's religious doctrine. The precision and economy of its language are particularly striking: every word carries meaning; no word is redundant. The book's artistry lies in its rich use of suggestion, symbolism, ritual, and metaphor. Its allegorical framework and figurative language give shape to a ritualized narrative, vividly animating the dialogue and emotional tension. It expresses complex theological ideas through gestures, symbols, and poetic imagery—parody, exaggeration, irony, and references to nature and animals. It often highlights inconsistency through deliberate repetition, ironic descriptors, and contextual argumentation (spatial, temporal, and social). Like a Greek tragedy designed for oral performance, the prose of the prologue contrasts with the poetic structure of the main text, which enhances memorization, musicality, and dramatic impact. The poetry of the main text, based on rhythm, gives diegetic continuity to the tale.

b) Ritual Language and Procedural Order

It is striking that the speakers in the drama of the book of Job take the floor according to a rigorous ritual orchestrated by the narrator—one in which procedural and penal laws are scrupulously observed. The book's structure emphasizes that the foundations of social order are staged not only through the pursuit of justice but also through proper procedure and etiquette.

In the prologue, the narrator presents a divinity who incites Satan to accuse Job without asking permission: ויאמר. It contrasts sharply with later scenes: acquiescence is not required in the dialogue between Job and his wife, nor when the divinity addresses Eliphaz of Teman and his two comrades (42:7). Job and his three friends—in their intervention and reply in each of the three cycles of dialogues—begin their intervention with the expression ויען as a praiseworthy approval of the narrator.

Even divinity, when addressing Job in the theophanies, respects ritual formality, asking permission to take the floor (ויען), subordinating to a systematic debate and lawful procedure. This subtle linguistic cue underscores the book's broader critique: that divine legitimacy is not rooted in arbitrary power but in reasoned and orderly dialogue. The presentation of Elihu disrupts this formal symmetry. The narrator initially introduces him as the son of Barachel, from the family of Buz and the lineage of Ram (32:2), thus anchoring him in a genealogical tradition. However, in the introductions to his second (ch. 34, on authority) and third (ch. 35, on servitude) speeches, Elihu is referred to simply by name, with no mention of his origins. This erasure symbolically portrays his speech as uprooted and his authority as unanchored.

On some occasions, the narrator explicitly marks a speech as redundant or superfluous through the use of ויסף (and he added), which I have interpreted as an unnecessary speech. He accuses Job and Elihu of talkativeness. ויסף (and he added) is said of Job twice (27:1; 29:1). In the first instance, the narrator rebukes Job when he affirms that divinity does not guarantee justice in its time (Job incorrectly affirms it wiser to fear the Lord), and when he describes his ideal of a patriarchal society (third sacrificial order). And ויסף is also said of Elihu twice. His fourth and final speech (chs. 36–37) begins with ויסף, which is described as redundant wordiness, when Elihu accuses Job (36:1) and when he imagines a tyrannical Providence who teaches through pain.

c) Prologue as Compendium

It is fair to affirm that Job lives in a timeless tradition, in an uncertain and indeterminate place, without identifying whether he is Jewish or gentile, personifying the development of a coherent theory on guilt and responsibility. The supposed incoherence of the book of Job likely reflects a skeptical and critical debate on the meaning and coherence of Scripture, which the prologue aims to raise and address through an allegory. The prologue debates the supremacy of a person over authority (Satan's first audience) and individual responsibility over dogma as the origin of a social organization (Satan's second audience).

The challenge of the prologue lies in discerning its ethical and dogmatic implications without being seduced by its literary elegance. In Scripture, a fable, allegory, or symbol often precedes historical and doctrinal narrative, as the Lord announces from the beginning what is going to happen (Isa 46:10). The prologue of the book of Job is particularly relevant as it determines the dilemma of guilt, summarizes its personal and collective identity, debates the historicity of responsibility, and anticipates its conclusions.

Indeed, the prologue exhibits the same inspired poetic, ritual, and symbolic precision that permeates the entire text. The literary and dogmatic unity between the prologue and the main body—evident in shared orthographic archaisms and thematic coherence—argues strongly for an authorial and conceptual consistency of the poetry of the main text with the prose of the prologue.

The prologue must be interpreted as a dream that rationalizes Job's past. However, Job, *in all this* (despite instituting the dogmatic sacrifice), did not sin and *did not blame his fall* on the Lord (1:23); *in all this* (despite instituting the dogmatic of patient submission), Job did not deny the marital freedom of the servant and, therefore, *did not sin with his lips* (2:10). The prologue's conclusion affirms Job's righteousness and denies the doctrine of collective guilt to justify his punishment. It explains Job's servitude and exile as expressions of his (personal) responsibility.

II.

The Storyteller Presents Job

2.1 FLAWED PROSPERITY OF JOB

a) Job's Praise and Reproach

There was a man in the land of Uz. Job, his name (1:1). Job does not succumb to social disorder—he has a name. However, the narrative makes no mention of his origins (his family, lineage, or wife), suggesting that Job constructs an authoritarian social realm.

And the man lives (ויהי). This phrase implies both praise (he lives) and threat (the storm). The dual characterization—Job and the man—describes Job's (personal) merit within an unstable social order. The passive, impersonal formulation (*and the man*) highlights the artificial fragility of his estate: he tries to build a family and social order in the chaotic land of Uz by abusing wealth and instituting servitude.

The narrator both praises and reproaches Job—he applauds his monotheism while simultaneously criticizing his corrupted social identity.

b) Critical Irony of Job's Four Praises

The introduction proposes a systematic praise of Job, enumerating four qualities in him: honest (תם), upright (וישר), fearful of divinity (וירא אלהים), and fleeing from evil (וסר מרע). The divinity twice ratifies the praise (1:8; 2:3), almost literally, only removing a conjunction (and) between upright and fearful.

Flattery has an ambivalent meaning and conceals a limitation, as only divinity deserves praise (Pss 145:3; 148:13). Job is peaceful, yet he establishes servitude; he is upright for his time, nonetheless abuses prosperity; Job should love divinity, not fear punishment; he flees from evil, without fighting it. Simple, strict, fearful, and elusive; the flattery ponders his uprightness of intention but nevertheless describes a foolish, solitary man, dominated by messianic dreams, who seeks to conquer prosperity by sacrifice or submission to an imaginary divine power whom he pretends to represent.

It happened (ויהי) signals a reproach. There are four such reproaches (ויהי), which counterbalance the four praises: Job abuses prosperity and institutionalizes servitude, offers unjust sacrifices, and fails to take responsibility for public disorder. These critiques expose the arbitrariness of his authority, the sectarian nature of his sexuality, the inequitable distribution of wealth, and the idealistic underpinnings of his ethical order.

c) Job's Defective Farm in Uz

Seven sons and three daughters were born to him (1:2). The seven sons symbolize his merit, echoing the seven days of creation. Yet this also implies criticism—Job does not appear to value his wife, and the narrative omits his lineage. They were born *to him* in the past, which hints that they did not last long at Job's side and suffered ruin and exile (the double arrival of Satan).

The narrative distinguishes between sons and daughters. The seven sons parallel Job's seven thousand sheep, and the three daughters correspond to his three thousand camels. In the prologue—and throughout the book—animals symbolize social structures (or "divinities") rooted in violence, whether through sacrifice or submission. The animal imagery represents a flawed and dysfunctional social realm.

2.2 JOB'S ABUSE OF PROSPERITY

a) First Reproach

Job's first reproach refers to (the abuse of) his (disproportionate) wealth. The narrator describes him as a rich man, the greatest *among men*. Job meticulously counts the heads of his cattle by species (sheep, camels, oxen, and donkeys). He itemizes his livestock, sons, and daughters but notably omits to count his servants; he does not know their exact number, for they are innumerable. It hints that Job values wealth above the servants.

The animals symbolize deceptive and ephemeral prosperity—unconscious and collective disorder. The reference to specific animals (sheep, camels, oxen, and donkeys) symbolically reflects a stark gender separation. The reference to the infertile pairs—oxen and donkeys (five)—underscores a defective marriage, where sons and daughters lack full marital autonomy. Men work the land (sheep), while women overcome incestuous structures and receive a husband from a foreign land (camels).

This "animal farm" may also allude to Job's condition in exile, where the animals represent violent authorities, and the servants stand for foreign deities. The sheep may symbolize Job's labor, through which he overcomes the sin of unjustly exploiting the land (triumphing over the symbolic death of his brother). The camels may signify a free, consensual form of marriage (triumphing over the sacrifice of sexuality). Notably, the sheep and camels are not the first to be punished; instead, the oxen and donkeys are struck first—as an allegory of the sterility of his authoritarian and secluded prosperity.

b) Job's Unconscious Responsibility

And that man lived [ויהי האיש ההוא], and he was the most significant [גדול] among all men from the beginning [כל בני קדם]. After depicting Job's (disproportionate) wealth, the narrative hints at a reproach for instituting servitude to enjoy his wealth and authority.

The man, in the past tense (ויהי), is repeated a second time. Job establishes a masculine and patriarchal authority, and the repetition (Job and man) underlines a reproach and an irony. The man was *important among men* (not in the eyes of women or serfs) and *at the beginning* (only for the time being).

He lived, a verb in the past tense, pinpoints that his (unconscious) greed brought corruption to his lineage and authority, and his (collective) prosperity and servants evaporated without warning. The narrative points to human sacrifice as a root of both unconscious and collective guilt.

c) Second Reproach: The Banquets

And his sons went away (והלכו בניו). Where did they go? The abuse of wealth—the source of unconscious guilt—led to their exile. Each son departed from the land of Uz, searching for a domain to host a banquet—each in his house, on his appointed day. These banquets can be interpreted as pagan rituals, misusing religion to justify abusive wealth and social dominance, a reflection on the origin of collective guilt. The banquet symbolizes the conquest of prosperity through violent sacrifice (robbery) or patient submission (theft), much like the feast in which Esther, on her day, unmasks Haman. *Each one in his day* underlines the guilt of each son, and Job, as a father (and guarantor), is also (unconsciously) responsible for the collective disorder.

One by one, they called their three sisters. Though no mention is made of wine, the text distinguishes between the guilt of the sons and the daughters. The sons organize the feasts, eat and drink, and actively call the daughters, assuming authorship of the gatherings. The daughters, in turn, allow themselves to be persuaded and participate—suggesting complicity and concealment. The lack of wine in the first narrative hints that the sisters brought it as a gesture of gratitude for their invitation. There is a veiled accusation of incest, as will later be developed in the story of Lot's daughters.

However, the prologue concludes that Job *did not sin [in all this]* (1:22). The narrative carefully distinguishes between Job's responsibility and his children's guilt. Despite his flawed social order, Job is still praised for his righteousness—of intention, though not necessarily of justice. The statement that "he did not sin in all this" means he did not sin consciously—he did not partake in the banquets—but emphasizes his unconscious responsibility for tolerating and concealing the abuse of prosperity, which will corrupt his lineage (sons and daughters) and social realm (servitude). Even if Job does not obtain a personal profit,

Job's punishment highlights the unconscious responsibility for the abuse of prosperity and Job's collective responsibility as a guarantor.

2.3 JOB'S ABUSE OF DIVINITY

a) Third Reproach

And it came to pass [ויהי] after fulfilling the days of the banquets that Job sent and sanctified them; he rose early in the morning and offered sacrifices for all, for Job said to himself that maybe his sons had sinned in their hearts (1:5). The act of offering sacrifices constitutes the third—and principal—reproach against Job: ויהי, pointing to the justification of servitude and the abuse of prosperity in the name of divinity.

The tale now opens the door to the collective dimension of guilt (the abuse of divinity) as the imaginary mirror of the social realm's defective origins (Job's soul). Seven is a limit to the days of the banquet: the land conquered by violence (the First Temple) will fall by violence; the land conquered by servitude (the Second Temple), by sterility.

b) Job's Collective Responsibility (by Omission)

Job rises early to offer sacrifices. His diligence indicates that he makes an effort and does not seek personal gain from his wealth or servitude. However, Job abuses a social structure that perpetuates the privileges of his children; he justifies, in the name of divinity, that some men are authority and others are servants or slaves, where only a few enjoy the riches (banquets). This attributes Job's responsibility for imputing defective creation to divinity (by offering sacrifices).

Job (the accuser) triumphs among all men; still, he builds the farm by violent means (sacrifice and submission) and does not unveil and repair the mystery of the defective origins of the collective being (*the beginning*). The four subsequent punishments reflect the earlier sacrificial history of Israel and its varied forms: the sacrifice of life, sexuality, prosperity, and separation. Job is unaware that his sons drank wine (interpreted here as an abuse of both servants and sisters), thus incurring unconscious and collective guilt by omission. This guilt will be made explicit by the narrator during the announcement of the first punishment (1:13). Job will learn the truth from the fourth messenger, who recounts the destruction of his firstborn's house (his inheritance) by a desert storm (1:18).

Thus Job did every day (1:5). The narrator is scandalized because the first punishment should have served as a warning, hinting that Job was not diligent in preventing the crooked behavior of his children. Job offers sacrifices every day for every son, justifying and not avoiding the due punishment of the children's orgies. The narrative underscores Job's guilt in uprooting his sons.

c) Fourth Reproach: The Falseness of Submission

The fourth reproach refers specifically to Job. *His day* hints at a personal reproach (1:6, 13; 2:1) for the abuse of the divinity (not revealing evil and not instituting justice as authority). It happened on that day (ויהי, [1:6]) announces something past and refers to an imminent punishment. Through sacrifice and submission, Job manipulates divinity, presenting himself as a servant to subordinate the divine will and justify his children's banquets. In doing so, he exaggerates the role of Providence as complicit in human fault: *The pillars of heaven tremble and are astonished at his rebuke* (26:11). Satan will fairly accuse him: Job flees from evil and does not reveal it (by his sacrifice and submission)

No matter that Job did not institute sacrifice, which had existed before his days; he had a duty (of guarantee) as father and authority to repair his domain. Job was bound to denounce sacrifice (responsibility by omission) and redeem his sons, daughters, and servants (collective guilt). The fourth reproach underlines the pride of Job's supposed fear of the Lord, fleeing from evil and not denouncing evil. Job justifies the unjust benefit of prosperity, not assuming responsibility for the collective disorder and deceiving the innocent.

III.

Job's Trial in Heaven

3.1 PORTRAIT OF SATAN IN RELIGIOUS HISTORY

a) Eschatological Struggle Between Good and Evil

Christian and Muslim interpretations of the book of Job presuppose the collective guilt of humanity and conceive of Satan as a personal being—either opposing or serving divinity.

In Christian doctrine, Job is portrayed as the prototype of a saint's patient suffering. Gregory the Great, in *Moralia in Job* (also known as *Expositio in Librum Job*), an influential medieval work, explains Satan as a damned personal being—a rebellious angel who tempts Jesus (Matt 4).[1] Satan assumes a pivotal role in human history, justifying the sacrifice of the righteous. This interpretation presents an eschatological conflict between good and evil, where Job's suffering prefigures the church: the body suffers to save the soul.

Job was chosen to suffer due to his virtue in the context of an ontologically corrupted human nature—the doctrine of original sin. Suffering is framed not as punishment, but as instruction and a triumph over temptation. This eschatological struggle is reenacted in each individual, who overcomes original sin only by divine grace, confessing and renouncing temporal goods.

---

1. *Moralia* 147, 155, 158, 209.

Medieval Muslim and Jewish philosophy denounces Manichaeism as the Christian doctrine of Job, which denies free will. Amid criticism, Thomas Aquinas defends and develops Gregory's view in his *Expositio Super Iob ad Litteram*. Thomistic theology admits the existence of Satan as a personal being and also presupposes the power of evil in the face of a human nature corrupted by sin. Yet, Thomas Aquinas, in contrast to patristic pessimism (original sin), affirms freedom of will, upheld by divine Providence, giving coherent meaning to history as a trial and pathway to individual salvation. The prologue of the *expositio* interprets the book of Job as an allegory of Providence, interceding in personal and collective salvation, through the church's educational and social involvement.

Thomas Aquinas considers Job a just man, accepting suffering and assuming that divine Providence guides man; his imprudence lies in the excessive defense of his innocence, which risks causing scandal. Providence needs to intervene to enlighten free will in its path to salvation since man cannot (by himself) understand the true meaning of divine plans. The *Summa Theologica* (in q. 83) explains man's free will.[2] Man fails only in the material realm, not in his immortal soul. In the spiritual realm, divinity guarantees a future retribution of good and punishment, which overcomes the fallacy of a supposedly unjust creation that punishes without guilt. The history of salvation explains the submission of Satan, the spirit of evil, which has a root exclusively in the material world.

b) Firmness in Adversity

Islam conceives a religion founded directly on divine revelation and does not admit the concept of original sin: no soul bears the burden of another (Qur'an 35:18). Angels and devils, repeatedly mentioned in the Qur'an, obey divine Providence. Satan is a devil, always a servant of divinity, created or tolerated to tempt and punish man. The Qur'an does not mention the book of Job among the historical sacred books (the Torah revealed to Moses, the Psalms to David, and the Gospel of Jesus, which in their current version are understood to be corrupted).

Job (Ayyub) is recognized twice in the Qur'an as a prophet (4:163; 6:84). Ayyub is translated as repentance, a path to revelation, as he remains steadfast in adversity (21:83; 38:44). He acquires the status of a prophet because he participates in the contemplation of the divine presence. The

---

2. See Yaffe, "Providence in Medieval Aristotelianism."

Qur'an quotes Job four times. In a long quotation (38:41–44), Satan tempts Job with poverty and suffering, but the deity restores his family and wealth. Amid his tribulations, the Qur'an applauds Ayyub's persistence in faith. A time comes when divinity invites Job to strike the ground with his feet, and water springs forth, with which Job washes and drinks (celebrated as a fast on Ashura). Job is worried about the promise he has made to whip his wife a hundred times for trying to deceive him, but the deity invites him (*hila* [subterfuge]) not to beat her with a stick but to symbolically use herbs.

The Islamic tradition considers suffering a test of faith and does not affirm unanimously Job's guilt. A minority tradition (Averroes) stresses that Satan's accusation is in itself a punishment, and to tempt a guiltless Job would not be compatible with divine justice. Accordingly, this view acknowledges Job's guilt and affirms the justice of his testing. Temptation here unveils hidden faults, resulting from divine predilection.

c) Satan as Servant of Divinity

Calvin preached 159 sermons on Job (1554–55).[3] Calvin contradicts Thomas Aquinas, who conceives history as the triumph over Satan; Calvin presupposes that, before human history, Satan was submitted by divinity. Even if we cannot understand it, the apparent struggle between good and evil serves to evaluate individual freedom and responsibility— not to portray Satan's rebellion.

Calvin explains the conflict between divinity and Satan in the first two sermons on the book of Job's prologue. Satan is presented as a servant and messenger of divinity to correct Job. Job has fallen into sin, does not want to listen to the divine word, and sleeps during theophanies. In his first discourse, Calvin affirms that Job's inner battles against Satan are harder than all the adversities that men can suffer in life. He urges believers to overcome temptation through moral integrity and affirms the legitimacy of temptation to Job's test.[4]

Job overcomes Satan's accusations when he confesses sin and prays for his friends. Evil is not an eschatological rebellion in heaven that precedes man (Satan) but a dilemma in every man. He highlights that the discourse of divinity (42:7) does not criticize Elihu, whose arguments are similar to those of the theophanies. Elihu represents the Reformed

---

3. See Thomas, *Calvin's Teaching on Job*, 30–32.
4. Schreiner, *Where Shall Wisdom Be Found?*, 102–26.

Church, a religion founded directly on divine revelation in the sacred books. Calvin emphasizes that Job's rebellion against divinity, rather than divine confrontation with Satan, explains human history. Since divinity cannot be unjust or tolerate evil, Satan is a mere servant of divinity, a disguise in which man pretends to hide to elude the divine law.[5]

The book of Job, according to Calvin, stages the triumph of the divine will in history through the Reformed Church, the new Israel, a chosen people (referring to the universality of the Reformed Church, as opposed to the individualism and bigotry of Israel). Satan was expelled from the heavens, and the meaning of history is the submission of the eschatological animals, Behemoth and Leviathan, who personify the sins of flesh and pride.

Calvin presupposes that the spiritual judgment of every man precedes his creation (time does not exist) and thus resolves the a priori contradiction posed by the existence of Satan: the tolerance of evil by divinity and the legitimacy of temptation. Calvin is uncomfortable with the scholastic presupposition that divinity is unjust and delays justice until a future world. He highlights texts about divine justice and punishment in this material world. A nonexistent time resolves the contradiction of the postponement of punishment to its more convenient moment: God does not do these things with absolute power, but because he knows all the ways of man, and considers all his steps (sermon 18). The individual and collective punishments are attributed directly to divinity, and their meaning is teaching and saving man, for the Lord sees in a way that we cannot observe him. The divinity judges a man by his acts but knows his conduct and intentions even before his creation. Knowing good and evil, the end of man is found in a timeless divinity, directing events to guarantee the freedom and salvation of man, in no way condemned a priori but through moral accountability, according to his acts.[6]

d) Incoherence of Divine Tolerance of Evil

Jewish modern philosophy interprets the book of Job as a critical approach to collective guilt. Like most representative authors, Maimonides, in *The Guide of the Perplexed*, denies collective judgment and seems to conceive sin as imperfection or error, not as rebellion or collective damnation.[7]

---

5. Thomas, *Calvin's Teaching on Job*, 226.
6. See Schreiner, "Exegesis and Double Justice."
7. Harvey, "Maimonides and Spinoza."

Spinoza, in the *Brief Treatise on God, Man, and His Happiness*, argues that Satan, the antithesis of divinity, is incompatible with an eternal being.[8]

Leibniz raises the problem of evil tolerance by divinity. He develops Calvin's argument on the incoherence of Satan as a representation of evil, expressing his doubts and surprise that divinity might tolerate evil; he affirms the incoherence of man's a priori collective responsibility, supposedly born in sin. Since evil is not created and cannot persist in nature, he interprets evil as man's ignorance, error, and malice. Leibniz argues that man sins because of his vices. Free will is the cause of merit, evil, and guilt.[9]

Kant continues this line of critique. He denies collective guilt, asserting that divine will lies beyond human scrutiny. Kant opposes the coherence of Satan and the legitimacy of temptation. Practical reason justifies law's suitability to govern the social order, not divine revelation (critical reason). Worse than divine criticism, to justify moral rules in divinity proposes an arbitrary deity, and it imputes guilt to heaven. Practical reason formulates and develops an objective morality, not based on particular interests. According to Kant, evil qualifies individual conduct and is not institutionalized; Satan is a superficial justification of individual egoism and irrationality.[10]

3.2 ILLUSORY COURT OF HEAVEN

a) Collective Trial in Prophetic Literature

Many scholars view the prologue as an account of Job's trial. Divinity presides over the particular divinities, the sons of Elohim; Satan assumes the role of Job's accuser. It is plausible to conclude that the court of heaven in the book of Job stages a vision or dream in which Job rationalizes his punishment and tragic past as an accuser of divinity; it criticizes Satan as an accuser or server of divinity (as portrayed in prophetic literature), presenting Satan as Job's disguise.

Prophetic texts—particularly in Micah and Isaiah—supposedly describe Job's trial carried out through intermediaries or intercessors (angels, prophets, or mystics). The prophet Micah participates in the

---

8. Harvey, "Maimonides and Spinoza."
9. Leibniz, *Teodicea*, 41.
10. Kant, *Religión en los límites*, 49–53.

judgment of King Ahab. Sitting on his throne, divinity calls for a volunteer to trick King Ahab and make him perish at Ramoth Gilead, with the whole court of heaven standing by him (1 Kgs 22; Chron 18:18–22). Chapter 6 of the book of Isaiah presents a similar judgment by the heavenly court, and divinity orders Isaiah to mislead his people until their cities are laid waste.

The judgment against Ahab depicts a spirit of heaven, a servant of divinity, punishing a rebellious earthly king and legitimizing deception. Yet the premise is fallacious, for the Lord has no need of men, prophets, or angels to administer justice, nor can he employ, condone, or conceal evil. Thus, drawing an analogy between Job's and Ahab's trials is problematic. Judgment through pseudo-divinities, prophets, and mystics presupposes collective guilt, accuses divinity of tolerating and hiding evil (false deities), and imputes to divinity a defective creation, using defective means (creating, tolerating, or concealing Satan) to redeem man.

b) Incoherence of Pleading Job's Collective Guilt in Heaven

The prologue of the book of Job allegorizes an incoherence of Israel's former doctrine of sacrifice and submission as a collective accusation of men: that to accuse Job in heaven (a collective accusation) means to accuse divinity.

To accuse men in heaven is incoherent because no one can rebel against divinity, *for he is not man [or a spirit] like me, that I should challenge him: "Let us come together in debate"* (9:32). Satan (Job in disguise) makes two main allegations against divine authority in heaven, presupposing divine tolerance or concealment of men's falsified divinities. In the first audience, the challenge *Have you not given him?* (1:10) imputes to divine authority the injustice of Job's prosperity. The second accusation, *You will see how he denies you to your face* (1:11; 2:5), presupposes a collective accusation against man's false servility, obtaining benefits and abusing divinity as a servant, pretending to institute or inherit authority and prosperity on the day of the divine destruction of the false deities on earth (induces sedition).

Accusing Job of rebellion (first audience) or sedition (second audience) exaggerates Job's guilt and responsibility. Rebellion presupposes a violent uprising, but no rebellion might be exerted, and there can be no violence against divinity, which cannot be found to hurt or harm. And to pretend to represent divinity as a servant on earth by the accusation of men implies an inconsistent crime of sedition, as no one can speak for a generic (ideal or spiritual) character assuming a nonexistent collective identity. Both accusations presuppose an arbitrary divinity, enforcing his will by condemning innocents; and a lazy divinity, tolerating and concealing evil. Furthermore, Satan (the collective accusation in heaven) lacks an instrument (causality) to attribute and measure damage, guilt, and restitution; as there is no causality in heaven for a man's acts on earth, and Satan does not accurately identify Job's supposed crime, lacking exact evaluation of damage and enrichment.

The collective accusation against Job also blames divinity, imagining a violent divinity who punishes the innocent, condemning a man for other people's misdeeds, instituting social order over suffering and collective punishment, and not valuing individual and social identity. No evil can come from divinity, and no man can suffer without guilt to increase a supposedly future reward. Collective accusation disputes a hypothetical future to divinity with no future or past, accusing Job's future conduct (intention) without knowing the future.

In short, collective accusation presupposes man's creation as a serf and an organization that prevails over the individual (merit and guilt). Satan's collective accusation in heaven presupposes institutionalized evil, incompatible with creation. It denies the creation of man in the divine's image, and it legitimizes an authority (Satan) who rebels against divinity (accusing divinity of tolerating or concealing evil). The accusation in heaven against Job as a collective accusation is incoherent because divinity cannot create or conceal evil.[11]

c) Satan as Job's Disguise

Satan and Job represent two aspects of the same person (dissociative disorder) because Job shapes his social identity according to the divinity he imagines. Job's supposed divine inspiration separates him from established authority and social realm, conceiving history as a fight against

---

11. Collective accusation contradicts the personal origin or measure (proportionality) of guilt and responsibility. Collective guilt contradicts the three essential elements of guilt and merit (the intention, act, and result). The warning of the damage and its explanation by the delimitation and publicity of the damage are the three elements of the causality of the punishment (and of the retribution of merit) in its ideal origin, material reality, and causal imputation (for its restitution or compensation). Satan (Job in disguise) can judge Job (men) only by his acts (causality), not by his collective identity or supposed intentions.

(unidentified and nonexistent) collective evil through defective means (violence, temptation, or separation), rather than viewing authority and a social realm as the product of personal merit and individual labor.

Satan thus personifies Job's mask, used to justify a collective accusation against humanity and to legitimize either violence or submission.

In his first disguise, Job assumes divine authority and fights what he perceives as evil authority through violence, gaining prosperity through sacrifice and bearing unconscious guilt for having used corrupt means. In contrast, divinity unveils Jobs disguise: *Where were you when I laid earth's foundations?* (38:4). The earth's foundations refer to personal merit and guilt, the institutionalization of man's labor (as justification of authority and society).

In a second disguise, Job adopts the disguise of a submissive serf to a false divine image, bearing disproportionate guilt for collective misdeeds, and incurs a collective responsibility because the patient submission (to a supposedly divine will) incites violence (*You incite me to punish him in vain* [2:3]), and uses defective means (theft) waiting for the inheritance of prosperity. *Will your anger contest my justice? Will you condemn my justice to justify yourself?* (40:8). The doctrine of collective responsibility presupposes an unjust divinity. The dialogue in heaven conceives submission as accusing divinity of tolerating or concealing evil. Satan's disguise as a serf exaggerates man's guilt and manifests a desire to inherit the prosperity of a supposed damned authority.

In short, Job's trial in the prologue presents Job with a double identity: as a proud authority or a treacherous serf. In both trends, the sickly masochism of Satan (Job's formal doctrinal past) does not interpret punishment and suffering as teaching (a warning and explanation of punishment) but as an accusatory dogmatic that explains evil as a collective disaster and exalts suffering as a personal redemptive privilege. A sanguinary or self-abasing pseudo-divinity (Satan) governing on earth justifies Job's violence or falsehood against the instituted authority.[12]

12. The narrative rationalizes the incoherence of Job's former history, accusing himself without understanding why. Satan insists on an incoherent claim because he does not accuse conduct but presupposes evil in Job's future wrongful conduct (accumulating property, denying divinity). He presumes the unjust character of authority and prosperity (the institutionalization of evil), or as a serf disputes a hypothetical future to a divinity with no future or past. By accusing in heaven, Satan (Job in disguise) pretends to be elected by divinity to repair (with violence or submission) the (supposed) defective creation or the (presumed) corrupted world. This manifests a dissociative disorder (Manichaean confrontation between heaven and earth) that affects the social integration of man in a coherent social realm, exaggerates Job's guilt, and fails to identify and measure

d) Sons of Elohim Personify Job's Merit

Nevertheless, Job's unjust allegations against divine justice and defective means to fight evil are well-intentioned behaviors deserving praise, as through sacrifice and submission, Job aims to learn and compensate for the collective disaster and protect innocents. Job's trial announces Job's punishment and exile but also anticipates a future blessing.

In the wisdom literature, the trial of Job renews the supreme council of heaven—depicted in Micah and Isaiah—with the presence of the sons of Elohim, which personifies Job's merit that prevails over his defective violence and ideal falseness (Satan). Satan (Job in disguise) comes (בתכם) among them (1:6), highlighting Job's inner contradiction and right intention. The sons of Elohim weigh Job's individual merit, lineage, and social labor (his sons, wealth, and servants) as evidence of a personal, marriage, and collective ethic. The sons of Elohim signify that Job is not judged by his past or present (his unjust accusation and means) but justified by his future (building a social order), as his merit establishes a social identity. A future ethical and social realm underlines the historicity of Job's merit (the sons of Elohim).

The backdrop of Job's trial in the book of Job is the setting of an ironic allegory of the (collective) judgments of peoples and kings portrayed in prophetic literature and staging an individual judgment underscoring personal guilt and responsibility. In inventing Satan, Job seeks to destroy (through violent sacrifice) or submit to (through passive obedience) the deities of Canaan, Persia, and Greece—deities already nonexistent before their imagined origin (because a false divinity may not exist).[13]

---

guilt and responsibility for damage or restitution in its (personal) origin and measure.

13. The narrator refers to *its due time* as Job's overcoming the injustice of sacrifice and submission and solving the ethical problems that Satan raises in the prologue (and which the three friends and Elihu reiterate in the development of the plot). Dogmatic (Satan's accusations) means an ethical reference to a systematic doctrine that justifies authority and organization. The accusations of Satan in heaven foreshadow the three friends and Elihu's dogmatics, claiming divine inspiration and justifying sacrifice and submission; they also foreshadow Job's answers to the theophanies, submitting to an incoherent systematic of guilt and accepting his punishment and servitude without personal fault (warning or explanation). The book will develop a coherent theory of individual guilt and responsibility by elucidating and criticizing the former evolution of Job's dogmatic from sacrifice (the three friends) to submission (Elihu), unveiling and criticizing in the theophanies Job's formal, idealist, and violent theory of religion.

IV.

The Abuse of Prosperity

4.1 DIVINE ETIQUETTE AND ACCUSATORY QUESTIONS

a) Authenticity of Divine Presence

And divinity says to Satan (1:7). The divinity opens the dialogue with simplicity and education, not wrapped in majesty (demanding sacrifice) and not humiliating Job (demanding submission); arguments are more important than divine authority; and there is no effort to identify the authenticity of the divine presence.

The nuclear doctrine of the book of Job is the personality of guilt and responsibility. The narrative identifies Providence in history (*divinity says*) as an ideal sequence of accusatory questions and further inquiries into Satan's responses, which gradually expose Job's absurd disguises (before and after his punishment), whether assuming the role of a tyrant authority or that of a false submissive servant. The narrative opposes both sacrifice and submission as flawed attempts to establish justice through unjust means (violence, deceit, or passive waiting).[1]

---

1. *I will question you, and you must answer me* (38:3) explains Providence as a dialogue, and the accusatory question as a warning and explanation of punishment and servitude. Satan's collective accusation in heaven pretends to deny the direct relationship of divinity with every human being. Theophanies will develop the prologue and criticize the representation of an imaginary and arbitrary deity by violence or submission. The first theophany warns Job in the storm, referring to what Elihu pretends to

b) First and Central Accusatory Question

The first accusatory question (*Where do you come from?* [1:7]) mocks Job for presenting himself in heaven in the guise of Satan, as representative of earth in heaven or heaven on earth.

In idealism, there is no innocence or guilt, no cause or time, no imputable damage or restitution; the rightful accusations must be individual and founded on facts. In the first audience, divinity explains the unconscious and collective responsibility of the abuse of prosperity (the earth) and authority (heaven's representation) as the hidden motivation of Satan's (Job in disguise) exaggerated accusation in heaven.

Where do you come from? Through this nuclear accusatory question, divinity explains that attributing guilt presupposes identifying a culprit and measuring damage or restitution by a causal relationship on earth. In heaven, one cannot seek merit or denounce guilt, nor demand responsibility or institute authority (*Where do you come from?*) because there is no causal relationship between conduct on earth and damage in heaven.

This nuclear accusatory question foreshadows the substantial question of the first theophany (*Where were you when I laid the foundation of the earth?* [38:4]) and accuses Job of establishing an artificial social realm in pretended divine inspiration. This accusatory question opposes the legitimacy of collective accusations that deny (personal) merit and guilt. Authority reattributes merit by the construction of a social realm, and servitude punishes guilt for abusing divinity. It highlights that an accusation in heaven accuses the accuser only on earth, as there is no causal relation between evil and divinity.

---

hear in the night, and the second theophany explains to Eliphaz his punishment in daylight. In the first theophany, a warning to Job reveals unconscious responsibility (abuse of the land); in the second, an explanation to Eliphaz (42:7–8) rationalizes collective responsibility (as abuse of the divinities, the *nebelah*). Elihu exaggerates the accusation against Job. Asking for an explanation might be treated as an accusation against divinity, as Elihu argues, but it might also hint at an imputation of oneself. Warning and explanation of punishment are a personal duty of authority as a necessary element to fight against evil, elude tolerance and concealment of evil, and defend dependents. Three essential elements of guilt and merit (the intention, act, and result) are the three elements of the causality of the punishment (and of the retribution of merit) in its ideal origin, material reality, and causal imputation. Only through clear warnings and public explanations—by delimiting harm and providing compensation—can punishment be justified in terms of personal responsibility and proportionality. The first theophany points out that Job must listen to reality as a testimony of justice (38:4), not to a supposed night inspiration of a concealed divinity. Evil cannot be institutionalized; it exists only as a testimony of the defective social realm (as damage or restitution).

c) Responsibility of Collective Accusation

Satan accuses Job merely of being part of earth, not for his actions. But earth has no will or conscience, so to whom can guilt be imputed?

Imagining Satan reveals Job's disguise as an inconsistency or perversion of the accuser. Job incurs (unconscious) guilt for violently instituting serfdom (and abuse of prosperity), or (collective) responsibility for a false confession of serfdom (a separation from the social identity). In both roles (as a rebel against evil or as a seditious servant of divinity), his anger simplifies (dogmatizes) ethical problems by denying divine justice (40:8). Job conceives a divinity who tolerates evil, and he foolishly tolerates evil, pretending to be inspired (chosen) by divinity to suffer.

An important issue should be highlighted and addressed as soon as possible. Job's (personal) unconscious and collective guilt and responsibility for his exaggerated accusation in heaven are not unlimited and unconditional. Unconscious and collective guilt must be interpreted as delimited cases of extended personal liability for the abuse of earth or heaven, referring to the unjust enrichment or damages due to negligence or breach of a warranty duty; and by omission, for unjust impoverishment or for assuming indiscriminately collective debts. In short, Job's accusations against heaven do not incur guilt in heaven but rather assign him responsibility on earth. The responsibility of an accusation in heaven has its origins on earth as a false or erroneous claim.

4.2 SATAN'S REPLY, JOB'S COLLECTIVE GUILT

a) Satan Exaggerates Job's Guilt

In his first reply, Satan (personifying Job's unconscious guilt) fails to address the divine question rationally and instead doubles down on his collective accusation. He claims that *he comes from going around the world and walking on it* (1:7) and does not identify individual causality, a measure of damage and (personal) guilt. He intends to correct the unconscious and collective responsibility of men (as an ideal and collective identity), arguing that men abuse prosperity (wealth) and authority (instituting servitude).

Indeed, pointing out evil (*going around the world*) and fighting evil (*walking on it*) builds authority and society. It is like drawing a circle (*going around*) and identifying the target (*walking on it*). Satan correctly affirms the existence of a double unconscious and collective dimension of guilt and responsibility, but he exaggerates them.

Satan accuses *the earth* (or world), an ideal entity (authority, people, religion, or land) that has no conscience and will and, therefore, cannot be blamed for the collective disorder. Satan's response accuses creation, authority, and the social realm as a reality where men are born (created) condemned without (personal) guilt and inherit someone else's responsibility. It is plausible to interpret Satan's response as Job's dissociative syndrome in his dogmatic history, which the accusatory question diagnostics. *Going around the world* evokes the conquest of Canaan by violence; *walking on it* alludes to the conquest by Esther of the Persian king.

b) Satan Contradicts the Personal Origin of Guilt

This metaphorical journey, *going around the world and walking on it*, expresses a collective accusation of a nonexistent culprit: the world (or earth). It means exonerating real individuals who escape accountability for damage or unjust gain. Satan confuses Job's individual and collective identity. Even if interpreted as a social being, the thousand faces of earth (the origins, the world, the land, the lineage, the people, and religion) lack subjective identity; they exist only incarnated in the individuals who believe in them.

By accusing "the world," Satan undermines prosperity, sexuality, and religion as valid expressions of personal and social identity, justifies Job's abuse of prosperity (the banquets of his sons), and institutes undue punishment and servitude (the abuse of innocents and strangers). The defective means of a collective accusation elude (personal) responsibility in fixing the damage or restitution, and do not restore the collective disorder by (personal) merit (labor, hospitality, and individual justice).

c) Satan Dissociates Job's Individual and Social Identity

Satan (Job in disguise) accuses Job's social self of rebellion (in the first audience) and sedition (in the second), portraying him as a traitor to family and society. By promoting servitude and blaming a flawed creation, Satan denies Job's merit and responsibility, inflating his guilt.

Accusing in heaven, Satan (Job in disguise) confronts and dissociates Job's individual and social identity. Job breaches his (personal) duty as a social warrantor (father, husband, authority, author, proprietor, servant, or tenant), and he intends to (unjustly) profit from a supposed future inheritance (a messianic kingdom).

The warrantor's duty can be explained by the allegories of the first theophany, from the double perspective of respect for authority, working the land amid chaos (founding the house), and assuming social responsibility by receiving the lion cub and the raven chick (consolidating the house by receiving the innocent [his wife] and the stranger [his sons and daughters]), without trying to establish an alternative authority. Authority should be built on an aggravated personal responsibility (*officium*, as warrantor of a social statement) as social identity, not over violence or submission (rebellion or sedition).

V.

The Abuse of Serfdom

5.1 INCOHERENCE OF SUBMISSION TO DIVINITY

a) Defective Methods of Serfdom

Denouncing the assumption of the serf's disguise, a second accusatory question replies to Satan: *Have you noticed my servant Job?* (1:8). It criticizes servility and illustrates the legal terms of the duty to condemn evil. Job's admission of his servitude and submission (to a supposedly divine will) fail to fulfill his duty to condemn evil in the terms of his warrant's guarantee.

If the deity had said, *Job, my servant*, one might have doubted and taken the phrase as a limited reproach, even as a sign of appreciation. However, the phrase *my servant Job* suggests that Job is a recalcitrant serf. It denounces the false humility and pride of submission, which strive neither to overcome servitude nor to condemn evil when necessary. And *my servant* implies an aggravating inference—not merely a servant, but *my* servant—suggesting a grave crime, difficult to repair. It is not simply economic or sexual defiance, but rather a selfish idealism that has taken the name of the Lord in vain.

The divine reply formally articulates what was already implied in the nuclear accusatory question from the first debate: to assume servitude means to exaggerate collective guilt (it presumes a defective creation), to betray Job's social identity (as an accusation against authority and lineage), and to elude personal responsibility. It highlights that Job avoids his duty of guarantee (of innocents and dependents) under the guise of a servant. He incites divine violence to inherit the world in a messianic future and attempts to justify human servitude as divine will. The accusatory question blames Satan (Job in disguise) for pretending to be a servant of divinity, therefore accusing divinity of having created humans as servants.

b) Social Relevance of Servitude

No one like him on earth (1:8) is an accusatory inference. Job deceives himself by interpreting history and society as a struggle against external authority and social order, thereby evading his duty to uphold the system that sustains him.

Servitude is not a personal choice; it has social relevance (*the earth*), referring to servitude as a defective method to institute a social realm. Job does not liberate his servants; he assumes that servitude is divinely ordained and endangers the future of his sons and dependents (and implicitly his wife) by constructing an authoritarian and flawed society in Uz. The disguise of the servant (as submission to authority) is a veiled repetition of rebellion against authority, pretending to inherit wealth through temptation or separation, which, if done knowingly, constitutes prevarication.

Praise always conceals a reproach, and to repeat the praise of a servant (*no one like him*: a divine servant) magnifies the reproach. *My servant* refers to Providence unveiling Job's disguise and awakening Job from his idealistic dream. However, his impertinent accusation in heaven does not affect his divine image (divinity does not consider his impertinence) because, as explained, it causes harm only to himself on earth. *My servant* outlines a complex personality called by his name (flattered for monotheism), seeks the truth despite his corrupt idealism, and is not a servant of Satan (of his violent and twisted sacrificial illusion and dissociative syndrome).

No one like him on earth hints that Job will overcome the abuse of prosperity and build a house that will protect his lineage. *No one like him on earth* underlines that earth has no subjective identity other than as testimony of Job's limited virtue. Job's fear of the Lord and fleeing from evil attenuate his guilt, even if they do not justify his unjust methods, motivations, and messianism. In short, Job's insolence uproots him, but he lays the foundation for an ethical tradition.

c) Impossible Institutionalization of Evil

The reply to Satan's accusations then repeats, almost verbatim, the praises of Job uttered by the narrator: *honest [תם], upright [וישר], who fears punishment [ירא אלהים], and who flees from evil [וסר מרע]*.

The litany commends Job's good intentions, which foster an ethical tradition, celebrates the historical moderation of his submission, and highlights his growing social responsibility in combating evil. Each of the four praises means progress in constructing a social order. After each disaster, Job gradually overcomes his dramatic history and begins to fulfill, step by step, the terms of his moral duty to overcome servitude.

The divine insistence in rebuking *the servant Job* anticipates Satan's reply. It confronts submission, in its historical modalities, for despising foreign deities, kings, sages, and peoples. The divine insistence awakens Job by explaining the legal terms of a conflict between personal and social responsibility, referring to the duty to condemn evil and overcome servitude. *The servant Job* falls, again and again, into the vortex of collective disorder. Divine intervention denies the possibility of institutionalizing evil, whether as divine tolerance (Satan as a flawed deity) or as hidden malice (Satan as a supposed divine servant).[1]

---

1. The second accusatory question of the audience foresees the next hearing in heaven, confronting Satan's accusation of Job's wrong intentions. To judge intentions signifies the ideal institutionalization of evil (foresees the future triumph of evil). Affirming Job's right intention (*my servant*) and his efforts in establishing justice (*there is no one like him*) and overcoming servitude (*honest, upright, who fears punishment, and flees from evil*), the accusatory question, despising the serf, exonerates Job of rebellion or sedition against divine justice and pretends to contradict the ethic of temptation and separation that Satan will propose in the second hearing. In medieval doctrine, Maimonides and Averroes debate the dubious legitimacy of temptation. The Mutazili trend in Islam argues that divine wisdom tempts the righteous to acquire merit. As a doctrine contrary to free will, its criticism constitutes the purpose of *The Guide of the Perplexed* (temptation as a crime of arbitrary realization of divine right).

5.2 SATAN'S REPLY, THE DEFECTIVE CREATION

a) Supposed Divine Prevarication

Satan's second response is *Does Job fear God for nothing?* (1:9). Instead of acknowledging Job's flawed methods in establishing a social identity, Satan (Job in disguise) justifies Job's servitude through fear and accuses the whimsical arbitrariness of divine autocracy.

At the outset of the dialogue, Satan manifests his anger, insisting on divine fickleness. *Have you not given him?* (1:10); *Don't you see?* (1:11). This implies an accusatory inference, as not only has the rebellious Job received authority and prosperity in vain (as warrior or servant), but knowingly to ruin him. In short, Satan (Job in disguise) accuses divinity of prevarication and implies that divinity promotes serfdom to tempt the serf with prosperity and authority.

Satan identifies four steps or temptations (in divine prevarication): *toward him, toward his house, in everything about him, and around him* (1:10). The historicity of serfdom is a mirror of divine fickleness, a counterpoint to the four divine praises of Job. It presupposes a divinity who incessantly gives Job prosperity, family, authority, and serfs, only to punish him later, mocking his fearful and servile attempt to rebuild a coherent social order.

b) Legitimacy of Temptation

Satan's reply insists on portraying temptation as a defective creation. *You have blessed the work of his hands, and his livestock spreads over the land* (1:10). According to Satan, servitude manifests the divine social order as a divine temptation.

Temptation, by definition, means inciting a crime, with the instigator bearing moral and legal responsibility. The specificity of the new scenario is that Satan no longer discusses life and sexuality as human corruption but sees prosperity (cattle and servitude) as divine abuse, pretending to corrupt men. Satan accuses divinity of tempting Job and legitimizes temptation as dogmatic.

After the first audience, Satan undoubtedly attended the philosophy lectures of Maimonides and Averroes, criticizing the legitimacy and violence of temptation. Satan implies a subtle institutionalization of evil and temptation by *omission*, concealing Job's supposed wrongdoing.

Satan wagers the deity to reveal Job's evil intention, insinuating that Job has obtained prosperity and authority with torturous means that divinity chooses to overlook. In the second audience, Satan might be jealous of the false virtue of the aggressive and cunning Job, who knows how to deceive the foolish and lazy divinity, who closes (for some time) his eyes to his abuses to corrupt him.[2]

c) Separation as Delay of Divine Justice

But stretch out your hand and touch all that he has, and he will surely curse you to your face (1:11). Now, the issue at stake is separation as a delay of justice. After denouncing Job's (concealed) greed, Satan (Job in disguise) proposes punishment—exile and a softened sacrifice of prosperity—against a groveling servant who does not renounce prosperity or patiently waits for a messianic future.

According to Satan, divinity institutionalizes evil (for a time) by tolerating the unjust prosperity of the servant Job (even if divinity does not give Job unjust prosperity). By delaying justice, divinity has committed (last but not least) a crime of omission (concealment of evil). Satan's collective accusation pretends to underline that timing is decisive in instituting justice.

Satan argues that Job's prosperity is not a sign of Job's virtue but a delay (separation) in divine justice. Job promotes submission not as loyalty but to overcome authority through temptation (*take all that is his*) or through temporal separation, waiting for a messianic collapse of foreign gods and kings (*you will see*). Satan (Job in disguise) induces and legitimizes violence by omission.

d) Wager Against Divinity

And you will see how he denies you to your face (1:11). As I have underlined, every time the narrator repeats an argument, it unveils its

---

2. Who is responsible for a violent death, the one who tempts and incites the murderer, or the executor of the murder? Undoubtedly, both are guilty of murder, but the ideal author (he who tempts and incites) is the (first and principal) responsible. The material executor (like the soldier in war) does not want the death (of the enemy) but the money of the ransom (or the glory of the nation). Death is a felony murder (in the executor), and the principal author is the inducer.

inconsistency. *The face* refers to the appearance of virtue, the defective time of divine justice, and *to see* alludes to Job's wrongful intentions.

As the debate develops, Satan insists, with increasing shamelessness, on accusing divinity alone and justifying the fear of the servant and resigned Job. The second round of Satan's accusations against Job in heaven (violence and emotional manipulation) concludes with a confrontation between Satan and divinity, like two party-going and ill-matched friends who contend with each other about Job's virtue and submission.

By inducing divinity to punish Job's intentions (*you will see*), Satan accuses divinity of delayed justice and Job of supposed future wrongs or errors (not for his actions but for his intentions). Satan, as a servant, questions a divine delayed justice, but Satan cannot formulate collective accusations against divinity (and Job in heaven) without knowing the future.

VI.

The Punishment of Job

6.1 SUPPOSED INSTITUTION OF SATAN

a) Dogma of Submission

And the divinity says to Satan: Behold, all that he has is in your hands; only upon him do not stretch forth your hand. And Satan left the presence of the Lord (1:12). It is not a coherent reading of the text to conclude that the first scene in heaven ends with the institutionalization of Satan. It is more plausible that the accusatory questions of the first audience in heaven utterly explain the personal origin of guilt (and the punishment on earth).

The first dialogue in heaven does not establish the undeserved punishment of an innocent man, nor a trial or education of Job through suffering. Rather, Job's servitude results from his (own) actions, unconscious responsibility for the abuse of prosperity, or collective responsibility for failing to condemn evil, as would be mandatory as father or authority (from his role as guarantor).

All that he has is in your hand refers to the normative punishment of patient submission (exile, poverty, and serfdom); and *do not lay a hand on him* (1:12) praises abandoning the sacrifice of life and sexuality. Applauds Job for his right intention (*upon him do not stretch forth your hand*) but reproves his submission (*all in your hands*). This passage suggests that, after renouncing the bloody sacrifices of life and sexuality (which the heavenly dialogue symbolically condenses), Job's sincere intention preserves his identity (lineage and marital status) and limits the scope of punishment resulting from his unjust submission.

And Satan left the presence of the Lord, explaining that divine inspiration does not inspire temptation and separation. Satan is not an envoy of divinity but Job's disguise. A collective accusation—by temptation or separation—exiles Job, and he leaves the divine presence. His submission as a serf presupposes imputing a defective creation to divinity.

b) Personal Responsibility of Submission

It happened that day [ויהי היום], sons and daughters eat and drink wine at the house of the firstborn (1:13). *That day* refers to Job's guilt and punishment. Evil is not instituted, tolerated, or concealed by divinity as a collective sin but revealed and punished at its (personal) origin.

Is it coherent to punish Job for the sins of his sons and servants? No. His punishment results from an omission rooted in his (individual) responsibility. His submission evades his duty (of guarantee) as father, authority, and tenant (he abuses authority). Job's punishment symbolizes the earth taking revenge for his undue submission to evil. Job tolerates his children's indulgent use of wealth (symbolized by the feasts) and fails in his duty to free the servants.

The sons abuse prosperity and live without deserving it; the incestuous daughters, when choosing a partner, admire the joy of their brothers and despise the yoke of the servants. The servants take advantage of the banquet leftovers and feel contempt for foreigners. Job does not participate in the feasts and is unaware that his sons and daughters drink wine (he has no conscious personal guilt); however, he tolerates and conceals the abuse of the children (unconscious responsibility) and the abuse of servility (collective responsibility). Furthermore, his submission also abuses divinity because he imagines a divinity complicit in the abuse of prosperity of his sons and servants (sacrifice of sexuality and prosperity, temptation and separation, as personal responsibility for collective guilt).

Job fails to fulfill his duty as a guarantor of his sons and servants. He is punished as a father (for the abuse of his sons), as a proprietor (for the submission of his servants), and as an authority and religious man (for not fighting evil and offering submission to an imaginary deity). Only at the end of the turmoil will the fourth messenger reveal to Job, as the nuclear reason for his punishment, that his sons drank wine (1:18), thereby establishing the analogy between sacrifice and wine.

c) Arrival of the Messengers

Sacrifice and submission are two faces of the same coin (a collective accusation). The messengers rationalize the violent and Manichaean past of Job in exile. They explain his punishment due to the incoherent Job's sacrificial and servile doctrine while also praising his tortured construction of an ethical tradition (the rationalization of his past).

The messengers arrive simultaneously, and their messages follow one another in an illusion of immediacy. *An angel informs Job*. This timelessness evokes the sudden awareness of a history of violence and tragic submission. The arrival of the Assyrians and Chaldeans seems likely a historical reference to the doctrine of collective guilt developed in the prophetic literature. The servants—formerly sacrificial deities—are slain by the swords of the Assyrians and Chaldeans, alluding to the incoherence of a dogma built on collective guilt. The Assyrians and Chaldeans symbolically represent the religious dogmas of the First and Second Temples.

The four pillars could refer to the dogma of the three friends and Job's final monologue (the destruction of sons, animals, serfs, and the house crumbling). Job successively assumes the incoherence of sacrifice (the three friends) and patient submission (Job in the monologue that closes the dialogues). The *desert wind* destroys the four pillars of the house. The destruction refers to the social order (the farm in Uz) that Job has built on shifting sands. It stages an allegory of Israel's historical dogma and presents the messengers as the embodiment of Job's narcissistic theology of divine election. Punishment destroys the firstborn's house (that refers to his inheritance) but spares Job's lineage.

6.2 JOB'S CONFESSION

a) Virtual Character of Job's Punishments

It is reasonable to interpret that Job's punishments describe the destruction of his authoritarian social order built on sacrifice and submission. The setting of the messengers refers to a virtual death of the sons (the foreign kings) and servants (the foreign divinities), not an effective physical death. It is consistent to interpret that the messengers do not give testimony of the death of animals, servants, and lineage, but they announce and explain it. The messengers describe a virtual death, like that of Isaac, which an angel (messenger) avoids at the last moment. The messengers ritualize the development of a critical conscience about the incoherent ideals of sacrificial dogma, which degrades men (authority) and their servants (divinities).

The narrator emphasizes an exaggeration because *a strong desert wind* (רוח גדולה) seems redundant. It means that the wind did not destroy the house but only its four pillars; not all sons died, only the servants (his former sacrificial divinities).

Indeed, the cold, detached manner in which the messengers describe the events is striking. Instead of arriving breathless or in panic, the first messenger calmly explains that the oxen were plowing and the donkeys were grazing. And how did the second messenger know that the fire came from heaven? Full of calm, the third messenger describes the arrival of the Chaldeans. Without tact, the fourth takes its time to mention the children's eating and drinking. Later, in the debate with his friends, Job does not grieve over the death of his sons but laments that they despise him (Job 19:18), implying that they are still alive (Job 19:13–19); and, above all, in the epilogue, Job has seven sons and three daughters after being rehabilitated. What a happy coincidence! Would he have the strength to rebuild, after the tragedy, the same numerous descendants? Furthermore, in the epilogue, his brothers, sisters, and old friends offer him their condolences in an extravagant way, not on the death of his children but when he has other children and has been rehabilitated (42:11). The moment of grief is curiously displaced, almost theatrically delayed.

b) Ritual of Confession

Job rose (1:20). After Job's punishment, the narrator praises Job for gradually becoming aware of the unconscious and collective responsibility of sacrifice and submission. The ritual precedes the confession and allegorizes the pride and foolishness of sacrificial dogma. Job tears his cloak (renounces authority), cuts his hair (renounces his servants), prostrates himself on the ground (renounces the sacrifice of prosperity, receives a woman), and speaks (renounces his Manichaean polytheism and ceases to accuse supposedly foreign deities).

Naked I came from my mother's womb, and naked I will return to it (1:21). The narrator intends to underline the merit of renouncing the sacrificial dogma but also the foolishness of patient submission. Job justifies his confession in a cumbersome way, singing a popular song learned in the tavern of the drunken sailors.

The Lord gave me, the Lord took away. He manifests verbosity and stupid pride in his supposed election. Job does not directly accuse the divinity of causing the collective disorder but presumes and conforms to an imaginary deity who tolerates and conceals the foreign kings to purify and punish him without guilt. He pretends to be innocent and accuses the divinity of (unjustly) giving and taking away his prosperity.

It is coherent to deduce that Job's confession overcomes sacrifice but assumes the dogma of submission to the supposed divine will (Job assumes collective guilt and ceases to proclaim himself innocent). Nevertheless, Job does not know what (collective) crime he confesses, does not identify the terms of his (social) debt, exaggerates his responsibility, and incurs collective responsibility. We witness the transition from sacrificial dogma (of life, sexuality, and prosperity) to patient suffering and an implicit accusation against the divinity of tolerating and concealing guilt.[1]

c) Assessment of the Confession

The narrative of the trial record, ostensibly authorized by the Judge, concludes that in *all this, Job did not sin and did not impute his fall to the Lord* (1:22). Job acted with upright intention to defend the innocent (exculpatory or attenuating error), as he did not sin *in all this* (consciously). He repents of bloody sacrificial theology and accuses himself. The phrase *he did not sin* refers to revealing the violent sacrificial dogmatic, which is a

---

1. Job (the accuser) triumphs among all men; still, he builds the farm by violent means (sacrifice and submission) and does not unveil and repair the mystery of the defective origins of the collective being (*the beginning*). Four punishments explain the former sacrificial history of Israel and its different modalities (sacrifice of life, sexuality, prosperity, and separation). Job must prevail over violence and submission, and he must overcome the interpretation of exile as a Manichaean conflict between divinity and Satan (sacrifice and submission as a collective accusation of men); nevertheless, by submitting to an imaginary divinity (not denouncing evil), he fails to rectify the flawed origins of a foreign land and does not construct a coherent social being founded in personal merit and guilt.

limited excuse because *not sinning* is formulated as an attenuating excuse (*in all* of *this*). *In a contrary sense*, he did sin by assuming patient submission that incites violence (temptation and separation).

The confession accuses Job of abusing divinity by instituting himself as a servant (spiritual sin), pretending to destroy the foreign social order from within, or patiently waiting for its destruction in its contradictions (messianism). In both scenarios, the false submission or the purifying separation induces violence. Job claims to be innocent, and the collective confession is also a claim of individual innocence that instigate violence. Ultimately, he condemns the world in the name of his idealist dogma, individualistic, messianic, and exclusivist.

In conclusion, *Job did not attribute his fall to the Lord* (1:22). Not to attribute his fall to divinity praises Job's right intention (exonerating divinity); nevertheless, his undue and exaggerated confession attributes to heaven the concealment and toleration of evil.

VII.

Satan's Second Hearing

7.1 HYPOSTASIS OF SERFDOM

a) Satan Reiterates Collective Accusation

The second hearing results from Job's confession. Satan no longer appears as a rebel in heaven (in an eschatological struggle against authority) nor as the violent servant of the divinity sent to purify men through suffering. In his new role, the accuser seeks to absolve the divinity of all guilt and instead accuses the *sons of Elohim* as a social realm (he walks among the sons of Elohim). Satan, the accuser, does not conceal himself: he walks among them and stands before the Lord (2:1), stripped of the mystery that sacralized him in the first audience in heaven.

Divinity confronts Satan and scandalizes. *Oy! How have you come back?* (2:2). Satan did not pay due attention to the nuclear accusatory question of the first hearing (*Where do you come from?*). In his renewed accusation against men, the accuser insists on affirming his innocence (now as a serf) and repeats the same argument of a supposed collective responsibility (for the defective origins) already contested in the first hearing. The second hearing creates an atmosphere of repetition, underlining the dogmatic analogy between sacrifice and submission, as servitude institutionalizes an authority founded on a collective accusation of men. Furthermore, Job candidly expects to inherit authority and wealth (messianism) after divine wrath destroys the greedy kings and their false divinities (supposedly perverse).

The procedural irregularity of Satan's second accusation in heaven is evident: it reflects stubbornness. Satan pretends to extend Job's punishment, after the culprit's release, for the same offenses for which he was tried and convicted in the first hearing in heaven. Satan, as a public prosecutor, pretends to prolong Job's prison without alleging new criminal facts, on mere suspicion, with the pretext that the detainee has not redeemed himself, supposing the detainee's intentions.[1]

b) Job Persists in Collective Accusation

Have you considered my servant Job? Divinity repeats the rebuke formulated in the first hearing, assimilating submission to sacrifice. The repetition underscores the aggravated reproach of Job's collective accusation.

The divine reply reiterates the foolishness and vanity of submission as an attenuated accusation of collective guilt projected upon humanity that (Job supposes) purifies him by intercession and separation. With his new intercessory disguise, Job accuses divinity by inference of tolerating or covering up the collective evil (*he stands before divinity*).

There is no one like him on earth (1:8; 2:3) praises Job for overcoming the sanguinary sacrifice (of life and sexuality) and also for exonerating the divinity of the earth's collective disorder (interpreted as an abuse of prosperity). However, although Job has overcome the logic of sacrifice, he imagines a violent divinity who commands submission. The praise thus carries a veiled, intensified reproach: Job unwisely continues to present himself as innocent, chosen to suffer servitude by an unjust deity.[2]

---

1. The second collective accusation of Satan (Job as intercessor) is particularly reprehensible. Satan accuses without identifying Job's conduct and damage. The divine reply reproaches Satan for not demanding the correct punishment from the beginning; it contradicts the principle of legality since it incurs a *mutatio libelli* (a fundamental alteration of the "cause of action" or the "subject matter of the dispute") permitted only exceptionally in criminal proceedings. Furthermore, the *mutatio libelli* occurs after the final execution of the sentence, which criminal justice does not allow: it violates the accusatory principle and restricts the right to defense.

2. In the second hearing, temptation (and separation) define submission (exile) as a fight against foreign deities and kings (supposedly consented to and concealed by divinity) and presuppose a defective creation that man has to overcome by servitude. It stages an organization that prevails over the individual (merit) and describes a rebellion against authority (Behemoth) and submission to an organization (Leviathan).

c) Serfdom as Incitement to Violence

The most significant argument of this second hearing, compared to the initial divine rebuke, is the repetition of the litany of Job's praises, *honest [תם]*, *upright [וישר]*, *fearful of divinity [ירא אלהים]*, *and who flees from evil [וסר מרע]*, accompanied by a nuanced compliment as the specific reproach of this second hearing: *he perseveres in his virtue* (עדנו מחזיק בתמתו). The divinity acknowledges Job's right intention but adds an aggravated reproach, indicating that Job's persistence in his virtue reflects a greedy and prideful morality.

You incite me to punish him in vain (2:3). An explanation is added to the reproach of persisting in (pretended) virtue: vainly inciting (חנם) the punishment of men. The reply points out the violence of submission as incitement to violence. Job's exaggerated confession of guilt incites rebellion against authority and contributes to the destruction of the established social order—without safeguarding the innocent. It is important to note that the divinity does not claim to have allowed punishment without cause, rather that Satan (Job) provokes violence (ותסתני) without presenting any concrete accusation.[3]

7.2 SATAN'S REPLY

a) Overcoming Sacrifice

Divine accusations foresee Satan's responses, and the confrontation of the second hearing unveils Satan's anger that incites violence. Satan (Job the serf) answers and says (ויען, ויאמר), challenging divinity he assumes

---

3. *Incitement* to crime refers to temptation (and separation as an incitement by omission). Job renounces the sanguinary dogmatic (of violence and emotional manipulation) and respects life and sexuality, but employs the sacrifice of prosperity to tempt and patiently submits to evil, waiting for the destruction of the foreign realm. Temptation and separation do not identify an individual imputation of damage and unjust enrichment, and mean an unjust collective accusation (of innocents and the social order). The narrative underlines the responsibility of incitement. The accusatory question teaches Job that his unjust confession, assuming collective sin (*persisting in his virtue*), hides an unfair accusation against authority, undermines the duty of guarantee (as father, author, and authority), and is a crime of incitement to violence (against an innocent). It reiterates the reproach of Job's wife (*bless divinity and die* [2:9]). Submission (to divine will) is the supposed greatest virtue of the servant Job, but, as incitement, excuses Job from assuming responsibility for his acts (causality) and his social responsibility (duty of guarantee toward innocents and dependents).

the same role and divine representation denied in the first hearing: *to go around the earth and to walk through it* (2:2).

Satan argues: *Skin for skin, as a man gives everything for his soul* (נפש [2:4]). Satan once again accuses man's collective identity (skin and soul) without identifying a personal crime. He justifies submission (skin) for the defense of life (soul) and prioritizes systemic organization (the soul) over individual autonomy (the skin). *Skin for skin* envisions a world where order—legal or inspired—prevents chaos and subjugates both ruler and servant alike. Satan is currently accusing both the people (intercession) and the false divinities (separation) of being an artificial (fictitious) creation of man's violence.

Skin for skin questions the violent Mosaic sacrificial law (*eye for eye, tooth for tooth* [Exod 21–23]) and institutes collective violence that justifies authority and organization as submission of personal violence to institutional violence. It means to limit the sacrifice (as retribution), which now does not aim to destroy authority or organization (*have you not given it to him?*) but to purify the soul (the individual) through poverty, exile, and suffering by inciting divine purifying violence (*strike him*). It might also pretend a necessary defense of a social order with defective origins through intercession or separation (wakefulness and inducement).

What relation do the soul, bones, and flesh have with the skin? This metaphor suggests a collective origin of the social order: skin, flesh, and bones serve the soul. It portrays a social identity grounded in (economic) servitude (through renunciation and intercession), which prevails over the violent sacrifice of life and sexuality. In this second hearing, Satan calls for blows against the bones and flesh (i.e., suffering) and denounces the social identity of a man—his lineage and tradition—as expressed through the flesh (sexuality, social order) and bones (tradition, prosperity, and authority).

b) Pretended Institutionalization of Submission

Perhaps if, at last, you stretch out your hand and strike him on his bones and flesh, you will see that he will disown you to your face (2:5), a proposition similar (*you will see*) to that formulated in the first hearing (1:11). Satan calls upon (tempts) the deity: please use your hand (שלח נא ידך)—in effect, asking to be used as the divine hand. He claims violence against the (supposed) collective disorder (of authority and serfs), indirectly imputing to the deity collective guilt for tolerating or covering up evil (foreign kings and divinities).

The accusation of incitement to violence foresees Satan's arguments (2:3). *Strike Job* refers to the dogma of temptation; *you will see* alludes to separation. Striking him in the bones and flesh promotes the temptation of sexuality and prosperity. By surrendering property and sexual freedom—acts of obedience and intercession—the serfs seek to build an order that overcomes the authority of foreign gods and kings through temptation and separation (inciting sedition).

There is a clear analogy with Elihu's arguments. Satan pretends to build an organization by (limited) violence; he refers to the bones and the flesh as a perverse inclination (of social disorder by greed and family corruption by sexuality). *Strike him in the bones and the flesh* means denying the tradition of property (social root, bones) and lineage (marriage, flesh). Instituting the ethic of temptation (and the simple separation), Satan (Job in disguise) incites social violence (intercession and collective accusation) that accuses the accuser as inducer (*you incite me to punish him without reason* [2:3]).

c) Second Bet, Inciting Divine Violence

In this second incoherent bet (*you will see*), Satan accuses Job of accumulating wealth and power (bones and flesh), a supposed rebellion against divinity (intention), which must be revealed not in the world of facts (causality) but in the idealism of subjectivity (divinity should have seen). Job supposes that divinity consents to the foreign (narcissistic) deities and (violent) kings so that he may reveal them (by suffering) and submit them (giving them a name). He incites divinity to destroy the foreign social order in his favor. The perverse inclination (flesh and bones) manifests the falseness of Job's greed and intentions (נפש).

Satan accusing Job in heaven means Job accusing the deity of breaching the duty of guarantee by creating, consenting to, or hiding an evil that men cause, which persists in the social realm (in the bosom of a defective creation).

I conclude that Satan's new collective accusation against Job is repeated and exaggerated (because he does not distinguish between guilt and responsibility). A collective accusation means to bet against divinity. Once again, Satan (as Job's disguised voice) presupposes an attenuated institutionalization of evil on earth through submission. He assumes a flawed creation rooted in greed (serfdom), sanctioned by divinity for purifying Job through suffering.

Satan cannot accuse alleged future acts (*you will see how he ceases blessing you*) without knowing the future and against a divinity who has no future or past. Furthermore, he asks for a new punishment without adducing new punishable acts, presuming Job's corruption, and reiterating a collective accusation already rejected in the first hearing in heaven.[4]

7.3 REJECTED INSTITUTIONALIZATION OF SUBMISSION

a) Satan's Unveiling

You have him under your authority, but respect his [נפש] social identity (2:6). The phrase signifies a rejection to institutionalize authority and organization through the proposed new dogma of attenuated submission, employing temptation and separation as instruments. The phrase *you have him under your jurisdiction* implies that social identity must be based on individual merit, and *respecting his [נפש] social identity* alludes to temptation and separation as an incoherent way to build a coherent social identity.

The accusatory reply—ordering respect for Job's social identity (נפש)—rebukes Satan's collective fight against foreign kings and deities in exile. Temptation and separation, while intended to purify, ultimately destroy the social structure that protects the innocent and the vulnerable. The fragile foreign social structure, though defective, must be respected (i.e., religious liberty) since it was established through both personal sacrifice and collective merit (submission). The divine answer denies the

---

4. Satan's answers in the prologue allegorize Job's answers to the theophanies and the divine rebuke of the three friends and Elihu, analogous debates that will explain the origin of unconscious responsibility for abusing prosperity and authority, and the origin of collective responsibility for abusing divinity (claiming to be a divine representative through patiently suffering evil). Collective accusations presume the corruption of prosperity, sexuality, and beliefs (authority and organization), undermine men's social identity, and challenge the notion of man being created in a divine's image and likeness. In the theophanies, the divine reproach of Job (40:8) will confront Job as Satan in disguise, as the former (dreamlike) representation of violence (of the three friends) or as the former apotheosis of submission (Elihu). Theophanies, framing a coherent doctrine on (personal) guilt, aim to answer Job's protest and recognize his right to a pertinent warning and explanation of his punishment and servitude.

legitimacy of collective accusations in heaven as incitement to violence; in a contrary sense, it affirms the duty to respect the merit of personal authority and the social functionality of a defective organization.

Satan receives authority after the second hearing, but divinity grants him only what he had already received in the first audience. Divinity recognizes Satan as an authority (achieved by submission) and gives him the indeterminate object that had already been given to him after the first hearing (the punishment of a personal fault of Job) without granting him man's social identity (נפש). Therefore, Satan was not given either Job's bones (authority) or his flesh (social marital order).

And Satan departs from the presence of the Lord (2:7). Satan withdraws from the presence of the Lord on both accusations (1:12; 2:7). To signal the failure of the new dogma of exile (submission) founded on temptation and separation, he is not mentioned again in the dialogues or the epilogue.[5]

b) Skin's Punishment

After supposedly receiving permission (inspiration), Satan *strikes Job with a malignant leprosy* (2:7). No organization subsists based on submission, only Job's idealistic corruption. This refers to the isolation that Job brings to himself by inventing a divinity a priori (Satan) and assuming collective guilt. Satan only dares to punish Job on his skin with malignant leprosy (רע), the mildest of the aforementioned justifiable objects (2:7), without daring to compromise the flesh and bones, and—much less—the soul or identity (נפש) expressly denied to him.

Accusing in heaven, Job condemns himself to isolation and exile. However, the skin torture seems to have been transitory and curable because, in the dialogues with his friends, Job has been relieved after scratching himself with a rake. In his countless subsequent laments (which refer to abandonment, injustice, loneliness, and social uprooting),

---

5. This refers to the prophetic doctrine of the Second Temple as a fight against foreign deities. Satan is authorized to accuse man (and authority) only for his acts, not his skin, flesh, bones, and soul as elements of collective identity. The response to Satan defines the limits of the right of rebellion (collective accusation) to legitimate defense or in the duty of guarantee as father, authority, author, or holder. The reply insists on refusing the collective punishment of Job, through poverty (temptation and intercession), and without (individual) guilt. *Respect his* נפש orders to respect Job's social order (even his nonexistent false divinities) as a (defective) merit of man that must be corrected and improved, not accused or destroyed.

he does not complain about the itching of his skin. As I will elaborate later, the reproach of separation is less severe than sacrifice or economic temptation; it is considered perverse only when the separation fails to fulfill obligations as a guarantor (as a father, author, or authority) or when it unfairly exploits wealth.

c) Trial of Job as Representation of Israel's History

The accusatory questions anticipate the debates with Job's three friends and Elihu. The temptation (sacrificial) is the crime of authority (unconscious responsibility), and incitement (ideal) is the sin of the servant (collective responsibility). These two perspectives converge in Job as an individual, wearing two disguises; a successive narrative in which violence submits to servitude and the servant, in turn, institutionalizes violence.

Satan personifies Job's dogma of sacrifice and submission and allegorizes the former sacerdotal and prophetic trend in historical Judaism. The violent conquest of the land (First Temple) and the conquest by affective submission (Second Temple) might represent the two hearings of Satan in heaven. Satan conquers ephemerally Canaan and Persia and subdues divinities and foreign kings with his strenuous virtue (sanguinary sacrifice), which the book of Job pretends to explain, as guilt has a personal (and not eschatological or collective) origin.[6]

---

6. Job disguises himself as an authority or servant to inherit or leverage prosperity by violence or submission. He abuses the wealth, even if not for his benefit: *Have you not given to him?* Or preaches the virtue of renunciation: *You will see how he denies you to your face,* which attributes to divinity a defective creation or to men a wrongful intention. Job imagines a social order founded on accusation of authority (violent sacrifice) or abusive silence (patient submission). In both profiles, Job offers himself as a divine servant and abuses servitude.

VIII.

The Foundation of a Separated Social Order

8.1 AWAKENING FROM A DREAM

a) The Rake and the Ashes: Allegory of Collective Accusation

Job takes a rake [חרש] to scratch himself with it and sits in the ashes (2:8). After the double unmasking of Satan (the foolishness of violence and the falseness of submission), Job awakens from his dogmatic dream into despair, pathetic isolation, and poverty. We witness a change of scene and Job's awakening to the dramatic reality of his supposed divine inspiration.

The allegory of the rake and the ashes summarizes Satan's accusations in heaven, referring to sacrifice and submission as the two identities of Satan. Scratching himself with a rake could be read as an allegory of a collective accusation (violence and temptation); sitting in the ashes ironizes and reiterates his pretended innocence (submission and separation). Job invents Satan (rake, collective accusation) and supposes that the divinity has delivered him into exile (ashes, unjust punishment).

Job awakens from a sacrificial idealism to an intimate narrative about suffering divine injustice, scorned by his wife and persecuted by his three friends. *Sitting in the ashes* mocks the vain response to his wife and his silence regarding Elihu's accusation (isolation). Fatuously (from the ashes), he feels like a saving hero, unjustly mistreated by pretentious friends, a crosspatch wife, and a lazy divinity. *Sitting in the ashes* could illustrate the patient and vain servant who consents to his servitude and trusts that the divinity or their contradictions will destroy the (invented) foreign divinities and (supposedly) corrupted kings.

b) Rationalization of Exile

The rake and the ashes represent the first step in the discovery of monotheism: to institutionalize divine authority while neglecting personal freedom and equality as manifestations of the divine image in humanity.

Rake and ashes are an allegory of Job's repentance from his doctrinal past of violence and submission. Job scratches himself (asking for an explanation) and wakes up (in Greece), deceived (ashes) by his deceptive imagination. The (aggressive) rebellion against the divinities of Canaan and the kings of Persia results in Job's torture and isolation (the invention and punishment of an accusatory and separated Satan). This image of Job—docile, patient, yet vain—represents a servant who consents to his (own) servitude, hoping the divine contradictions will destroy foreign deities and corrupted kings. He accuses divinity of evil while benefiting from the earth's order, revealing the contradiction between his monotheism and messianism.

The rake and the ashes allegorize Job's doctrinal and dogmatic past. The rake and the ashes are signs of an authority and an organization determined (doomed) by his violent and submissive origins. The rake symbolizes the first Satan (authority), and the ashes represent the second Satan (an organization). It seems plausible to interpret the rake and the ashes as Job's dissociative syndrome, a contradiction between Job's ideal (sacrifice and submission) and his crude reality (servitude). His conduct is foolish (scratching), and his end is barren (ashes). Job naively sees himself as the protagonist of an eschatological conflict between good and evil, and brandishing a rake or trident, he patiently waits in ashes for a divine victory over evil. *Scratching himself* with a rake satirizes Job's collective accusation, and the ashes refer to his submission to an evil that, supposedly, divinity employs to purify him.

c) Oneiric Image as Self-Definition

Job defines his ethics according to the divinity he imagines. He conceives a bloodthirsty divinity to conceal his violence and a submissive authority because he is false. To base social order on supposed divine inspiration and not on justice, means abuse of divinity and deception of man (servitude), participating in or concealing violence (the ashes).

The rake and the ashes might represent the three friends and Elihu as reflections of Job's past and present. The rake refers to the three friends who institute authority in their land with violent sacrifice and will end up scratching themselves in the ashes of servitude. The rake personifies a trident: the violent, the servant, and the isolated tyrant. The ashes embody Elihu's confession and Job's despair in exile. Job confesses collective guilt without understanding what he confesses, and signs a blank check that ruins him as a serf, persecuted and abandoned by his divinity.

Job protests against divine justice by inventing Satan (40:8). Employing a disguise of authority or serf, Job asserts his messianic idealism and evades his social accountability (as the responsible or warrantor of his family, serfs, and state). It is not in heaven that Satan rebels and accuses, but he accuses himself on earth, destroying his social identity. The rake and ashes illustrate that outer reality reflects inner conflict: by accusing humanity in heaven, Job is ultimately condemning himself on earth.

8.2 ROLE OF JOB'S WIFE IN JOB'S AWAKENING

a) Religious Tradition on Job's Wife

Three different traditions interpret the role of Job's wife. Jewish tradition portrays her as a helper and supporter. Her words show virtue and loyalty to her husband, whose suffering and agony she shares. In the Muslim tradition, though Satan deceives her, she ultimately aids Job and becomes the instrument of his redemption after his confession. Patristic and scholastic traditions, presupposing an original sin, see the woman as an agent of Satan. The traditional Christian interpretation supposes that she curses Job. Augustine of Hippo, Gregory the Great, and Thomas Aquinas maintain that Satan uses the woman to tempt Job.

A psychoanalytic interpretation assimilates the woman to chaos. Job faces the dark shadow of the feminine element of his psyche, which, like the divine experience, means facing the illogical and paradoxical. It is not an intellectual discovery that leads us to assume the hidden shadow of the self, but the encounter with the feminine and the divine as the personification of the collective unconsciousness. The beauty of his daughters and the exaltation of music (feeling) and dance (ritual) will later show Job's merit in protecting the feminine identity.

The modern and most common interpretations tend to vindicate Job's wife. She remains with Job despite the catastrophic loss of land, children, and dignity. She identifies herself with Job's fate, embodying the spirit of his household in exile and symbolizing the foundation of a separated yet coherent social order.

b) Reproach of Idealism and Isolation

After awakening from his dogmatic dream, Job's wife speaks to him while *sitting in the ashes*. There is no ritual presentation of Job's wife as there will be of the three friends. The narrative describes her as his wife.

The feminine presence in the prologue illustrates Job's development of an ethic of marriage and social responsibility. The dialogue with his wife portrays Job's merit in tilling his property in Uz and establishing a family (respecting marital freedom). He dialogues with his wife (overcoming sacrificial dogma) but shows an authoritarian attitude and limited respect for her freedom (establishing servitude).

Job's consort represents an awakening from idealism, the shift toward a collective identity through personal merit and not through submission to the divinities, building a marriage on personal labor and freedom (marital freedom). The wife asks, *Do you still hold fast to your integrity?* (2:9), and challenges Job's adherence to sacrificial dogma, particularly concerning life and sexuality. *Holding fast to his virtue* refers to the sterility of submission and the criticism of the dogmatic confession of guilt. Job imagines a nonexistent divinity who preaches poverty and isolation (renunciation and temptation). *Your integrity* denounces his separation, committed to paying a nonexistent collective debt (idealism, all debts are personal), and falling into insolvency (Job speaks foolishly).

There is a clear analogy between the divine reproach to Satan (Job in disguise) in the opening of the second hearing in heaven (2:3) for persisting in his (stingy) virtue (עדנו מחזיק בתמתו) and the feminine reproach (2:9) for persisting in his integrity (עדנו מחזיק בתמתך). The wife's allegation foreshadows the first theophany, as she promotes building a house in the desert amid the spiritual wilderness imposed by violent, foreign authority. She teaches Job to assume a family and social responsibility and offers a response to Job's complaints against divinity. Marriage signifies a relationship with divinity and authority. The feminine (family and social) ethic means the preeminence of personal freedom, merit, and responsibility over Job's collective dreams of violent and submissive redemption.[1]

c) Rebuke of Job's Persisting Anger

Bless the Lord and die (2:9) must be interpreted as a critique of Job's sacrificial and submissive dogmatism, not as a literal curse. This text echoes the divine rebuke of Job's anger in the second theophany (*Would you discredit my justice?* [40:8]). Job does not learn from the punishment and persists in criticizing the arbitrary divinity and offering himself as a servant instead of building his house through his work and hospitality. It has a clear analogy with the divine interpellation after the first theophany. *Will you continue to rebel against the Almighty?* (40:2) reproaches Job for persisting in an attenuated dogma of submission (messianism). She unveils Job's anger and criticizes his view of the divine as a flawed Creator—thus, in effect, cursing creation.

This is an expression analogous to the threatening second accusation of Satan: *You will see how he blesses you* (2:5). Similar to the book's conclusion, Job is blessed but dies (42:12–17). Job's wife denounces the foolish violence of authority and the false submission of the servant, which hides anger in Job's supposed divine inspiration. She points out that divinity does not bless unjust violence and submission since our fatigue adds nothing to the enrichment of divine blessing: *The blessing of the Lord brings wealth, without painful toil for it* (Prov 10:22).

---

1. Job's wife signifies Job's conscience of the inaccuracy of his accusations of (foreign) men in heaven. His wife unveils to Job that patient submission and separation mean anger and tempt divine justice. The woman spurs Job to build a coherent social order and does not curse him. Divinity blesses building a coherent social order (which the woman and the children represent). She sums up for Job the content of the two theophanies: the blessing from the Lord (not the blessing to the Lord) defines the origin of man on earth (first theophany), and the fight against evil by the construction of a coherent social order (not supposed divine authority), builds life (prevents death) (second theophany). Job's anger condemns justice (40:8). In a free translation, in analogy with the first theophany, she says to Job (2:9): *Wake up, you idiot, where were you when divinity founded the Earth? Will those meaningless words* (confession) *give you life? Squeeze your kidneys like a man.* Integrity goes beyond discipline and purity, referring to building a community (family and social realm) and being a part of it (paying debts in their hierarchy). The woman fulfills the same function as Peninnah for Hannah: she teaches Job to overcome his idealistic violence and sterility (sacrifice and submission).

Her demand for Job to assume social responsibility challenges his complaint that God permits evil. The woman chooses Job individually and values him personally; in a defective society of violent origins, she establishes a separate but coherent social order. The wife's accusatory questions promote establishing a house, protecting the innocents (their children), and overcoming the violent condemnation of evil or passive submission to divinity. Job receives a wife when, in monotheism, he overcomes Satan's two accusations in heaven and builds a society on personal freedom. Her critique offers a rational expression of what Job had only vaguely intuited, pushing him to reconsider his social role and responsibility.

8.3 JOB'S RESPONSE TO HIS WIFE

a) Job's Replies Prefigure His Responses to the Theophanies

And he said to her (2:10). Job employs an authoritarian expression similar to divinity when addressing Satan. Although Job has built a house in Uz, his wife remains unnamed, suggesting a symbolic anonymity or subordination. He fails to engage with her argument and instead commands her, treating her as an inferior.

There is an analogy between Job's answers to his wife and his responses to the theophanies. Job's intemperate words express his anger and collective accusation, for he judges her feminine condition (collective accusation), not her actions. Still, he accuses her of tolerating and concealing evil, nevertheless attenuating his imputation and exonerating her of causing the collective disorder.

b) Alleged Falsehood (נבלה) of the Woman

You talk as a disgraceful woman (2:10). The narrative explains that unconditional submission to divinity means an accusation against family life and lineage (*nebelah*). Here, *nebelah*—often translated as "disgrace" or "folly"—symbolizes a collective accusation. Job's use of it implies condemnation not of an act or negligence but of his wife's nature. He demeans her, which reflects his unresolved anger (see also 40:8). Despite this affront, the debate with his wife and his answers to the three friends credit Job's right intention (42:7–8), preluding his final blessing.

Job's rebuke lacks specific accusation; he suggests she has been seduced by the prosperity and pleasures of foreign deities and has submitted to their hidden violence (paralleling Satan's two claims). Ultimately, *nebelah* is linked to an incorrect understanding of divinity (42:7–8), reflecting Job's error: attributing divine complicity in tolerating evil as a form of purification. Job's relationship with his wife reproduces his relationship with the foreign peoples and divinities, as she represents the foreigner, doomed to be a servant of Job's virtue. Job sees divinity and his wife as his servants.

c) Job's Accusatory Dogmatic

Shall we accept the good from divinity and not evil? (2:10). Job conceives evil as a personal or collective being, not a personal and social limitation. Job justifies the rebuke of his wife by accusing foreign deities and societies of evil (a collective accusation), and submits to evil as coming from divinity (at least as tolerance or concealment). He still conceives guilt as a collective and social disorder that only renunciation and intercession redeem.

Job does not recognize merit in the history of a (foreign) social order (in his wife); he thinks of an exclusive masculine tradition (of renunciation and intercession) and a feminine (collective) servitude. He supposes that good in women will prevail over evil (in a messianic future) and abandons the dogma of the sacrifice (of Esther) but builds a new ethic of temptation, accepting the good from divinity, and separation, suffering evil from a foreign divinity (*dust and ashes*).

Job's answers do not assume that evil has no substance, cannot collectively institutionalize, and cannot come generically from his wife. His error lies in assuming evil can be institutionalized or personified, and that it can be countered by virtue alone through separation. He conceives of a creation founded on punishment, submission, and violent redemption, assuming the dogma of purifying submission based on confession (*I know, you can do everything* [42:2]).

Through his interaction with his wife, Job's understanding of divinity begins to evolve. The dialogue sets the stage for the book's eventual conclusion: the immorality of Job's initial accusation (sacrifice) and confession (submission). Divine innocence is incompatible with tolerated evil or inherited guilt. Job must confront both the unconscious roots of personal guilt and the limitations of attributing responsibility to collective disorder.

d) Nuanced Praise of Job

As I have mentioned, the first summary judgment of Job concludes with limited praise: *In all this, Job did not sin by attributing his fall to the Lord* (1:23). The text changes subtly in the second summary judgment (after his wife's rebuke): *In all this, Job did not sin with his lips* (2:10). I think that not to *sin with his lips* refers to his right intention, but *in all this* underlines his defective means (submission and contempt), as he did not revoke his formal confession. Job's harsh treatment of his wife implies a sin of the heart: an internalized collective accusation stemming from omission. By attributing evil to divine concealment or tolerance, and by holding his wife responsible, Job indirectly blames God (and her wife) for his downfall.

His wife talks to him. In his reply, Job *does not sin with his lips* but does not reveal the secret mystery of foreign divinities (that do not exist). He attributes divine tolerance or concealment of evil (spiritual sin), and he does *impute his fall to the Lord* (by accusing his wife as a collective accusation). He persists in affirming his innocence, considers his punishment unjust, and attributes the collective disorder to his origins without recognizing any formal merit in his parents and authority. Nevertheless, he will be blessed because, step by step, he will assume his family and social debts.

The narrative values the new dogma of submission and intercession. *He did not sin with his lips*, which means he did not abuse the earth (does not attribute to Job unconscious responsibility). Job spoke as a sign of hospitality, but not justly or wisely (*he did not sin with his lips*). Language means a social realm; he did not sin, but he did not speak wisely, as he did not unveil the nonexistent foreign deities. Job did not respond to his wife's accusatory questions, as he would not answer correctly to the two divine interpolations in the theophanies. He did not sin with his lips because he did not confess (as Elihu did); however, he did persist in his illusory exaggeration of guilt (the accusation in heaven) because he did not revoke his limited confession.

IX.

The Dogmatic of Authority

9.1 THREE FRIENDS' AUTHORITY

a) Rabbinic Tradition

Who are the friends who come to accompany and console Job? Rabbinic tradition interprets the three friends as foreign princes who respect Israel in exile if it complies with the law and testify that the Jewish people fulfill the Torah (Avodah Zarah 3a, 9). The gathering of the gentiles will bear witness to the Jewish people (in a messianic future) and will attest to their righteousness.

Eliphaz and his friends do not identify guilt as a cause for punishment, deny Job the right to rebel against a supposed divine will, and condemn human nature. Rabbinic tradition takes into account Gen 36:12 and considers Eliphaz father of Amalek, persecutor of Israel. Eliphaz's concubine, Timna, was not admitted as a proselyte, and this explains Amalek's persecution; Sanhedrin 99 b attributes Job's lack of hospitality to the rootless foreigner.

The three friends came to accompany and comfort Job. They represent the effort to find and justify religious tolerance as a consolation to serfdom. They elude divine condemnation. The Spirit shines on them, and Job prays for them (Qoheleth Rabbah 7:2–4).[1]

---

1. In my interpretation of the rabbinic tradition, the debate with the friends presents Job as a man justly exiled because he has abused the land and did not responsibly

b) Three Friends as Individual Virtue (Maimonides)

The suffering of the righteous due to collective sin is an incessantly discussed problem in medieval Islam. Maimonides explains the debate with the three friends as a nuclear discussion on (collective) guilt.

According to Maimonides, the book of Job seeks to overcome (with the notion of divine Providence) *old* opinions about suffering as a collective doom: justice, wisdom, and the unfathomable divine will, which the three friends personify. Eliphaz represents the traditional (sacrificial) religious position that attributes suffering to sin (Maimonides quotes Job 22:5). Bildad personifies the Kalam Mutazilite, who maintains that man suffers to gain merit and ascend in wisdom (to make him worthy of a reward [8:6–7]); and Zophar symbolizes the Kalam Al Ashari, who conceives an unintelligible divinity and maintains a predestinarian position (11:5–7).

It is plausible to conclude that Maimonides, rooted in rabbinic traditions, sees Job as a representation of the people of Israel guided by Providence and the three friends as a personification of the peoples among whom Israel lives in exile. According to Maimonides, the axis of the debate between Job and his friends is not on sin and the justification of suffering, which presupposes the existence of Satan and the divine tolerance of evil, but on the sense and meaning of Providence, as supreme wisdom of the revealed law (*Guide of the Perplexed* 26.3). The three friends are steps in Job's moral elevation, overcoming the material essence of egoism. Maimonides identifies Israel with Elihu, who personifies moral purity and spiritual elevation (illumination) by (hearing and complying) the divine word. In contrast to an authoritarian religious dogma, Maimonides identifies revelation with a personal ascent in virtue. People do not exist as the reality of divinity but as the imperfection of their laws, which Israel redeems with collective revelation as the testimony of individual virtue in interpreting and living the law.

The uniqueness of Israel does not lie in its submission to divinity but in its service to the law as the reality of wisdom (since Satan does not exist but rather signifies a lack of merit and wisdom). The people of Israel, chosen after accepting to become witnesses to the divine word, experience the reality of the revelation (Providence). Job experiences the work of Providence as he ascends the moral ladder. Providence gives sense to

---

build his house, land, and justice. Satan, the accuser (who leaves the presence of the Lord), refers to Job himself exiled for unjustly accusing men.

history and makes freedom compatible with personal merit because revelation enables solving the contradiction between individual and collective identity in man. Israel accepts fulfilling the law; this does not imply the blind acceptance of a mandate, but rather the study and teaching of its purpose in building a social order.

Providence carries out the divine will through individual and moral perfection. Maimonides comments in ch. 5, *they saw the Lord of Israel under their feet*, as a critic of the three friends' authoritarian dogmatic; he affirms that moral virtues are the basis of rational aptitudes and revelation of the laws (*Guide of the Perplexed* 33). He denies collective judgment and seems to conceive sin as imperfection or error, not as rebellion or collective condemnation. He develops the same idea in ch. 17, where he states that Providence watches over individuals in particular: *Providence contemplates all their steps* (Job 34:21), and the Providence of the species is proper to animals (defined by their origin, as they lack free will). In his interpretation of the book of Job, in defense of free will, Maimonides contradicts Aristotle's negation of Providence with an individual human being, a fundamental error of philosophical and theological thought of medieval Islam, which Maimonides interprets as a collective doom and denial of free will.

c) Three Friends as Irrationality of Individuality (Kant)

Kant uses another terminology but, as Maimonides, seeks the foundation of the social order in the (coactive) law, denying the coherence of Satan and the legitimacy of temptation.[2] The three friends do not fully understand that the divine will and word are unfathomable, and they judge a priori. They appeal to divinity to justify their authority and resolve practical justice, as they put their particular interests before the general interest of the law.

The law governs the social order with a practical reason as a collective morality, not based on particular interests. The fundamental difference between Job and his friends lies in his authenticity (*Aufrichtigkeit*). His friends represent the state of nature, and Job the transition to rationality and universality of the law, which coordinates and overcomes particular interests.

Job conceives a (coactive) law founded on rationality and justice as the principle of practical morality. The three friends interpret laws as

2. Kant, *Contienda*, 18.

ideal realities that benefit them, and they do not assume rational principles to build a coherent society. The hypocrisy of the three friends confronts collective justice because they do not rationally discern between good and evil. *Will you defend divinity unjustly?* (Job 13:7–11). Ethics must prevail over a critical reason based on idealistic principles. Friends accuse divinity of evil by claiming to detent a divine representation; they invent Satan and lack practical morality. Since the will and submission to power (coactivity) constitute the only morality they understand, the three friends justify the means to the end (justify temptation and irrational violence).

9.2 COLLECTIVE SIN AS JUSTIFICATION OF AN ORGANIZATION

a) Gregory the Great, Friends as Unjust Authority

Gregory the Great presents the three friends as the secular world; Job lives a religious experience of faith that symbolizes the church.[3]

Job, the hero of faith, confronts the three friends, who represent the proud egoism of power and prosperity. Job is condemned a priori by the original sin, redeemed from collective sin by divine incarnation. A patient Job finds himself in an unjust world (the friends), confesses his sin, and is redeemed from collective guilt by divine grace. The divine presence in history realizes the supremacy of (religious) faith (organization) over egoism (the individual).

Gregory the Great interprets the debate between the friends and Job as the violent conflict between the material world of pride, lust, and greed (of the three friends), confronted with the search for divinity and repentance. The friends explain suffering as punishment. To consider wealth and power as a reward for merit (of violent sacrifice) constitutes the error of the friends, defenders of the theory of retribution. According to Gregory the Great, the friends believe that Job suffers for his sin, but Job denounces their pride and gains merit through suffering, progressing in detachment. By accepting the injustice of the world and renouncing the world, Job ascends in virtue and contemplates the authentic wisdom of the divine work.

---

3. Schreiner, *Where Shall Wisdom Be Found?*, 43–45; Cabello, "Libro de Job," 27n129.

The three friends are fools. They did not know the meaning of affliction. They thought that Job suffered because of his sins, and they tried to prove that God had been just in afflicting him, not knowing that suffering praises divine glory, increases merit, and does not punish sins that Job never committed. Nevertheless, the three friends quickly obtained forgiveness because they sinned more through ignorance than malice.

b) Thomas Aquinas, Defense of Free Will

Thomas Aquinas, the father of systematic theology, represents the transition from the authoritarian church to an organized and hierarchical church built on the doctrine of sacraments, the assessment of individual salvation, and the value of free will.[4]

The three friends live in a material world where the reward of merit and punishment of the wicked have no meaning. They face the contradiction of conceiving an unjust divinity. The friends ponder only the deceptive material reward and are unaware of salvation in eternal life. The dialogue with the friends shows divine Providence inspiring Job as human wisdom and Providence walk hand in hand as stages in revelation.

Thomas Aquinas limits the power of Satan to a temporal world. Sin corrupts the material being but not the spiritual being of man, redeemed and guarded by Providence. He conceives the church as the history of salvation from sin, which reproduces the singular judgment of man, condemned at his origin. He presupposes the existence of Satan in an eschatological conflict between good and evil, which every man reproduces. Given the power of Behemoth and Leviathan, man cannot claim to overcome evil with his strength. Retribution of merit and guilt does not have meaning on earth, as only an immortal soul can explain it.

c) Calvin, Building Tradition

Calvin did not write a systematic commentary on the book of Job, as he did on many other books of the Bible; however, he preached 159 sermons

---

4. Schreiner, *Where Shall Wisdom Be Found?*, 72; Cabello, "Libro de Job," 39–41. Yaffe posits in Thomas Aquinas the supremacy of moral perfection over intellectual rationality, corrupted by sin; while Maimonides considers that through wisdom, moral perfection allows one to achieve intellectual perfection (Yaffe, "Providence in Medieval Aristotelianism," 65–66).

on Job during six months in 1554–55. His sermons provide an exegetical commentary that systematically approaches the numerous references to Job in his *Institutions of the Christian Religion* and *Commentary on the Book of Psalms*.

Evil has been deleted before the beginning of time to manifest divine glory. Even if Calvin does not question the figure of Satan, prince of the world, the accuser loses a leading role in justifying the incarnation and explains the church as preaching and intercession (Elihu), not as a fight against evil through suffering and temptation. Calvin presents Satan as the servant of divinity in the judgment of the individual man, and suffering teaches man to confess and be saved by faith.[5]

In his first sermon on the first chapter of the book of Job, he explains the meaning of suffering and reinterprets sacrificial dogma. Far from identifying suffering as a privilege, a test, or a temptation, he views suffering as a teaching. Due to original sin, the three friends do not want to listen to the divine word and see suffering and servitude as the reality of sin. There is no contradiction or injustice in individual suffering, but rather the very essence of Providence. Justice carries out the divine will, identified with divine law, which gives meaning to history and the transcendent justice of punishment and retribution. The transcendence of the divine will, the confrontation of social disorder with a rebellious man (Job), realizes history itself as law (predestination), which the church concretizes and teaches, and man cannot understand in his immanence.

Calvin explains the dispute between Job and his friends as a debate about Providence and immortality. The three friends identify sin with suffering; they do not understand its unintelligible meaning, not a punishment or tolerance of evil. Suffering leads to acceptance of divine will, teaches wisdom and divine justice, and enables the salvation of a rebellious nature. Even though man does not want to listen, the immutable divine law guarantees his freedom and intends his salvation. The friends have no conscience of a soul and his final judgment; they do not understand justice in the spiritual realm, the resurrection as a reality of the Reformed Church, where history glorifies divinity as reality, founded on man and his judgment. Christ takes on himself the evil of the world and provides man with the means for salvation despite his rebellion.

---

5. Calvino, *Calvino sermones sobre Job*, 18–21, sermon 1.

9.3 THREE FRIENDS' ARRIVAL AT THE COUNCIL OF HEAVEN

a) Three Friends Personify Sacrificial History of Job

Job's debate with his three friends summarizes his allegations against divine justice and illustrates his gradual overcoming of sacrificial dogma. The dialogue of Job with the three friends explores the origin, evolution, and incoherence of authority founded on sacrifice or submission, allegorizing Israel's tragic history.

The three friends justify authority (and servitude) in sacrifice or submission to the supposed divine service. The three friends personify the three modes of sacrifice: life, sexuality, and prosperity. The three friends imagine a narcissistic divinity who grants them prosperity and authority as a reward for their virtue (sacrifice or submission). *There were three friends, and they heard all the evil that befell Job* (2:11). They resume Job's sacrificial history (Canaan, Persia, and Greece). The ensuing dialogue deconstructs Job's dogmatic past, challenging priestly and prophetic models of religious thought.

The friends hear Job's exculpatory arguments—parallel to Satan's accusations—criticizing a history in which human suffering is idealized as merit; and, as a result, they acknowledge evil in humanity (thus exculpating divinity) and ultimately recognize Job's righteousness (32:1). Through the dialogue, Job teaches them a less dogmatic vision of authority and tradition—one that affirms economic, marital, and religious freedom. *They heard* manifests the praise of the three friends because they overcome the tendency to attribute the origin of evil to a supposed rebellious angel; it also means a reproach, as they fail to acknowledge individual guilt and responsibility, and to free the oppressed.

b) The Friends Justify Servitude

In conclusion to the dialogues, the three friends will find Job just in their eyes (32:1) (they will institute religious freedom). They will overcome sacrifice (of life, sexuality, and prosperity), and divinity weighs their efforts and blesses them for having listened to Job's arguments (42:7–9).

They came together seems to allude to their meeting in the council of heaven (as sons of Elohim). They renounce sacrificial authority and instead seek to build a more coherent social order to legitimize their own rule. The friends *console and accompany* Job; they respect his property and family (establish their authority on the social and religious autonomy of the serfs).

Each of the three men went out of his place, which hints at the three men repenting from violence without achieving a coherent social realm. *Each of them* refers to the historicity of Job's doctrine. The three friends *went out*, a phrase that explains the gradual transition from the dogma of sacrifice to submission. *Going out* of their place symbolizes overcoming Satan (sacrifice) without freeing Job from servitude and without instituting a coherent marriage. The friends will attribute punishment not to divine will but to collective guilt stemming from the abuses of Job's ancestors. They interpret Job's servitude as a form of divine justice.

c) They Do Not Discern the Causes of Social Disaster

The friends *lifted their eyes from afar but did not recognize him* (2:12). They debated in idealism without understanding the personal basis of collective guilt. *They hear* the arguments (against sacrificial dogma) but are far from discerning the deep causes of social disaster (which Job had not adequately rationalized either). They *lifted their eyes*, meaning they accepted monotheism but did not recognize Job as free and equal. They fail to construct an ethic grounded in dignity and freedom, and they accuse Job of collective guilt. *From afar*, it refers to the desert, like Moses, who did not enter the land of Israel. *They did not recognize him* as equal and instituted Job's servitude.

They lifted their voice and wept (2:12). *They lifted their eyes*, referring to Eliphaz, who ponders Job as a servant; they *shouted*, alluding to Zophar, who built an aristocratic sexual morality of servants and lords. They *wept* (the three friends) and *sat in silence* when they failed to organize a coherent society (justice) and blamed divinity for tolerating and concealing the collective disorder (assuming Bildad's predestination doctrine). The three friends will mourn the doom of their kingdom.

The debate between Job and his friends tracks the historical development of a theory of guilt and responsibility. Divine wrath arises against sacrifice as a collective punishment that chastises the innocent and does not retribute personal guilt and responsibility. A second reproach accuses the three friends for submitting Job as a servant, which also means a punishment without guilt. The epilogue will affirm the principle of personal guilt and responsibility (as human identity created in divine image and likeness) and despise the three friends *for not speaking correctly about me, like the servant Job*. In my opinion, the epilogue depicts that the violent man (Eliphaz) necessarily ends up submitting to his servant (to the plate of lentils, with which Job feeds him); it also explains that the servants (Bildad, Zophar, and Job) end up equally destroyed by the violence of submission, which causes sterility and the decomposition of the social order.

9.4 JOB'S AFFIRMED INNOCENCE AS A COLLECTIVE ACCUSATION

a) Abuse of Divinity

The friends *tore their garments and threw dust into heaven* (2:12). Job's arguments force them to improve their social organization and soften their (sacrificial) violence. *To tear their garments* refers to renouncing personal authority (sacrificial dogmatics). The three friends evolve, grounding their legitimacy on a social order that respects life, marital freedom, and property; still, they abuse divinity by justifying servitude in the supposed sins of their servants.

The friends threw dust into heaven, and the three friends manifest their foolishness by basing their authority not on justice but on the invocation of divine inspiration. Job also accuses the divinity of concealing or tolerating evil, concluding that he must accept a servitude that purifies him.

b) Silence Justifies Servitude

Job and his friends were *silent for seven days and seven nights* (2:13). Language means a social order; silence alludes to the sterility of submission and solitude that institutes serfdom. Job's friends were unsuccessful in constructing a coherent social order.

Silence is also an allegory of Job abusing divinity by affirming innocence. The narrative underlines the seven days of silence, each of the seven nights of Job's anguish and despair (mourning for the loss of his children and farm). The three friends deceive themselves by identifying their authority with divine favor, and Job also deceives himself by blaming his servitude on divine unjust punishment (*they keep silent*). The three friends' silence abuses prosperity (an abuse of the earth), and Job's silence submits to evil (an abuse of heaven).

Job renews the council of heaven by silently accusing divinity in the presence of the great inquisitor. The eschatological struggle between Satan and divinity in the court of heaven evolves into an alternative cunning vision of an immoral divinity triumphing over evil by choosing the righteous for silent suffering. The debate between the friends and Job represents the overcoming of sacrifice but falls into the sterility (silence) of an alternative servitude justified in a supposed collective guilt.

c) Coherent Institution of Social Order

The debate between Job and his friends constitutes the core of the book of Job, an allegory of sacrifice and submission as similar paths to institute servitude (assume collective evil). Job's silence (confession) incurs a commission by omission (of the due fight against evil). Affirming innocence without assuming responsibility (not guilt) for the collective disorder (in defense of innocents), Job blames divinity for tolerating or concealing evil (breaking tradition).

The friends correctly contradict Job's innocence because pretending innocence means denying responsibility for the collective disorder and accusing divinity of tolerating and concealing evil. Job's silence suggests in both scenarios, as authority or servant, that Job's affirmation of innocence means an accusation against divinity (creates an imaginary and accusatory Satan).

The friends' silence stands in contrast to his wife's rebuke, which functions as an allegory of divine interpellation—the dramatic turning point in the first theophany. His three friends and Elihu allegorize the sons of Elohim in the council of heaven and the need to institute a coherent social order, one grounded not in collective guilt but in personal responsibility to overcome foreign disorder.[6]

6. Elihu will show the incoherence of the debate, and the theophanies will conclude that Job must look to himself in the foreign lands (peoples, kings, and divinities) and see in them the responsibility (not the guilt) for his violent past, pretending to represent divinity. Instead of fighting against himself (tempting and separating from a foreign authority), he must elude a new exile by assuming a duty of guarantee to the foreign land, acknowledging Providence in his tragic uprooting, and recognizing the incoherent sacrifice and submission that led him to exile. The theophanies will develop in detail that Job's (unconscious and collective) responsibility does not mean the duty to assume

collective disorder unconditionally, because unconscious and collective guilt and responsibility are delimited cases of extended personal liability (for unjust enrichment or damages or injuries due to negligence or breach of a warranty duty as a father or authority). The authenticity of Job (*go to the servant Job*), who speaks with righteousness (42:7–8) but does not act with righteousness, refers to ceasing bloody sacrifice (response to the first theophany) and, by separation, renouncing the bloodless sacrifice of prosperity (response to the second theophany). Sacrifice kindles divine rage, and Job is praised and blessed for overcoming sacrifice in his answer to the second theophany.

FIRST ACT

The Debate with the Three Friends

X.

Job Curses His Day

10.1 JOB LAMENTS DIVINE HEDGE

a) Job's Despair

Job's laments mark a turning point in the rejection of violent sacrifice in its three modalities: life, sexuality, and prosperity. Job wakes up in exile (the ethic of suffering), and shows remorse for his accusatory past against foreign deities, the foreign social realm, and his destiny.

Three parts divide the laments and prefigure the three sessions of the dialogues: the imprecation against day and night (original guilt), against the social order (collective guilt), and the lack of hope after his unfathomable guilt and his inexplicable punishment and servitude, supposedly tolerated by the divinity (unconscious guilt). Job imagines a defective creation (*curses his day and social identity*) that he must repair by suffering (*curses creation*). Surprisingly, the narrator has previously explained that he did not curse divinity or creation because *he neither accused divinity* (1:23) nor *sinned with his lips* (2:10).

The narrative appears to mock Job's protests: in the past, Job had countless servants, but now, he dares to accuse divinity of tolerating and concealing his servitude and submitting him to foreign deities, peoples, and kings. *Now, when it comes to you, you weary; it touches you, and you are frightened* (4:5). *Who was innocent that perished?* (4:7)

b) Job Protests Divine Servitude

Job proclaims his innocence and shows contempt for the foreign kingdoms in exile as a reality of religious violence, yet he does not rebel. He laments (suffers) but trusts in Providence. The central argument criticizes the authority—human and divine—that imposes slavery (עמל) and servitude (מרע נפש), from which only death (3:18)—divine will—frees the servant of his master.

Placed systematically after showing Job's faithfulness to his wife and his submission to foreign authority (receiving the three friends and debating with them), Job's laments, strikingly, do not focus on the death of his children, his wife's betrayal, or his material losses. What does Job curse? Plausibly, the laments repudiate his past marked by violence, which led to servitude and divine abandonment, as an intuition of the unjust means of his former priestly and prophetic doctrines, which once sought to combat collective evil through violence and submission.

c) Job Demands an Explanation

Why did the Lord give him light and life? (3:19). He criticizes the Lord, who hides everything from him, asking for an explanation (3:11). Job argues that it is an injustice to create a man from whom divinity hides the path and raises a hedge around him (3:23).

As in the prologue, the narrative of the dialogues will praise his right intention (speaking), as he seeks an explanation without (directly) accusing the divinity, in his despair (1:23), without sinning (consciously) with the lips (2:10). Although the narrator criticizes the intemperance of his language (*opening his mouth*), his protests search a path to rationalize his tragic destiny and assume that his conduct (sacrificial and submissive dogmatic) might have subjected him to worldly tyrannies (3:26).

Job's laments reveal a key insight into a doctrinal contradiction. In the dialogue with the friends Job will repeat the reasoning of the laments: he has not committed a misdeed, and divinity tolerates and hides evil, *not lifting the black fog that surrounds him* (23:17). Job insistently demands explanations, particularly in the first cycle of dialogues (6:24; 7:20; 9:12–22; 10:14; 12:6; 13:23; 23:17; 30:20) and when he discusses Providence in ch. 23. In his despair, Job does not curse creation (1:23) (as the kingdom of Satan) but laments his defective social identity (2:10). He alleges his uprightness of intention and does not deny his (possible) guilt (7:17–21; 9:15, 20–21).

He willingly faces the divinity's wrath, assumes its consequences (13:13–18), and does not exclude his ignorance or even his possible negligence; therefore, his protests might not be considered a rebellion against divine justice. He protests against punishment and servitude but respects divine and human authority and does not sin with his lips (intentionally).[1]

10.2 HISTORICITY OF JOB'S LAMENTS

a) Jeremiah Inspires Job's Protest

Job's arguments in the laments (and dialogue with his friends) seem similar to the lamentations of Jeremiah about the prosperity of the wicked (12:1–3): *You have planted them, they have taken root, and they have even produced fruit* (12:2). This hides a messianic dream of the destruction of the wicked and triumph of Job's (individual) virtue: *You see me, and you try my heart with you. Draw them out like sheep to the slaughter, and prepare them for the day of slaughter* (12:3). The entire third chapter reflects a doctrine of collective guilt and seems inspired by Jeremiah's words: *And the Lord said to me in the days of King Josiah: Have you seen what backsliding Israel has done?* (12:6). *Through the lightness of her harlotry, she polluted the land* (12:9). It hints at redemption by suffering (20:14–18): *Cursed be the day in which I was begotten; the day in which my mother bore me shall not be blessed* (20:14).

However, Job's laments should not be seen as a repetition of Jeremiah's laments but rather as a dawn of the day of Job's restoration from the ashes. In the debate with his three friends, Job conceptualizes his prophetic past as a criticism of the biblical dogma of sacrifice. He recalls Jeremiah's complaints but goes beyond them: while Jeremiah denounces

---

1. Theophanies will explain Job's incoherence by formulating a coherent theory of unconscious and collective guilt as personal guilt and responsibility. The book teaches Job to work the land, receive a wife (first theophany), overcome servitude (second theophany), and establish a coherent social realm in a foreign land. He must build a house and elude temptation (of foreign kings) and separation (from servitude to imaginary deities). After speaking these words to Job at night, criticizing Elihu and his intercessory doctrine of collective guilt as an abuse of divinity, reality will explain to Eliphaz and his two cronies (42:7–8) the unconscious guilt for establishing the sacrificial and submissive dogma as an abuse of the land through violence and servitude: lacking innocence does not imply a duty of assuming collective guilt.

the people of Israel, Job questions himself. The narrative in the book of Job stages an awakening. His words must be interpreted as the beginning of the rationalization of sacrifice and submission as incoherent ways to build a social realm.

b) Laments as Counterpoint to Creation

The litanies of laments review the horrors of his past suffering, the despair at his current servitude, and the uncertainty about his future. *Job raised his voice and said* (3:2). The laments do not subdue him; on the contrary, as his wife's words, Job's protests should be seen as a desperate counterpoint to his former sacrificial and submissive dogma. The laments are not a monologue into the void; Job objectifies his dogmatic past as rational arguments within a historical discussion on personal responsibility.

He has an intuition that the collective accusation against a man (authority) is an accusation against divinity, who did not close the doors of his mother's womb and did not hide suffering from his eyes (3:10). Job evokes in his laments the protest of a solitary rebel, disappointed because his former kingdom is in ruins (3:14), subjected to an arbitrary destiny (3:19) despite his efforts (3:20). He underlines that it makes no sense to create a man to make him suffer (3:20), a man whose path is hidden and who is imprisoned (3:23). Punishment takes precedence over reward (3:24). The arguments hint at criticism of his former biblical accusatory dogma, which does not rescue man or the social order (3:20–26), disappointed by his past of ephemeral treasures (3:21) and a party-going divinity who deceives him (3:23) and tyrannizes him (3:26).

c) Crisis of Methodology

It is plausible to conceive Job's protests as the despair of the hardworking Job after the destruction of the Persian Empire, assuming the distressed experience of the uselessness of Esther's sexual sacrifice.

In his laments, Job rationalizes the violent (sacrificial) theology that has justified his fight for personal identity in Canaan and Persia, which has brought only misfortune upon him and the conquered peoples. The despair of the laments is not a dialogue of the deaf; on the contrary, they are arguments of a historical discussion on personal responsibility (historicity of the dialogues). As a counterpoint to Job's laments, the book of Genesis and the theophanies present a creative process determined by the divine Providence and the guarantee of men's personal labor and social identity.

The laments relate his awakening in the face of Manichaeism (the dogma of original and collective sin) and the despair in the face of Greek conquerors and their decomposition. Job intuits that to accuse divinity means that he is accusing himself in a triple dimension of guilt: personal, social, and doctrinal. Job rationalizes his social guilt in the debate with the friends, and his doctrinal responsibility in the divine critique of Elihu's doctrine. The prophetic doctrine of submission to divine inspiration (*try my heart*) will be presented in the monologue of Elihu as a reiteration of the doctrine of collective guilt, justifying the use of unjust means (pretending divine inspiration) as dogmatism that condemns the (foreign) social realm instead of defending the innocents and dependents. His laments are a first step in the critique of the doctrine of submission, as based on an attenuated sacrifice of land (temptation and separation) that condemns foreign deities and reproduces a diminished dogma of Satan (Job's disguise) accusing in heaven.[2]

---

2. The first theophany might be interpreted as a response to the laments (of ch. 3) in its very nuclear question (*Who darkens?* [38:2]), responding to the reference to darkness with which Job begins his lament (3:4–5). As in a Greek tragedy, after the debate with the friends and Elihu's monologue, deus ex machina, the divine presence on the stage, will resolve the moral dilemma of Job's laments and deny the divine persecution of Job by tolerance or concealment of evil. As an alternative to the laments, the allegories of the first theophany present creation as a hospitable home by the sea and an animal farm that receives and protects life and cleans and removes the corrupted corpses, underlining the sterility of patient submission (as a collective condemnation of foreign gods and peoples) and the personal character of merit, guilt, and responsibility. In similar terms, the nuclear question of the second theophany (*Will your anger denigrate justice?* [40:8]) answers the nuclear lament that the divinity hides everything from Job and punishes him without guilt and explanation (3:23).There is an undeniable analogy (Clines, *Job 38–42*, 1101) between Job's judgment in the Council of Heaven and the creation account in Chapter 38, which is attended by the morning stars singing and the sons of Elohim shouting for joy (38:7).

XI.

Job Confronts His Violent Past

11.1 MORAL DILEMMA OF THE DEBATE

a) Job Reiterates His Innocence After His Punishment

As previously noted, the characters in the book of Job represent Job in his past. The three friends personify Job's prosperity in Canaan, Persia, and Greece, an optimistic version of Job affirming his innocence (idealism) before Satan's accusations and punishment.

This first cycle formulates the nuclear dilemma of the entire book: his allegation of innocence and demand for an explanation. Strictly speaking, Eliphaz's first intervention and Job's first reply raise the core of the debate. Zophar and Bildad will insist on Job's guilt and justify the social realm in divine inspiration. In the second and third cycles, Job confronts a diluted but persistent violent sacrificial dogma, insists on his innocence, and reiterates the demand for an explanation.

Confronting the three friends, Job reiterates his innocence and claims that his friends neither aid the needy nor guide the lost—they do not liberate the oppressed. Repeating the doctrine of the laments, he assumes the wrath of a vengeful divinity who tolerates evil (the foreign deities and kings) to purify him from the collective sin of institutional violence. However, by submitting patiently to suffering as a form of purification, Job falls into a different version of a collective accusation—an attenuated doctrine of submission, institutionalizing servitude.

After the debate with his three friends, in his final monologue, Job ratifies the doctrine of the laments (his innocence). Job advocates respect for life, marital freedom, and the dignity of the serf; and he proposes patient submission to divine designs. He waits patiently for foreign violence to destroy itself in its contradictions and waits to inherit the messianic future that his virtue deserves. The murderer, the adulterer, and the thief personify the three sacrificial kingdoms of the three friends. He declares himself innocent—punished not for personal guilt but for humanity's inherited sin—and laments that his virtue has not spared him from divine wrath, presuming that divinity tolerates and conceals violence.

b) Friends Justify the Ethic of Sacrifice

The dialogue presents the three friends abusing prosperity and authority; and Job abusing servitude. In the dialogue with the three friends, Job confronts their violent methods and their abuse of authority, sexuality, and prosperity. He insists that his three friends uphold servitude, justify arbitrary violence, and invoke the name of the Lord in vain to legitimize their disproportionate and unjustified wealth.

However, the narrative will also criticize *the servant* Job because he intends to conquer prosperity by submissive violence and take advantage of the three friends' inexorable damnation (he abuses divinity to a private end).

It is likely that the dialogues were composed by a single author or school and arranged intentionally in their current canonical form, with coherent content and a close connection between their inner arguments and the development of the plot. Of course, the final draft might have been a canonical formalization after centuries of doctrinal debate on unconscious and collective guilt. The purpose of dialogues is to show (and later overcome) the twofold logic of a Manichaean doctrine founded in sacrifice (the three friends) and submission (Job's patience).

c) Dialogues as Critical Approach to Manichaeism

In the opening of the debate, Eliphaz expresses outrage at Job's laments: *Who was innocent that perished, and where were the upright destroyed?* (4:7), arguing that *he who sows violence and lies, perishes in them* (4:8). Eliphaz establishes a collective accusatory inference: *Man cannot be just* to *[demand justice of] the divinity* (4:17). Eliphaz presupposes the wickedness and guilt of men, of every man, denies Job's innocence, infers that Job's servitude is based on his (collective) guilt, and refuses Job an explanation, arguing that *corrupt men cannot claim justice* (4:12–21).

The narrative will conclude that the three friends correctly contradict Job's innocence, because pretending innocence means denying coherent unconscious and collective guilt (man's unconscious and collective identity). However, guilt and innocence are not strictly opposites, nor are they necessarily correlated; Job cannot claim pure innocence, but neither can the friends convincingly declare him guilty. Job's unconscious and collective guilt does not mean the duty to assume the collective disorder unconditionally, as the three friends argue, because unconscious (social) and collective (doctrinal) guilt and responsibility must be interpreted as delimited cases of extended personal liability (for unjust enrichment, damages or injuries due to negligence, or breach of a warranty duty as a father or authority).

11.2 DEBATE ON SUPPOSED DIVINE INSPIRATION

a) Mystical Vision of Eliphaz

Eliphaz experiences a mystical vision (4:12–21), raising the question of its authenticity.[1]

Eliphaz does not attribute to Job any specific punishable act. However, following a cryptic and contested allegation of his mystical experience (4:12–16), it is revealed to him that guilt (Job's haughtiness [4:21]) is inherent to the condition of man. Eliphaz's doctrine of collective guilt is based on his supposed mystical evidence: Servitude does not sanction personal guilt, as Job presupposes, but punishes a creation corrupted by man. *He does not trust his servants and casts reproach upon his angels* (4:18).

The narrative subtly criticizes Eliphaz's vision through a foolish rhetorical question, surrounded by mystery and prosopopoeia that imagines divinity as human: *Can a mortal be more just than divinity, purer than*

---

1. Bamidbar Rabbah 20:12 compares Eliphaz's dreams and visions to Balaam's. A widespread approach in Jewish tradition (Rashi and Maimonides) interprets them as defective inspiration to a gentile because the divine manifests only to the Jewish prophets. A Jewish tradition considers false a mystical inspiration or revelation to a gentile and attributes the supposed Eliphaz's vision to Job.

his Creator? (4:17). It intends to show the idealism of Eliphaz (and of Job) and presents a subjective certainty (dogma) as a supposed divine revelation.

b) Eliphaz Denies Explanation of Job's Punishment and Servitude

After a doxology of divine greatness and contempt for the foolishness and naivety of men, Eliphaz concludes that man is born for pain (5:7), pain submits to the divine will (5:8–27) since suffering educates (5:17–26), and only the Lord heals the wounds (5:18). In short, Eliphaz and his friends (and later Elihu) argue about the axiomatic character of collective guilt and exaggerate personal fault to justify an ethic of suffering.

Throughout the dialogue with the three friends, Job repeatedly insists on the nuclear argument of the first dialogue with Eliphaz, asking for an explanation of his punishment (*allow me to understand where I have erred* [6:24]). Job argues that to deny warning and explanation means founding an organization on arbitrary authority (sacrifice), and not on rationality.

c) Rationality (Warning) and Proportionality (Explanation) of Punishment

Job confronts Eliphaz's alleged (mystical) authority and reiterates his innocence and divine persecution (*my spirit drinks divine venom* [6:4]).

He insists that his servitude is not due to his guilt, blaming the institutional violence and falsehood of the false inspiration of Eliphaz and his cronies. He concludes that the violence imposed by the friends, in the name of their inspiration, conceives a bloodthirsty and false deity, which reflects their wickedness: *Anyone who withholds kindness from a friend forsakes the fear of the Almighty* (6:14). The three friends institute an inspiration (they imagine from divinity) that agrees with their evil violence and unjust prosperity (*they do not know the ways and get lost* [6:18]). Job asserts the irrationality of the violent imposition of authority in the name of a supposed collective sin (*like wind, words of futility* [6:26]).

He insists that only through warnings and explanations can authority and social order be legitimized, avoiding tolerance and concealment of evil (6:27–30). He argues that a warning sustains the rationality of commands, and that explanation justifies the measure of punishments. It separates from evil, thus establishing a coherent social order (6:30).

Job then shifts the argument to the absurdity of punishing humanity based on its inherent fragility (proportionality of sanctions) *as the wind that goes away like a cloud* (7:8–9). Why would divinity pay attention to a man? (7:17–19). As part of the demand for an explanation, Job alleges his upright intention to correct any damage. Job does not deny his possible guilt, claiming (7:17–21) his upright intention that does not justify a disproportionate punishment. Warnings and explanations achieve the proportionality of punishment, which constitutes an essential element of the warrant duty of authority: *Why have you made me crooked, so that I have become a burden to myself?* (7:20). Job insists on the lack of causality between heaven and earth (ch. 7) and concludes that there is no causality of acts on earth and damage in heaven to justify a disproportionate punishment: *I have sinned; what did I do to you?* (7:20). *Soon I will lie on the dust; and you shall seek me but I am not here* (7:21).[2]

11.3 DIVINE DUTY TO BASE CREATION ON INDIVIDUAL JUSTICE

a) Lineage and Offspring

Bildad and Zophar support Eliphaz's statements, adding arguments (the delay of justice and the excellence of wisdom) that pretend to confirm an authority instituted by divine inspiration and justify sacrifice in the unworthiness of men.

Bildad scolds Job's answers to Eliphaz: *How long will you repeat this [foolish] talk?* (8:2). Justifying divine justice, Bildad introduces the theme of justice in his due time, which involves debating the rationality of justice and the collective damnation. According to Bildad, the retribution of the righteous and the punishment of the wicked might be postponed for a while; however, *would the Lord betray justice?* (8:3). If you are truly pure, justice will be fulfilled in its due time (8:5), even if it is not immediately evident. He presupposes that the time of justice is not based on personal

---

2. Guilt and merit are human acts, proportional and personal, the three elements of the rationality of the punishment (and of the retribution of merit), as an individual act, which damages or enriches. Only through previous warnings and public explanation can harm or enrichment be delimited and compensated, and punishment be justified in terms of personal responsibility and proportionality.

guilt and subtly introduces the value of lineage and offspring (tradition) as collective merit and damnation.

He assumes that merit and guilt are perpetuated in the lineage and authority (the sin and merit of the fathers and the land). Perhaps his children's sin might explain Job's punishment (8:4). He also refers to the beginning and end of generations and days (8:7–10). Consciousness is only a shadow of the personal and collective identity and guilt (of lineage and land): *We come from yesterday and forge in history; our days are only shadows* (8:9). Bildad imagines human history and personal identity as entangled roots, *beside the fountain* (8:17).

b) Irrationality of Delayed Justice

Job asserts that the exact time of justice maintains causality (rationality and proportionality) as an essential element of divine retribution, and opposes Bildad's reference to lineage as the origin of collective excellence and damnation. Job denies that (by lineage) divinity might conceal or tolerate personal injustice (9:3–14); *no one can oppose divine justice and remain whole* (9:4), *no one can hold him back* (9:12); *will he condemn me being innocent?* (9:20).

It makes no sense for divinity to deny (individual) justice to condemn evil, as evil condemns itself. The Almighty does not need the help of man (intercessor) to establish justice (9:5–12). Furthermore, man cannot assert the authenticity of the divine word: *if he spoke to me, I wouldn't know who answered me* (9:16). The due time of punishment supports rationality (individuality) and proportionality of sanctions, attributing merit and punishment to the author and the responsible. It also guarantees proportional imputation of damage and correct restitution of unjust impoverishment. Collective guilt denies causality that identifies the origin and quantifies the damage and qualification of sanction and restitution (proportionality). Postponed punishment is a collective punishment that violates the rights of the individual and condemns the innocent, *punishing both the just and the wicked* (9:22). Collective condemnation means instituting arbitrary authority and legitimizing (unjust) temptation: *the earth is given over to the wicked, and he covers the faces of the judges* (9:24).

The due time of punishment determines the legitimate exercise of authority (the righteousness of creation). Postponed justice means the persecution of the righteous (the defective retribution of merit and guilt). Collective damnation is an act of arbitrary terror: *I know that you will not declare me innocent* (9:28). Job must overcome the fear of the Lord: a powerful divinity does not need terror to impose himself (9:34). *I will speak and not fear him* (9:35). The correct word (inspiration) means building a coherent social order that prevails over violence. Job confronts sacrifice and submission as a collective accusation of men; and, at this point, opposes the interpretation of exile as an accusation.[3]

c) Divinity as Guarantor

Job argues that an arbitrary divinity who delays and does not justify justice must be a false divinity, which Satan and man can legitimately challenge. *I will say: do not condemn me; let me know why you quarrel with me* (10:2).

Justice postponed for a time institutes or tolerates an a priori (arbitrary) authority, which does not protect the innocent (justice for each man) and contradicts divinity as a guarantor. *Will you reject the toil of your hands?* (10:3). Job argues that delaying justice means tolerating evil, denying responsibility and personal merit, executing collective sentences, arbitrarily punishing the innocent, and failing to fulfill the authority's warrant duty (teach, warn, and explain). *Are his days like the days of a mortal, or are his years like the days of a man, that divinity should search for my iniquity and seek my sin?* (10:5–6). An incoherent logic, since *no one can save [me] from your hand* (10:7).

The warrant's duty defines divine authority: *Have you not formed me, and will you destroy me?* (10:8). *You made me like clay, and you will return me to dust* (10:9). *You have granted me life and kindness, and your providence watched my spirit* (10:12). Power is justified by authorship. There is a divine responsibility to base creation on individual justice: a manufacturer must teach how to use a product, care for it, and repair it.

Bildad imagines an incoherent false divinity who punishes him arbitrarily, instituting collective punishments that deny divine Providence. Will you not care and repair your labor: *would you not cleanse me of my iniquity* (10:14). Furthermore, Job claims not have done wrong to divinity: *If I dealt wickedly, woe is to me* (10:15), and there is no sense in punishing

---

3. He reiterates his uprightness of intention (9:15, 20–21), *washed with snow water and cleansed hands with purity* (9:30), and calls into question the uprightness of Bildad, using unfair methods to conquest authority and prosperity (his rhetoric justifies his selfish motives).

a dependent and weak innocent: *my days are but a few; stop tormenting me so that I may breathe* (10:20). *For numbered years will come, and I will go on a way from which I will not return* (10:21).

11.4 DIVINE WISDOM AS PUBLICITY OF INDIVIDUAL JUSTICE

a) Zophar, the Supposed Mystery of Wisdom

In response to Job's criticism of Bildad, Zophar raises his voice and asserts the supposed mystery of divine justice, as only wisdom creates authority. Zophar attributes to Job the claim that he is pure and clean (11:4). He introduces an idealistic presupposition and an implicit accusation (the purity of renunciation and confession). *Can you find out the mystery of divinity; can you find out the limit of the Almighty?* (11:7).

Zophar affirms that divinity is the only holder of truth that knows and judges the wicked: *For he knows deceitful men* (11:11). It is implicit in Zophar's argument that confession of smallness and impurity constitutes the ideal foundation of a society (sacrificial dogma). Zophar preaches unconditional submission to divine will: *Prepare your heart and spread out your hands to him* (11:13).

b) Incoherent Violent Divinity

In his long and emotional reply, Job sums up the central argument of his response: Zophar affirms the inscrutability of divine will to invent a divinity who legitimizes the violence of his authority. A sophism lies in submission as recognition of sin (the corruption of the material) that becomes an essential element of justice, excluding the request for an explanation. Another fallacy lies in submission as messianism: *the eyes of the wicked shall fail, and they shall have no way to flee; their hope shall result in intense grief* (11:20).

Job reiterates his innocence, accusing Zophar of wordiness (12:2–5). In a long doxology that closes the chapter (12:7–25), affirming his trust in divine wisdom, Job underlines that men cannot scrutinize the mysteries of divine will (12:6). All creation recognizes heaven's wisdom, which reveals darkness (when he pleases), exalts and destroys kings and peoples.

Again, Job asserts his innocence. He argues that asking for an explanation means to deny evil as a being and to conceive evil as the result of ignorance, error, or individual guilt (destroyed when revealed): *I wish to reason with divinity* (13:3); *will you contend with him?* (13:8). Job denies hidden wisdom (13:18). To hide wisdom means to tolerate evil. The deities that Zophar imagines are not wise, as hiding does not teach or warn and *strikes without teaching; let me know my transgression* (13:23). He manifests the foolishness of the supposed mystery of wisdom (that denies Providence's duty of guarantee). The institutionalization of evil is incompatible with a perfect creation and contradicts the duty of guarantee of divinity as Creator and manufacturer.

Job insists on asking for an explanation and affirming the publicity of wisdom, the two main accusations against Eliphaz, Bildad, and Zophar: *Explain my transgressions and guilt* (13:23). Job argues that a priori submission to a *supposed* wise divinity presupposes a responsibility by omission: not to reveal, denounce, and fight against evil when it is mandatory to the protection of dependents and innocents. The categorical argument is the perfection of creation. Creation is ontological publicity that unveils a false divinity for not answering or explaining the punishment. If creation is perfect, man cannot be guilty of its defects nor held responsible for collective transgressions.

Job insists that Zophar falls into an ontological fallacy, presenting human inability to comprehend divine mysteries as proof that divine punishments must be just, reiterating the Manichaean foolishness of comparing heaven and earth. Reality, not man, unveils evil because man cannot correct a perfect creation: *Would you intimidate a leaf that has fallen from a tree?* (13:25).[4]

c) Personal Nature of Guilt and Responsibility

In ch. 14, Job reiterates that it makes no sense for the divinity to hide and pursue Job, the work of his hands, and even less to attribute him the (collective) guilt of men, given his smallness and limitation. Creation

---

4. Zophar's supposed wisdom denies tradition and the merit of man, signifying a narcissistic submission to an imagined divinity (that justifies arbitrary and disproportionate punishment). In the second and third cycles of the dialogue, Job and his friends accuse each other of rebellion against divine justice. The friends deny the servant's right to rebellion, and Job affirms the duty of authority to respect the social identity and confront servitude.

is perfect, and he cannot be bound to correct a defective creation (the divinity imagined by Zophar is incoherent). He insists on the foolishness of collective guilt, which imposes a responsibility disproportionate to the life and nature of man, of *short days and full of fears* (14:1), without being able to go beyond his limits (14:5), who falls and does not rise, who does not wake up from his sleep (14:12).

Evil cannot exist in a perfect creation: it flourishes and is cut down, like a passing shadow (14:2). What sense does it make to open his eyes to judge me? (14:3). Unconscious and collective responsibility must be interpreted as an extension of individual responsibility, in a limited being that cannot cross its boundaries (14:4–21). What basis can there be for his anger? (14:14–21).

The first cycle closes with a desperate protest by Job: *Only in the flesh is suffering felt, and only for himself does man grieve* (14:22). It is the central argument of the book: the personality of guilt and responsibility. A collective being is not a subject with conscience and will, and cannot be imputed guilt. Guilt and responsibility are necessarily personal and not collective. Collective responsibility is a kind of individual responsibility; only the concrete individual—with a name and a face—can be a rightful subject of justice. As warning (rationality) and explanation (publicity) are essential elements of punishment, only the individual man suffers and is responsible. The warning reveals unconscious social responsibility (abuse of the land), and the explanation rationalizes collective doctrinal responsibility (abuse of the divinities, the *nebelah*).

This first cycle encapsulates the spirit of the book and raises all its central issues. Job seems to have understood the nature of personal guilt and responsibility by denying collective guilt and the institutionalization of evil. In any case, Job does not address the inscrutability of providence raised by Zophar, and opens the way for Elihu's argument, insisting on collective condemnation and man's intercessory path (listening in the night and suffering). Job criticizes bloody sacrifice and the notion of collective guilt, but then insists on his innocence and fails to explain the foundation and limits of unconscious and collective guilt and responsibility.

XII.

Servitude Confronts Social Identity

12.1 SECOND CYCLE: THE ABUSE OF AUTHORITY

a) Violent Foundation of Three Friends' Ethics

Eliphaz opens the second debate by accusing Job of wordiness (15:2–4) and rebellion (15:5–6, 26). Pretending innocence, his tongue condemns Job (15:6). Job's initial protests against Eliphaz's authority now expand to denounce the three friends' immorality and their institutionalized violence. Job's insistence on proclaiming his innocence scandalizes his friends, who intensify their accusatory rhetoric and cease providing him comfort and support.

Job argues that the three friends impute evil to divinity, justifying sacrifices and failing to acknowledge the personality of guilt. Job contends that rebellion against divine inspiration stems not from his peaceful protest but from the sacrificial ideology upheld by his friends, which distorts justice and perpetuates oppression. He argues that the collective disorder might not be attributed to the servants but to the three friends, who, through the violence of sacrifice, build a defective authority and profit from false divinities.

Job insists on his innocence and demands an explanation, denying his alleged rebellion against divine justice. The three friends are accused of constructing an ethical framework centered on authority to justify the unequal distribution of wealth and the abuse of servitude.

b) Eliphaz, Job's Rebellion

According to Eliphaz, social order is based on authority and servitude; a servant has no right to question either human or divine authority, especially since Job was not created before Adam (15:7) and lacks ancestral knowledge of his origins (15:7–14). Eliphaz emphasizes the unworthiness of a servant who does not participate in the divine council (15:8) (he does not assume responsibility for the social order).

Eliphaz presupposes that only divine inspiration saves man. *Man is not innocent, the son of a woman is not just* (15:14); not even the heavens are pure in his eyes (15:15). Man is abominable, impure, and drinks injustice like water (15:16). Eliphaz reiterates his supposed inspiration, he affirms man's corruption (15:16–19) and Job's perversion (15:20–24).

Eliphaz concedes that injustice can endure for some time and authority can abuse wealth; however, this does not tarnish divine justice, as the days of the wicked pass in anguish, and the years of the tyrant are measured (15:20–35). The impious has raised his hand against divinity (15:25), and his face is full of fat (15:27); he will not attain lasting prosperity (15:29). Eliphaz concludes his dissertation by accusing Job of greed (15:28–33) and hypocrisy (15:34).

c) Falsehood of Friends' Divinities

Job reiterates a lament (*my pain does not cease* [16:5]; *his wrath has torn me, my adversary sharpens his eyes upon me* [16:9]). He accuses Eliphaz of abusing authority (*heaven delivers me to a fool* [16:11]). Because of his disordered origins in violence, Eliphaz will fall to the unavoidable justice of the earth (*which will reveal the spilled blood* [16:18]).

Job denies rebelling and affirms that the alleged rebellion of the servant seeks only to institute serfdom: mere talk (16:2–7) and disdain for men (16:10); *they gather together, and the Lord delivers me into the hands of the wicked* (the deities whom Eliphaz imagines) (16:11).

Insisting in his laments, Job assumes patient submission: he renounces violence (rebellion) and lives in the shadows of death (16:16); he only prays (16:17). Job suffers the divine wrath that destroys him (16:9), he accuses the divinity (imagined by Eliphaz) of complicity with crime, of protecting violence. No injustice stains his hands, and his prayer (his intention) has always been pure (16:17). Instituting serfdom, the three friends destroy man's labor as tradition and social identity; still, *his witness is in heaven* (16:19).

d) Personal Freedom and Warrant's Duty of the Social Realm

Job denounces the corrupt origin of the three friends' authority in sacrifice; they abuse wealth and serfdom, and will inexorably fall. *You did not want to understand and will not be exalted* (17:4). Their false beliefs, false authority, and flawed ethical doctrine deny man's social identity. *His hands are clean, and he grows stronger and stronger* (17:9).

Job accuses Eliphaz and his friends of abusing their authority and falsely claiming divine representation to justify servitude, acting as tyrants rather than liberators of the oppressed. In Job's view, they should build personal freedom and liberate the servants (as the authentic meaning of prayer). He states, *All of you shall not return, and [when I will come back] I will not find any wise man among you* (17:10). Their arbitrary authority does not honor fundamental aspects of human identity and social identity, such as freedom of religion, marriage, and property rights. They neglect their warrant's duty toward innocents and dependents, illustrating a failure to fulfill the duty of freeing the oppressed (17:5, 14), and he compares them to a father who abandons his children.

Yet Job finds himself in a pit of despair, calling out to the worms: *You are my father, mother, and sister* (17:14), and he concludes that the three friends lie in the dust (17:16).

12.2 SUPPOSED SOCIAL IDENTITY OF EVIL

a) Bildad, Divinity Roots Social Identity

In his response, Bildad identifies divinity with the foundation of authority and social order (marriage and property). Therefore, Bildad imputes rebellion to the servant Job and condemns him to isolation and poverty.

Bildad affirms that anger carries Job away (18:4). Job's wicked individualism justifies his punishment. He emphasizes that the wicked (Job) falls into his trap (18:8), a prisoner of terror (18:11). Job's rebellion destroys his social identity: children, servants, and wife (18:12), a sin punished with hunger, ruin, and skin disease (18:12–13). The rebel is barren, *the prince of death shall devour his branches* (18:13), his roots will dry up, and his branches will be cut off (18:16). The rebel against authority does not take root (18:13–20), and his memory (property) and name (family) are erased (18:17).

b) Perversion of Social Values

Job challenges the identity, affirmed by Bildad, between divine authority and social order. Only the labor of a free man builds marriage and property, not authority. He reaffirms his righteousness and blames the three friends for the perversion of social values (marriage and prosperity).

Their pretended divine authority is an unjust violence: *I cry out [concerning] violence* (19:7). Their authority persecutes the individual and prevents men from freely constructing a social identity. He complains about his unjust persecution (19:10), as servants, friends, and relatives consider him an intruder and despise him (19:13–18). He implies that anyone submitting to a false authority, founded in sacrifice, participates (is complicit) in the injustice of tyrants and their divinities. Job employs the image of the disintegration of the body, skin, flesh, and kidneys to prefigure the decomposition of authority instituted by sacrifice (19:20, 26–27).

Job concludes that the sword will punish an artificial social order built with sacrifices that abuse sexuality and wealth. The abuse of authority, family, and prosperity (unconscious guilt) makes the three friends guilty of the same punishment as Balaam: the sword that punishes (collective guilt due to) violent origins. *Fear the sword because you display stubbornness, a crime that deserves it, to learn justice* (19:29).

c) Zophar, Heavens Reveal Evil

Zophar, the most subtle of the three friends, closes this second cycle. He recognizes the possible and precarious responsibility of the authority (that Job claims); still, he considers it exceptional and temporary (20:5–17): *the triumph of the wicked is short; the joy of the flatterers is but a moment* (20:5), *his food will turn into the venom of cobras within him* (20:14). The wicked disappear like a dream (20:18) because they steal a house they have not built (20:19).

The triumph of the rebel is an instrument of his slumber and demise amid the relentless triumph of divine authority (20:18–26). *The heavens reveal iniquity, and earth rises against it* (20:27). Zophar concludes that heaven cannot participate in evil or conceal evil and is obliged to reveal it. The fight against evil justifies authority, as the earth rises against iniquity when the divinity reveals it (20:27).

I think that this approach of Zophar is the best argument of the idealism of this second cycle, concluding the debate on authority, servitude, and the supposed rebellion of the servant or the authority. Zophar condemns rebellion because he supposes divinity is the ultimate guarantor of the social order and the destroyer of any authority that becomes corrupt.[1]

d) Job, Supposed Divine Tolerance of Evil

Job answers with empirical evidence: perverse authority institutionalizes because the heavens do not reveal evil; *the wicked establishes, progresses, and asserts himself in his strength* (21:7).

Job alleges an argument ad absurdum: the social evidence of the institutionalization of evil: his descendants inherit from the tyrant (21:8), there is peace in his estate (21:9), they rejoice with the drum, the harp, and the sound of the flute (21:12). They do not want to know anything about divinity (21:14–15); however, they last for long (21:17).

Job opposes the dogmatism of the perverse authority (institutionalization of evil) to the friend's doctrine of the *wicked servant*. Job presupposes that evil (the lie) is also instituted in the heavens (among the divinities), not only on earth. The heavens tolerate and conceal evil, at least until they all perish by divine wrath (21:20). *What does he care [the violent tyrant] about his house after him?* (21:21). *Who will tell his way to his face?* (21:31). Job concludes that the wicked man is led with honors to the grave (21:32).

The second cycle closes with a grim conclusion: the friends are stupid for not recognizing the evidence of the possible institutionalization of evil—namely, violent authority and a corrupt religion built on false divinities. Job points out the perversion of authority as an expression of their sacrificial divinities. He concludes that their consolation is foolish, and their assertions of authority are fallacies (21:34).

---

1. Zophar assumes that the idea predestines reality, and denies tradition as the foundation of social order.

12.3 THIRD CYCLE, DIVINE IDENTITY OF COLLECTIVE REALM

a) Eliphaz, Human Origin of Evil

The affirmed institutionalization of evil poses the dilemma of justifying the divine toleration and concealment of evil, which will be discussed (and unresolved) in the third cycle. Eliphaz no longer justifies his authority in divinity and concludes that, due to divine transcendence, evil must have its origin in men; he justifies his authority in fighting evil. Eliphaz must have attended Kant's philosophy lectures, and now he stresses divine transcendence, the immanence of wisdom, and the material and moral perversion of the foolish and selfish Job (22:5).

Eliphaz accepts that evil does not affect divinity and concludes that earth reveals evil and judges corruption through personal virtue. Wisdom reveals evil in its origin on earth and not in heaven (he conceives Satan as a servant of divinity, the messenger of evil's unveiling and submission). He presupposes that man's greed causes evil (the impurity of his hands). Eliphaz accuses the servant Job of *taking a pledge from your brothers for naught and stripping them naked of their clothes* (22:6). It is not the social realm that is now confronted but the corruption of earth by Job's perversion.

The importance of this third speech of Eliphaz lies in attributing a role to Providence (as an acknowledgment of Satan's incoherence) in the foundation and development of the social order and history. He conceives a righteous divinity who institutes the earth as a test of Job (not as a testimony of justice), Satan as a servant of divinity. Authority educates and subdues man's corruption by personal virtue, temptation, and punishment. Eliphaz accuses Job of oppressing the poor, failing to feed the hungry, and denying aid to the orphan and widow; he ceases to accuse the divinities, the woman, and the social realm (22:6–7).

This third cycle conceives social order as the institutionalization of the wise (religious) man who reveals and submits evil, and not as the institutionalization of evil. Prosperity and authority reveal the evil servant and unveil Job's former pride, greed, and abuse of the stranger, widow, and orphan (22:7–9). Eliphaz interprets life and history as a test of man; he argues that Providence institutes authority to defend the weak (22:8) and servitude to condemn man's corruption (by greed). Eliphaz insists on Zophar's argument that the earth unveils evil and rebels against corrupt (unjust) authority. Job has abused prosperity, *traps are around you, and sudden fear terrifies you* (22:10). Job is supposed to have caused evil (corrupted the earth) with his (former) abuse of authority and prosperity, he should reveal his unconscious and collective guilt with the purity of intention (interpreted as renouncing prosperity).

The third cycle is limited to Eliphaz's intervention, who is the only one to whom the divinity will later refer by his name (42:7). In this third cycle, the focus shifts from pride and rebellion to the sin of greed, which Eliphaz now considers the essence of human evil, as submission to earth: Man harms himself with his greed, and Job benefits by his merit. Eliphaz admits that the heavens do not disclose (immediately) evil but (in due time) *the innocent one mocks them* (on the corrupt authority) (22:19). Eliphaz affirms that man (not divinity) must unveil evil (*return in repentance* [22:23]), as divinity will be *the judge of his adversaries, will give him prosperity* (22:25), *and will save the humble* (22:29). Eliphaz asserts that the virtue of a wise man (unveiling evil) benefits him, not divinity (22:2); he concludes that man will be saved by *the purity of his hands* (22:30).

Eliphaz imagines a false divinity as an objective reality materialized (instituted) on earth. He ultimately preaches renouncing prosperity, viewing it as inherently prone to perversion.[2]

b) Test of the Innocent

Job denies his unconscious responsibility for abusing the foreigner, the orphan, and the widow. He insists that a just divinity would not persecute the innocent (23:4–7), and a powerful divinity *would not place coercion upon me* (23:6).

---

2. Eliphaz innovates the foundation of social order by discovering Providence (personification of wisdom) and confronting the eschatological conflict between divinity and Satan. Evil has its origin on earth, in the corruption of man. Providence protects life (confronting the tyrant who takes advantage of divinities and monopolizes prosperity). Eliphaz accuses Job, who thinks that the Lord, beyond the clouds, does not see him (22:14). The epilogue measures the reproach to Eliphaz, who, although he renounces the bloody sacrifice of life and sexuality (42:7), does not institute a coherent ethic. Eliphaz interprets evil (the sin of man) as greed (*the gold of Ophir* [22:24]), which provokes sexual perversion and inspires the violence of false divinities. He does not justify life or sexual sacrifice but presupposes intercession. He affirms that renouncing prosperity earns the delights of the all-powerful and constitutes authentic wealth (22:26). *The Lord comes to the aid of the one who humbly lowers his eyes* (22:29). This refers to the renunciation of wealth, which institutes and supports a social order of unjust origins (in violence).

He feels despair confronting the divine tolerance of evil (23:2–6). Divinity does not condemn the alleged wealth accumulation, for divinity is not found in the east, the west, the north, or the south (23:8–9). A deity cannot be found on the left (condemning evil) and not seen on the right (rewarding good) (23:9). He denies having abused the weak and assumes suffering as an instrument of his trial and purification. He presumes exile to test his endurance and purify him (he institutes the dogma of separation), and after his test, he expects to be reborn *pure as gold* (23:10).

Job insists on declaring himself innocent (23:11–12) and describes divine Providence (wisdom) as unintelligible. The divine inspiration of the three friends is an instrument for justifying the institution of evil and their violent (arbitrary) authority. Who can oppose him? (23:13). He claims to be afraid (23:15) and disheartened (23:16). He has not committed the misdeeds attributed to him, and he concludes that the divinity tolerates evil and hides in darkness rather than exposing it, *not lifting the black fog that surrounds Job* (23:17).

c) Supposed Tolerance and Concealment of Evil

Job concludes the debate by contrasting his supposed realism with the idealism of his friends: the divinity hides, and the timing of judgment remains unknown (24:1). He accuses the divinity of tolerating and concealing evil and not rewarding his merit by imposing exile and servitude without personal fault.

Job denounces the foolishness of the sacrificial dogma. Since evil is hidden, Providence allows the abuse of the weak and the needy (24:3–10). *They rob from the breast of the orphan, and they take a pledge from a poor man* (24:9). The murderer rises in the light, the thief steals in the night (24:14); the eyes of the adulterer scan the twilight, *no one will see me, he says to himself* (24:15). He refers to the murderer, adulterer, and thief as a triple allegory for the sacrificial divinities of the three friends (sacrifice of life, sexuality, and prosperity). Eliphaz does not unveil the terrors of the shadow of death (24:17); with everything they accumulated, the conquering empires of the earth and their divinities will fall suddenly (24:24).

Job concludes that the foreign gods (of the three friends) purify him: *They are taken away in a second and are no more, like what they have gathered in* (24:24). It is not in heaven or earth that Job must triumph over evil (through temptation), but within himself, revealing his evil (through separation). He must triumph through submission or separation from evil until its destruction by divine wrath or in its contradictions. Job overcomes the sacrificial doctrine but assumes the fallacy of a tolerated false divinity, presuming the divine toleration and concealment of evil on earth.

d) Bildad, Denial of Right to Rebellion

Bildad concludes the discussion with a final statement similar to its beginning, which affirms a collective sin, institutionalized evil, denying the right to rebellion (referring to a social order): *Can a man be just before the divinity, can the son of a woman be pure?* (25:4).

The Lord makes peace on high (25:2). This presupposes that the earth hides evil, a Manichaean vision of good and evil: *A mortal cannot be just before the Lord, one born of a woman cannot be innocent* (25:4). The moon and the stars are not pure in his eyes (25:5). This presupposes that men corrupt the creation. He denies the virtue of women (the social order). *Man is nothing but rubbish; a son of Adam is but a worm* (25:6).

Bildad does not accuse Job but seems to agree with his despair (ch. 3) and justifies his servitude because of the divine's tolerance and concealment of evil (separation of earth). Nevertheless, he concludes that Job's protest is illegitimate, and his demand for an explanation is unfounded. He denies his innocence.

Zophar has remained silent in this third cycle, presumably not knowing what to reply. Indeed, the debate actually ends with the refutation of Zophar's claim that the heavens reveal evil, which constitutes the foundation of the sacrificial doctrine (and also of the doctrine of submission). Job does not take his argument to its ultimate conclusion: that the origin of evil is in each person (not in men) and that man corrects it by redeeming the earth, because his actions affect the earth, not divinity.[3]

---

3. Bildad's response foreshadows the arrival of Elihu, who dogmatizes and justifies exile as a self-accusation of collective guilt. In the new model of accusation that Bildad proposes, Job is no longer a warrior who conquers the land or a mystic who renounces sexuality (the *servant* of divinity who repents and listens with fear at night) but a man who builds a farm on servitude and corrupts his lineage by his greed and pride disdaining legitimate authority. Elihu will conclude that the three friends (and Job) presuppose collective guilt but do not correctly explain ontological guilt on earth, which only divine inspiration at night overcomes.

XIII.

Job's Messianism

13.1 JOB REITERATES COLLECTIVE DAMNATION

a) Job Insists on His Innocence, Trusting in Providence

After the debate with the three friends, the narrator gives the floor to Job, who uses the expression ויען (take the floor [26:1]).

In a conclusive monologue, Job reaffirms his innocence and repeats his request for an explanation, still, trusting in Providence and justifying his ethical stance of patient submission. Job criticizes the (miserly) Providence outlined by Eliphaz and his friends: *How do you help the weak and support the weaklings?* (26:2). He underlines the warrant duty of Providence: *How do you instruct the ignorant and spread knowledge?* (26:3). *To whom do you speak these words, and whom do you represent?* (26:4).

Despite his frustration, Job portrays an idealistic and scatological conflict between good and evil, in which divinity reveals and punishes evil: *Hell is naked before him* (26:5). Providence protects and directs nature (expands science) and history (institutes personal merit) (26:5–14), assuming that light and darkness have an end (26:10). Job presupposes a temporal institution of evil to test him and achieve a greater good. The heavens are corrupted and tremble at his rebuke (26:11). He concludes that Providence hides (26:9) to shake the pillars of the earth with reproach (26:11).

According to Job, Providence assigns a destiny to humanity and establishes the social order. Divinity rules the sea with power, subdues pride, and strikes down Rahab (26:12). His spirit covers the heavens, and his hand controls the serpent (26:13). He defeats the tyrant, subjects the divinities to the thunder of his greatness (26:14). The protagonism of Providence reflects the perplexity of Job, who criticizes the sacrificial dogma but has not developed a coherent theory of guilt and responsibility.[1]

b) Job Supposes Divine Toleration of Evil

After his doxology on Providence, Job assumes a dogma of purification by separation (and hopes to witness the spectacle of the destruction of evil). Job insists on accusing divinity of concealing evil in its proper time (*it deprives him of his right and embitters his soul* [27:2]) and assumes an ethic of resignation (*his tongue will not protest* [27:4]), reiterating his innocence *until death* (27:5). He hopes that the divinity will destroy his wicked and unjust enemies *in due time* (27:7).

Job insists that divinity concealed evil: the hypocrisy of the thief (27:8), who receives a share from the wicked man (27:13). The tone of his speech presents a cruel divinity letting evil grow to destroy it in due time (the corrupt tyrants and their foreign land). *If their children multiply, it is only to perish by the sword, and their descendants will suffer hunger; the multitudes that survive, the plague will bury them, and their widows will not mourn them* (27:14–15). The righteous will inherit and distribute their goods (27:17), while the house of the wicked will be destroyed (27:18); terror will pursue them (27:20), their misfortune will be applauded, and they will disappear amid mockery (27:21–23).

The narrative now uses ויסף to ponder Job's monologue as servile, criticizing his pretended innocence (the accusation of collective guilt) and the supposed divine toleration of evil. Job's idealism imagines a cunning divinity who conceals (uses) evil to purify man. He conceives a righteous divinity who institutes the earth as a test of man (not as a testimony of justice) and considers that suffering educates and purifies man through (unjust) punishment. In his long monologue (ch. 27 and following), he concludes that the sinner is not punished (in his time) for his wicked acts. He does not deny the retribution of the righteous and the

---

1. He reiterates a collective accusation to foreign deities, preaching a resigned submission to a righteous but violent Providence who (he supposes) directs nature and history from a distant hiding place, concealing evil.

condemnation of the depraved, but he affirms that it does not happen in his time but in due time (when men shall purify). Job humbles himself because he patiently waits for a messianic future when Providence will destroy the foreign kingdoms (the serpent) and he will restore his prosperity and authority.

The doctrinal difference between Job's monologue and the doctrine of the three friends refers to renouncing sacrifice and overcoming temptation as an attenuated sacrifice of prosperity, which can be inferred from Bildad's doctrine. Job affirms that unveiling evil overcomes it; still, only Providence submits evil, destroying the false deities without warning.

c) Wisdom as Separation and Hiding

Chapter 28 displays the apotheosis of wisdom as Job's dogmatic doctrine. Job outlines his vision of virtue as resigned submission with faith in a messianic future. He portrays wisdom as the divinity he imagines, preaching separation from the world and hiding from evil.

Job contrasts the greedy optimism of his three friends with his experience of a more *authentic* divinity at the end of darkness (28:3), which he compares to the miner who searches for minerals in the center of the earth, digging for a treasure hidden in the shadow of death. Job proposes an objective religious conscience (the law) as an alternative to the moral subjectivism of his friends, a path (virtue) that proud beasts (reference to individual sacrifice) do not tread (28:8). Job concludes that wisdom is not to be found among the living (28:13) but in divine creation and revelation.

He affirms that divinity is unfathomable, and man (the rebel) is not worthy of understanding (divine justice) (28:12). Wisdom lies *hidden from the eyes of all living, concealed from the winged creatures of the heavens* (28:21). The criterion of the authenticity of inspiration is shown in the denial of sacrifice and in waiting for the revelation of divinity's creative will (a messianic perspective), which elects his people and gives them the land in due time when the divinity rescues Job, purified by his unjust exile. The creative moment (not the authority, as the identity of the social order) determines the origin, end, and substance (authenticity of the wise inspiration): *he has seen it, appreciated its value, marked a place, and penetrated it deeply* (28:27), which man attains by patient and messianic submission: the fear of the divinity (separation) and fleeing from evil (hiding) (28:28).

The fallacy of separation and hiding lies in creating nonexistent divinities (ideally) and condemning himself to servitude and exile. Separation, though it rejects sacrifice, reiterates collective damnation, which pretends to inherit prosperity and power from the divine damnation of foreign kings and deities.[2]

13.2 JOB DENIES RESPONSIBILITY FOR COLLECTIVE DISORDER

a) Supposed Unjust Means of Providence

In ch. 29, the narrator blames Job for a second time (ויסף) and criticizes his naive messianic talk. Indeed, Job begins his messianic discourse (29:2) by longing for the nights of his past (ירחי קדם), when he conquered the land on sacrificial presuppositions, yearning for a messianic future where *he will sit at the head of the congregation and will dwell as a king* (29:25).

Rather than viewing his suffering as a call to (personal) responsibility, Job interprets it as evidence of his election and moral superiority. *They abhor me, they have distanced themselves from me; and from my face, have spared no spittle* (29:10); *they pursue my nobility* (30:15). His foolish messianism means a collective accusation and submitting, by omission, to hoarding the land without correcting the disorder (without freeing the servants). Job implicitly accuses the divinity of using evil and presupposes a Manichaean conflict between good and evil; *I expected good and received evil* (30:26), *thrown into the mire* (30:29).

However, he claims to receive unjust evil with patience until the triumph of good (30:26) (which Job naively intends to represent). He exaggerates the protagonism of Providence, condemns the world, and separates himself from it (awaiting its destruction), denying his responsibility for the social disorder and the universality of man as the end of

---

2. As a conclusion to the debate with his three friends, Job expresses the substantiality of his fear and fleeing from evil. *Fear of the divine* means patient submission to a damned social order founded on sacrificial violence; *fleeing from evil* refers to unveiling evil (naming false divinities) and separating from the established social order. The reference to Job's pretended wisdom reiterates Job's praises of fearing the Lord and fleeing from evil (1:1). The ironic conclusion of the narrative is that Job has not learned from the earth's punishment as a testimony of justice and proposes separation to overcome foreign divinities. Job condemns himself to exile and servitude by accusing the foreign divinities (*he crosses their limits and closes the doors* [38:10]) without revealing their defective origins and repairing the social disorder.

creation. The hinted reproach of the narrative, ויסף, underlines that divinity does not use violence to purify men and does not justify the test of men (temptation). Evil does not redeem, because it means nonexistence and deceit. Job judges himself by judging divinity; he conceives a divinity who conceals evil, and he (foolishly) tolerates and conceals evil, pretending to be chosen by divinity to suffer and inherit a future messianic age.

b) Institutionalization of Marriage

The dogma of patient submission institutes marriage (*the covenant of his eyes* [31:1]) as the social ethic of separation and hiding. Job distinguishes himself from his friends (and from Elihu) by the institutionalization of marriage, a sign of his separation ethic in exile. A wife personifies a personal ethic in the foundation of a separated social order upon leaving Persia; the authentic response to the ethics of friends and Elihu, who remain without a coherent doctrine of marriage.

A wife announces Job's blessing after overcoming the accusations of Satan (the sacrificial dogma of violence and sexual submission). The narrative shows Job living in a monogamous marriage (as a social identity of monotheism), not in a polygamous family (typical of polytheism); the woman converses with Job, as divinity converses with Satan. Marriage gives testimony of the separate ethic of not enticing his heart to a (foreign) woman (31:9), seen as a fire that consumes (men) until destruction (31:12), lurking at the neighbor's doorway (31:9), because not to separate and hide causes lewdness and iniquity deserving punishment (31:11). It displays an analogy of foreign women and deities, and he accuses women of the collective disorder (*nebelah*, as the institution of false doctrines).

He establishes separation, overcoming sacrifice and temptation, believing that evil is temporally concealed to purify him. He overcomes unconscious responsibility but not collective responsibility (the doctrine of an unjust divinity).

Separation builds a social realm founded on marital freedom amid a supposedly corrupt world, trusting that evil will self-destruct. His insistence on not depriving the disinherited of clothing (31:19) refers to not abusing the servant and the weak economically or sexually. Marital morality also prefigures a retributive economic justice. His social commitment advocates welcoming foreigners and not abusing wealth

(31:24–28), as well as not taking the produce of the land without paying its price (31:39).[3]

c) Social Responsibility of Servitude

From the perspective of a theory of guilt, the woman manifests the first step toward awareness of social responsibility. In a monogamous marriage, the woman speaks and urges him to assume his duty toward his family and collective realm (and overcome the cunning and Manichaean dogma of isolation). The system is doomed if Job pretends to build a society on violence, consecration, or submission to the divinities (and not to respect his wife). The words of Job's wife summarize the message of the theophanies, while Job's words to her summarize the response to his three friends and his answers to the theophanies.

The narrative states: *Here, the words of Job end* (31:40), mocking the inconsistency of Job's final monologue. Job opens the floodgates of self-accusation and self-condemnation. He is an accomplice, not an abettor, covering up the institution of servitude. He respects as a false servant the social order constituted by servitude (founded on sacrifice), waiting for the divinity to destroy it and to inherit the earth (messianism). A messianic kingdom means to institutionalize a new authoritarian, elitist, pseudo-sacrificial morality of submission (to induce violence) by separation. He becomes the servant who pretends to be king and the servant who displaces her mistress, which makes creation tremble (Prov 30:22).

As said in the prologue, *Job did not attribute his fall to the Lord* (1:22). Not to attribute his fall to divinity praises Job's right intention (exonerating divinity); nevertheless, his pretended innocence and undue collective accusation attributes divinity to concealing evil. His exaltation of wisdom, intended as a critique of the sacrificial dogma, rejects bloody offerings of life and sexuality, still upholding a messianic ethic of separation—an ethic the first theophany will soon confront.

---

3. In particular, ch. 31 proclaims his strict ethical code, far beyond the unfounded accusations of Eliphaz and his friends. As the culmination of his monologue, he calls the divinity to witness his upright intention (31:35–37). As explained in the allegories of the first theophany, Job's wife signifies overcoming the unconscious responsibility of abusing prosperity. If a man treats the woman as a servant, the systemic violence of male authority (personification of a violent and manipulative totem) establishes a society divided into lords and servants. Job builds a house by the sea to offer hospitality to a family (and strangers); amid a collective disorder, his wife provokes Job to stand, prevent, and minimize the inexorable vengeance of a defective social system founded in submission.

SECOND ACT

Collective Guilt

XIV.

Dogmatic Traditions on Elihu

14.1 DEBATE ON THE ORIGIN OF COLLECTIVE GUILT

a) Versatility of Elihu

Elihu views evil as a collective disorder (an institutionalized evil) that arises within the corruption of humanity. Elihu opposes Job's innocence because it implies an accusation of divine tolerance of evil and insists on overcoming corruption through suffering, personal confession, and individual intercession.

A positive evaluation interprets Elihu's doctrine as an expression of faith, praising Elihu as the spokesman of direct divine inspiration. Elihu teaches Job to take upon himself the sin of the world as a *mediator*, chosen for his virtue. Elihu explains to Job the educational function of suffering, preaching patient resignation, moral purity, and right intention. Elihu prepares the theophanies, which will ratify his doctrine.

A negative trend denies Elihu's inspiration and presents him as a foolish and asocial anarchist. His speech is a mere repetition of the arguments of the three friends who condemn Job. Elihu despises man's labor and merit and presupposes collective guilt, denying free will and personal responsibility. He exaggerates the unconscious and collective guilt and condemns men because of a supposed (collective) sin of his origins, not for his acts.

I will try to explain that both unilateral trends are unacceptable. Elihu lays a fundamental pillar for a coherent theory of guilt because he imputes to men the responsibility for the collective disorder, not blaming divinity (or authority). Still, his supposed divine inspiration lacks authenticity and cannot justify a doctrine of human collective guilt. He conceives an incoherent, solitary, neurotic, and vengeful divinity who establishes or redeems by intermediaries the collective order in the night (by confession and intercession), promoting a persistent and unjust punishment of the righteous (torture) by suffering and renunciation. Elihu's doctrine of an exaggerated damnation must be interpreted as an ironic counterpoint to the supposed overstated innocence of Job, as antihero or alazon, showing the dependence of the book of Job on the literary structure of a Greek tragedy.

b) Elihu in Jewish Tradition

An ancient tradition interprets Elihu as testimony of the revelation on Mount Sinai. The discourse on Elihu begins after the narrator states, *Here the words of Job come to an end* (31:49). In a flattering interpretation of his speech, ancient doctrinal testimonies of many Tannaim and some Amoraim affirm that Elihu wrote the second part of the book of Job, as a witness of the divine word and representative of Israel.

In contrast, in another and later trend, some Tannaim and many Amoraim downgrade the consideration of Elihu and even consider Elihu as a personification of Satan, the spirit of the tyrannical Persian divinity who *comes to an end*, responsible for the exile, or later of Rome, destroyer of the temple.

Irving Jacobs places the controversy over the character of Elihu in the very awakening of rabbinical thought as a coherent movement.[1] Rabbi Akiba justifies Job and his swaggering language on suffering, and he compares Elihu to Balaam, who intends to curse but blesses Israel (Sotah 5:20d). The school of Hillel, contradicting the sacrificial school

---

1. Jacobs, "Book of Job," 23, 73n17. The canon, in the context of whose formalization the Book of Job seems to have been written, replaces the catastrophic and sacrificial vision of the history of Israel: GORDIS, *Study on Job*, 144, overcoming of the polytheism of the Manichean conception of the Persian gods, and highlighting concern about the value of the individual (209). The core problem of the canon is raised by Rabbi Akiba and the school of Hillel, who propose to interpret suffering not as atonement for a past sin, but as an awareness of personal guilt. Rabbi Yohanan ben Zakkai, a tannaim disciple of Hillel, petitioned the Emperor Vespasian (Gittin 56b) for freedom of worship and advocated replacing sacrifices with prayer.

of Shammai, ends Phariseeism (sacrificial theology), rejects separating Israel (by reconstructing the temple), and consolidates rabbinic Judaism. History and social order are no longer a conflict between good (Israel) and evil (peoples) but a defective human work.

The portrait of Elihu as a prophet of the gentiles is not unanimous either. The Gemara considers Elihu either one of the seven gentile prophets or a Jew who teaches the foreign peoples (Baba Batra 15b). And in Sotah 5:20d, Eleazar ben Azariah, of the second generation of the Tannaim, identifies Elihu with Isaac, who does not protest his unjustified sacrifice (he gives himself as a propitiatory victim).[2]

c) Medieval Christian Philosophy

Patristic thought and scholasticism consider Job just for submitting to divinity (accepting his destiny) and confessing his sin. Job does not bear any personal responsibility for losing his property or leprosy that corrodes his skin. Since Job has no fault and it is ontologically impossible to attribute guilt or injustice to divinity, only men cause collective disorder because they have corrupted nature.

Despite his pertinent reply to Job's pretended innocence, Elihu personifies spiritual pride that does not recognize history as the reality of the divine incarnation. Man cannot claim to find the truth in an objective revelation to a people or in a personal experience of perfection and purity because unveiling truth comes from redemptive suffering and awakening in the resurrection. The Epistle of James 5:7–11 praises Job as a model of patience that represents the church.[3]

---

2. Later rabbinical interpretation takes distance from any extreme evaluations of the figure of Elihu, who is neither exalted nor condemned. Bamidbar Rabbah (20:11) interprets illumination (by analogy with Num 20:20) as the revelation of Balaam, and also like the speech of Eliphaz (4:12–13). In my opinion, the Gemara identifies Elihu with foreign religions, which may have their origin in the earth (greed) or in Israel (the search for divinity). As their deities do not exist, they cannot be condemned. Until the day of their (ideal) destruction, Satan has the right to his share (to condemn man, to fix the earth, and to take it for atonement of personal sin). Avodah Zarah 3a interprets the three friends and Elihu as personifications of the peoples and their gods who testify that Israel (Job) has fulfilled the law.

3. Collective sin will have its institutional formalization in the epistles of Paul of Tarsus. The interpretation of Job in the Pelagian heresy, its hero par excellence, is fought by Augustine of Hippo, and condemned in a consolidated Christian dogma. Human nature is defined as corrupted by original sin, and grace alone saves men. Gregory the Great describes Job as condemned by original sin, who patiently assumes suffering. He

Thomas Aquinas develops the ideas of Gregory the Great and explains that Elihu accurately reproaches Job for not believing in divine justice (first lesson of ch. 34, the divinity is just with every individual); furthermore, Elihu rightly considers the immortality of the soul and the existence of another life where justice will be manifest, in contrast to friends who only believe in material retribution. Nevertheless, Thomas Aquinas affirms the educational and preventive function of suffering and censures Elihu for boasting. He criticizes Elihu's excessive pride, asserting that he can resolve the conflict between Job and his friends despite not understanding the inscrutable divine wisdom.[4]

d) Lutheran Dogmatics

In his preface to the book of Job, Martin Luther criticizes the medieval tradition of a patient Job and praises his rebellion.[5] In Luther's thought, Job ceases to represent the church and personifies an individual in despair. Luther depicts Job as a fragile sinner who cries out to the Lord as a sign of his saving faith. As the Lutheran Sebastian Münster affirms, Job slept during theophanies.[6]

Even though Luther presupposes original sin as a collective guilt and corruption of human nature, he exalts Job's rebellion as a testimony of faith. In his private conversations, he presents Job as the paradigm of faith, a man who trusts in his salvation through grace alone. In his own rebellion against Rome, Luther sees himself as Job.

Luther considers Elihu, in line with traditional Christian thought, the personification of spiritual sin, identified with Jewish pride. In his confrontation with the Anabaptists, he also identifies Elihu as a rebel.

---

blesses the suffering of the just as redemptive suffering. The interior ascent to divinity is made possible only by suffering, which purifies man and frees him from material ties. Suffering does not mean personal punishment but an eschatological function, as an experience of the reality of sin and redemption. Repentance means becoming aware of sin, despising the goods and honors of worldly life, and climbing in wisdom. The *flagella Dei* (suffering) renews the soul and favors the contemplative life. The trial and purification of man explain the meaning of life and history. Elihu prefigures spiritual sin, of which Gregory the Great affirms that "there are many in the Church," referring to the sin of rebellion against divine justice (Glatzer, *Dimensions of Job*, 11).

4. Cabello Llano, "Libro de Job," 15; Keynes, "Trials of Job."
5. Clines, "Spirituality of the Reformation," 49–51.
6. Andersen, "Elihu Speeches," 76.

14.2 DUALITY OF STATE AND RELIGION

a) Medieval Jewish Philosophy

The Christian dogma creates the duality of state and religion. The medieval world witnessed the birth of a Jewish philosophy that explains Elihu as the personification of revelation. Medieval Jewish commentators study and criticize Muslim and Christian philosophy as Manichaeism.

Saadiah Gaon identifies suffering with exile. In a positive evaluation of Elihu, he affirms and repeats that divinity tests a just man and teaches him through suffering, which is not necessarily punitive.[7] Maimonides, the best-known Jewish philosopher, asserts that intellectual perfection overcomes material corruption. On the reception of Aristotelian idealism, he interprets prophecy as a personal experience of purity and illumination.

In the prologue to the *Guide of the Perplexed*, Maimonides expresses his admiration for the book of Job, which has a central meaning as a reasoned and systematic exposition of the principles of Scripture. He interprets Job as a tale about Providence guiding man in his struggle against himself. Elihu correctly explains prophecy as a natural consequence of virtue (*Guide of the Perplexed* 3.23), participation in the divine essence through moral conscience. He interprets the redeeming angel described by Elihu as the personification of the different phases in the ascent to prophecy, reached through renunciation and suffering. Elihu personifies the moral purity of Israel, the only repository of revelation that establishes moral law. In the context of his theory of emanation, Maimonides interprets intercession as a way to ascent in divine perception. The direct relationship with the Creator is exceptional, divinity is a remote cause of prophecy, Providence is unfathomable, and the intellect does not surmount material reality. A revelation transcends personal experience, chooses a virtuous man, and identifies a people as witnesses and testimony of divine Providence. He interprets the prophecies of Balaam and Eliphaz as a personal inspiration of a gentile prophet.

Commenting on the dialogues of Job and his friends, Maimonides underlines, as Elihu says, that divinity fixes *his eyes on man's way* (*Guide of the Perplexed* 3.23). As deprivation or lack of order, not as punishment, the reality of Providence deploys thunder, lightning, rain, and blowing winds, meteorological and social phenomena, famine, plague, and war manifesting the spirit of man as an attribute of divine justice. The

---

7. Eisen, *Book of Job*, 33.

reference to flesh and bones in Elihu, whom the interceding angel saves, may plausibly refer to Providence regarding social order and nature.

He interprets the divine intervention in theophanies as an allegory of the unintelligible divine power over nature and history. Chapter 18 of bk. 3 of *The Guide of the Perplexed*, concerning Providence, explains that Job suffers from intellectual and moral deficiency, and men enjoy providential inspiration to the extent of their perfection. The debate between Job and his friends is no longer at the center of the interpretation of the book of Job. Elihu unveils Providence's labor depending on the awareness of human limitations (repentance and confession) and the study of revelation.

Maimonides refuses to value Job as the experience of sin or the historicity of the formation of a people (and its conquest of the land). He interprets Job as the reality of Providence in history, building a social being as the work of divinity. Job, each man, personalizes history. Maimonides presupposes a legislative divinity who institutes a morality, which man understands through study and confession (as recognition of his imperfection). Depository of revelation and explaining the meaning of theophanies, Israel's virtue (Elihu) brings harmony to the personal and the collective realm of revealed moral law and natural ethics. Elihu overcomes the debate of the friends when he places the substantive question of sin as a deficiency and, on the contrary, understands wisdom as an instrument of morality (revealed only in its principles to Israel as a people of virtuous men).

Maimonides concludes that Elihu answers Job and rationalizes theophanies. Revelation is a vital aspect of Israel's constitution; its study and personal purity lead to unveiling the spiritual perfection of the law.

b) Elihu in Calvinism

Calvin pays particular attention to the commentary on the book of Job, underlining the importance of the Jewish tradition in Calvinist thought, which does not conceive Christianity as a break with Judaism but as its continuation and overcoming.[8] Once again (as in Gregory the Great, Thomas Aquinas, Maimonides, Kant, Hegel, and Kierkegaard) the book of Job lends Calvin the fundamental systematic keys to build his doctrine on human guilt and redemption, with a decisive influence on English

---

8. Schreiner, *Where Shall Wisdom Be Found?*, 92.

Calvinism (the Puritan and Pietist trend), which instituted religious freedom.

Calvin exalts, like Luther, the figure of a rebellious Job justified by his faith. Calvin no longer interprets Job as the representation of the church but rather as a man who does not want to hear the divine word and sleeps during theophanies. The divine reproach (*Where were you when I laid the earth's foundations?* [38:2]) is directed against Job, not against Elihu (as in the patristic and scholastic interpretations).

Calvin's sermons on Job are decisive in consolidating a doctrine on Providence, later expressed in the *Institutes of Christian Faith*. Calvin develops three ideas from Thomas Aquinas: the notion of original sin, the notion of free will, and the notion of Providence. According to Calvin, revelation presents a historicist (and rationalist) imprint, interpreting the book of Job as a treatise on Providence. Far from describing Elihu as the personification of pride, a manifestation of spiritual sin, Calvin considers Elihu, with the same approach as Maimonides, the introducer of theophanies. Elihu, not blamed in the epilogue, confesses sin and is justified by faith, assumes the role of depositary and preacher (by word and example) of divine revelation. Calvin finds in Elihu the meaning of revelation as an expression of the divine inspiration and the righteous directing history. He emphasizes confession as the reality of a saving faith, a path to virtue and wisdom. Calvin sees Elihu as a representation of divine election (the visible church) and no longer considers Elihu to embody spiritual sin. He presents Job as an arrogant man who disputes divine justice.

Calvin sees himself and conceives the church, with echoes in medieval Jewish thought, as the triumph of the incarnation in history through moral purity. Calvin considers the church the realization of Providence and saving predestination. Calvin characterizes Job as a gentile with Edomite roots. With a Jewish name, Elihu personifies the new Reformed Church based on confession and intercession. Although not from the lineage of Abraham, Elihu is saved by his faith when he confesses his sin and trusts in the resurrection. The Jews were chosen by their flesh, the church by the historicity of revelation as the redemption of man.

The church teaches the divine word to a Job who does not want to listen. This does not mean disdaining the importance of suffering, since Job, an imperfect man, is educated by suffering as a sign of election. Suffering is a means, not an end, as hospitality (charity) and preaching inform the very structure of functions in the church. Revelation is admitted both in the constitutional aspect of the church and in the personal experience of virtue.

c) Biblical Criticism of Eighteenth Century

The debate on Elihu's doctrine is an overall simplification of a more general dispute on dating the book, its coherence, and its patched, unitary, or progressive redaction.

For many modern authors, in the context of the biblical criticism of the eighteenth century, Elihu's speech was not considered part of the original tale but of a later addition (or two later additions), trying to repair the poor structure of the dialogues with the three friends, or an interpolated text, mending the scandal caused by Job's bold statements.[9]

Supposedly, Elihu's monologue has less literary quality, written with a monotonous and repetitive style without images or metaphors that spoil the symmetrical composition of the text, without representing a structured thought. Terms and expressions of Aramaic origin seem inserted by a later author, maybe scandalized by the dogmatic implications of theophanies, which undervalue Providence and do not concord with the original composition of the tale.

d) German Idealism

Elihu represents in Hegel the foolishness of seeking truth or justice in ideas. Job proclaims his innocence: Would it not be easier for the unjust to suffer misfortune and for the evildoer to be reproved? Let Job be weighed in just balances, and God will sign Job's mercy!

Hegel (answers Job in 33:12): Look! You are not righteous precisely because God is more than a man; why do you pretend to litigate against him? Since divinity does not accept Elihu's doctrine and his knowledge of divinity is pretended to be inspired or prophetic, Hegel asserts that Elihu must be considered a fool.[10] Elihu personifies a merely negative relationship with reality and a merely subjective relationship with the abstract being of the divinity, not with its concrete being, because in itself, the divinity is not ulteriorly determined.

---

9. Hawley, "Composition of Elihu Speeches"; Alter, *Hebrew Bible*, 3:459. According to Habel, Elihu repeats the arguments of the three friends (*Book of Job*, 182).

10. Hegel, *Filosofía de la religión*, 2:41.

Hegel criticizes Elihu as the nuclear point of his interpretation of the book of Job. According to Hegel, a religion founded on divine inspiration and revelation, the idea, is not objectified in reality because—according to Hegel—the divinity who exists in the imagination is created as the subjectivity of the interpreter that conceives it. Elihu explains divinity as subjection to power and at the service of subjective individuality (arbitrary power), which has no real essence and cannot guarantee freedom and justice. Hegel argues that Job, in contrast to Elihu, conceives divinity as the other and builds a religion of the sublime, determined by divine revelation (of his essence), which promises him (in theophanies), amid chaos (the storm), a particular land (to build a society), a farm, and a family.

Hegel identifies Job with Israel. In the duality of Israel as a state (Job) and as a religion (Elihu), Hegel assumes that (in the epilogue of the book), Job abandons his struggle for justice and lets himself be tempted by religious idealism; he abandons his claim to build a state (corrupted by the messianism of the land of Israel) and exhausts his essence in the criticism of the divinities of the peoples among whom he lives. Job submits to divinity (the abstract idea that exalts subjectivity), and only in his submission does he find his (excentric) happiness (the conquest of the earth as the chosen one).

e) Faith as Exception and Repetition

Kierkegaard opposes Hegel and presents Job as the exception and repetition, an expression of faith. He justifies sacrifice as the reality of faith.[11]

Kierkegaard poses evil as a test and the ontological confusion in man between good and evil as the essence of anguish. Spiritual repetition can never become as perfect in time as it will be in eternity, precisely the authentic repetition. Fear and trembling, the sacrifice of Abraham, the supreme test of man, justifies the exception, the supremacy of man over the system. And the temptation of Satan makes repetition a reality, which culminates in eternity as the repetition of the redemption of man. Kierkegaard presents Job as the prototype of the spiritual suffering of a man tempted (and condemned) by his divinity.

The friends submit to Satan through greed. Life, the test of Isaac's sacrifice, defines faith (fear and trembling). Job represents a man struggling to reach the confines of faith. Satan sowed discord between God and

11. Kierkegaard, *Repetición*, 42–53.

Job, a process that concludes with the recognition that it was all nothing more than a test. Job triumphs in the test because he does not bow down to God or Satan, which conspire together to subdue man. Eternity is a repetition. Only the children were not recovered by Job because a man does not allow this form of reduplication.[12]

---

12 Modern thought, freed from its dependence on an authoritarian theology, confronts the book of Job in the search for principles on which to base ethical coherence. Job occupies a relevant space in secularized literature. The Spanish Golden Age wrote many commentaries on the book of Job, and there is a direct analogy between Don Quixote and Job. Shakespeare, and *King Lear* specifically, has been interpreted as being inspired by the book of Job, debating the sterility of the religious wars in England. Victor Hugo considers the book of Job a masterpiece he would save from the hypothetical destruction of literature (Uzanne, "Conversations of Victor Hugo," 570). Goethe's Faust is a literary fiction of Satan in the book of Job, the loneliness of the tyrant, and a critique of the authoritarianism of Germanic culture. Job is mentioned in ch. 6 of Dostoevsky's *Brothers Karamazov* when the elder Zosima explains the story of Job and refers to the mystery of divine justice. Dostoevsky presents Job as an authentically Russian hero, skeptical of the elaborate Orthodox ritualism and a refutation of atheism and anarchism. Kafka depicts a prisoner trying unsuccessfully to reach the judge who condemned him and finally executed without knowing why—a literary allegory on the arbitrary divinity of Job, the lament of the Eastern European countries subjected to the maelstrom of the religious wars.

XV.

The Double Presentation of Elihu

15.1 NARRATIVE PRESENTS ELIHU

a) Elihu's Unjustified Anger Against Job

The narrative introduces Elihu by summarizing Job's dialogue with the three friends: *The three men ceased to argue, considering Job righteous in their eyes* (32:1). This introduction plausibly means that they overcome the sacrifice doctrine without liberating the serfs or restoring the social disorder.

Elihu argues that affirming Job's innocence means to accuse divinity of collective disorder. Elihu raises the dogmatic incoherence of the debate between the three friends and Job, and interprets the dialogue as a sterile reiteration of mutual accusations. Elihu is portrayed as a rebellious young man who pretends to be blessed by divine inspiration, criticizes the dialogue between Job and his friends, and fancies himself as defending divine innocence. He concludes that they are all condemned (the three friends and Job) by their violent nature and their rebellion against divine authority.

The narrative repeatedly (four times) underlines Elihu's anger (in 32:2 (twice), 32:3, and once more in 32:5. Elihu's rage against Job (who protests against divine justice) is (apparently) justified since, after Job's answer to the first theophany (40:4-5), The divinity assigns blame to Job for persisting in his rage against divine justice (40:8). However, Elihu's anger against Job will be described in the epilogue as unjustified (as an animal ferocity), since it contradicts the insistently credited Job's righteousness (42:7–8).[1]

b) Sarcastic Loss of Family Name

The narrator introduces Elihu as the son of Barjael, from the Buzi family, and the lineage of Ram (32:2). This seems to underscore an aristocratic background as his social origin.

Still, Elihu presents himself as the son of Barjael, of the Buzi family (32:6). The description of his roots is striking, as no other actor in the complex plot of the book of Job introduces himself; all other characters, including the divinity, are presented (and defined) briefly and exclusively by the narrator. This implies that Elihu separates himself from his people (the lineage of Ram) and uproots himself from a tradition.

In the second part of his monologue, Elihu will uproot his name from any social identity. He will radicalize his separation from foreign divinities, kings, and countries (34:1; 35:1; 36:1) and retain a rootless individual name (Elihu), pretending to be inspired and elected by divinity. As previously mentioned, the characters of the book of Job reflect a historical perspective of Israel's formal religious doctrine. Elihu seems a Jewish name, plausibly a self-criticism of the traditional historic Jewish doctrine of sacrifice, as a confrontation of men against divinity, pretending to build his messianic future over the ruins of the present world.

c) Unjust Delay of Answer

The narrator points out that Elihu waited to intervene, *as they were older than him and full of days* (32:4). The portrayal of Elihu as an antihero censures his silence and supposed divine inspiration as a form of violence and decay of identity (a name as social identity).

---

1. Job builds a social order (no matter how defective), receives his wife, prays for the three friends, and will be blessed in the epilogue (42:10). Despite his anger, even though he accuses the divinity of tolerating or concealing evil, Job also asks for an explanation and tries to fight against evil through separation. Job's anger does not deny divine justice, only obscures it (40:8). Exaggerating Job's guilt, Elihu's anger denies divine justice. A name underscores a social responsibility; Elihu loses his name (unroots) because he does not assume a social responsibility.

Elihu did not remain silent to understand the arguments of Job and the three friends and to reply to them (if he did not understand them or considered them erroneous). Explaining his inspiration (32:8–10), Elihu disavows the supposed older servants and tyrannical lords—Job and the three friends—to allow them to be destroyed by divine wrath or to melt in their contradictions. Elihu manifests (patient) aggressiveness; "to wait," expressing an unjustified challenge to the authority of the three friends and Job's doctrinal tradition.

The unjust delay (renunciation) presupposes a distortion of reality (intercession): the mulish waiting relies on the existence of instituted evil, supposedly tolerated and hidden by divinity to purify Job. This is a sophism and an ontological contradiction, as divine justice cannot be delayed because a postponed divine justice would mean an institutionalized evil (attributing evil to divinity).[2]

15.2 ELIHU PRESENTS HIMSELF

a) Elihu Claims to Be Inspired

Following the narrator's introduction (32:2–5), Elihu *raises his voice* (32:6) and rhetorically ponders the righteousness of his words, *waiting in*

---

2. Responding in due time means answering after overcoming anger, and recognizing evil by weighing the harm caused and the benefits derived from the unjust origins of violence and submission. Justice is realized in a timely response, and a name signifies the inherent responsibility of the social realm. A man without a name is a violent man, and the delay of an answer refers to the lack of warning or explanation of a punishment. Speaking in due time measures guilt (harm) and restitution. Elihu despises tradition and authority (the merit of Job and the three friends) and abuses silence (which he calls listening to the word in the night). He pretends to benefit divinity (separation) as a violent instrument (supposed inspiration) until the downfall of the established authority. Pretending to exonerate divinity by assuming collective guilt, Elihu accuses Job and the three friends unjustly and disproportionately (with anger), does not establish a coherent foundation for unconscious and collective responsibility (has not a name), and condemns Job without adducing facts, damage, or unjust enrichment (does not answer Job). The epilogue identifies unconscious guilt as the three friends' abuse of prosperity, and Job's guilt as collective responsibility for the abuse of divinity (servility). Job's unconscious and collective guilt does not mean the duty to assume unconditionally the collective disorder because unconscious and collective guilt and responsibility are delimited cases of extended personal liability (for unjust enrichment or damages and injuries due to negligence or breach of a warranty duty as a father or authority). Nevertheless, Eliphaz's anger defends his roots, and Job's anger saves his lineage; Elihu's anger, on the contrary, has no roots and is sterile. Elihu precisely points out the two causes of unconscious and collective responsibility: taking advantage of authority (friends) and not unveiling evil as a duty of guarantee (Job).

silence. The narrator points out a contradiction in Elihu's presentation: to simultaneously speak (raising his voice) and wait silently.

Elihu makes a long and confusing presentation of himself, affirming to be inspired (wise) by the divine presence: *for the spirit is in man and divine inspiration builds him* (32:8), *the spirit of the Lord gives wisdom* (32:9). It seems plausible that the narrative intends to conclude that Elihu confuses anger with inspiration. His supposed inspiration pretends to hide his wrath against Job and the three friends.

Elihu repeats twice אמרתי: to justify his (inspired) silence and long delay in (not) answering. He affirms, first אמרתי, that he is young (צעיר אני) and that he humbles himself before age (tradition) and wisdom (religion, authority), which could justify his silence (32:7). However, after the second אמרתי, his inspiration prevails over wisdom and tradition, and he urges everyone to listen to him (32:10), a repetition, אמרתי, which conceals reproach. His supposed inspiration pretends to prevail by silencing the elder (tradition) and wise (authority), not because of the suitability of his arguments.

b) Elihu's Unjustified Rage Against Job

Elihu affirms that the three friends do not know how to answer Job: *I waited, and behold, none of you brought convincing arguments against Job, any suitable answers against him* (32:12). He criticizes with anger the three friends' final silence (*considering Job righteous in their eyes* [32:1]) because they recognize Job's innocence and, in his view, attribute evil to divinity.

Elihu's speech, claiming divine innocence, deserves honorable praise in the book of Job for there is not and cannot be a causal relationship between divinity and evil. Attributing evil to divinity is an impossible crime because the fact of creation cannot contradict creation itself. Nevertheless, affirming divine innocence and denying Job's innocence does not mean, as a counterpoint, Job's guilt, as innocence and guilt are not correlative or symmetrical concepts. After all, as it has been repeated, only guilt has content (guilt of something); innocence is a negative concept (not being guilty of anything).

Elihu asserts that the root cause of social disorder must be in men, and he confronts Job (who accuses divinity by inference with his affirmed innocence and servility). He renews the individualistic and eschatological presuppositions of the theory of guilt established in the debate between Job and his friends. Elihu correctly concludes that the three friends stand without words (32:15–16). He correctly underlines that guilt and responsibility are not grounded on conscience and will, as Job argues, and have an unconscious and collective component. Elihu denies the legitimacy of sacrifice (the dogmatism of the three friends) and invites the three friends (and Job) to recognize unconscious and collective guilt; still, to acknowledge a deeper (unconscious), and shared (collective) responsibility does not mean a duty to assume unconditional collective guilt (as Elihu concludes).

c) Elihu Exaggerates the Three Friends' and Job's Guilt

Elihu's speech stages objective reasons to rebuke the three friends (the authority) as they unjustly abuse prosperity and take advantage of their social preeminence (32:18–22). Eliphaz has a belly full of words (32:18); *it suggests that* Elihu accuses the friends of filling their bellies with delicacies (abuse of wealth). New wine in jars (32:19); *in a contrary sense*, the three friends abuse the lineage. *Without partiality* (32:21–22), the friends tolerate violence to establish themselves socially and institute servitude (abuse of divinity).

Elihu's criticism of the three friends (the authority) is pertinent, as they abuse prosperity and enforce servitude, assuming supposed divine authority (32:21–22); however, Elihu overstates the three friends' guilt since he justifies the anger toward them for an erroneous reason. Elihu cannot despise the three friends for not condemning Job because the collective disorder is not imputed to the servant except for his unjust use of prosperity (or for complicity with authority in the servitude of the stranger). In the epilogue, divine anger is explained against the friends because they do not speak correctly about divinity, and Elihu justifies (erroneously) his rage against the friends because they do not condemn Job (32:3; 32:5). They (improperly) presuppose evil as an institutionalized being, creation of men as a collective identity, denying personal merit and guilt, in a defective creation.

Accusing men collectively, Elihu does not define the limits of Job's unconscious and collective guilt and exaggerates (unconditional collective) guilt of Job *for not listening at night*. With veiled irony, the narrator mocks Elihu's rhetorical enhancement and endless repetitions. Elihu amplifies the three friends' guilt for not condemning Job because there is no duty to condemn evil except in compliance with a warrant's duty to defend innocents and dependents (*officium* as a father, authority, or tenant). Elihu exaggerates an unconditional unconscious and collective responsibility that must be explained as personal accountability in specific cases: for abusing prosperity or for lack of diligence in revealing evil when it is mandatory (as a father, authority, or author, or in general, in the responsibility of guarantee). Elihu's rage manifests an inclination to prevail by submission and deceit (and not by dialogue and reasoning).[3]

---

3. As a fictitious and boastful character, Elihu is not presented in the prologue; theophanies respond directly to Job without paying attention to Elihu, and he is neither rebuked nor remembered in the epilogue. Elihu preaches self-condemnation by submission and separation and, pretending to exonerate divinity, still accuses heaven by denying a personal imputation of guilt, instituting collective damnation, and presupposing divine punishment without warning and explanation. Elihu's anger against the three friends for not finding an answer (32:3, 5) seems justified since divine anger rises against Job's anger (40:8) and the three friends, who do not speak correctly (42:7–8). Nevertheless, the epilogue will underline that the three friends admit the innocence of the servant Job without assuming their collective responsibility as an authority (which is bound to free the servant). The epilogue posits that the three friends and Elihu's accusations against Job are an incoherent imputation of heaven for tolerating or concealing evil.

XVI.

The Supposed Inspiration at Night

16.1 INSPIRED COLLECTIVE GUILT

a) Elihu's Pompous and Contemptuous Language

A lengthy and ostentatious narrative introduces Elihu, the antihero, as a petulant and boastful character marked by repulsive language. The prologue to Elihu's doctrine intends to ridicule his claim of divine inspiration, purity, and wisdom.

Elihu proclaims the excellence of his person and doctrine (33:2–5). He orders Job to be silent and listen to his words (33:1). He pretends to be noble of heart and clear of lips (justifying submission at night and confession of guilt) (33:3). Incessantly reiterating his purity and wisdom to justify his inspiration (*My words express the uprightness of my heart, and my lips clearly show my honesty* [33:4]), formed in the clay (33:6), he boasts his humility (33:7): *Therefore I say to you, listen to me, I will reveal my knowledge to you* (32:10).

Elihu (the pretended divine serf) manipulates words (the social realm) and humiliates and discredits the righteous Job (the personal merit and human authority). Elihu despises Job and repeats (like the three friends) that Job *is condemned by his tongue* (15:6; 33:12). He also presents a populist profile; he asserts not discriminating (32:21) and not flattering the powerful (32:22) (a hinted criticism of Job and his friends). As a master of verbosity and a skilled inquisitor, Elihu affirms representing the highest authority, abuses an intimate and friendly tone, redundantly repeats Job's name, and assumes camaraderie and friendship toward those he despises, intending to subjugate them and inciting rebellion (confess) against instituted authority.

b) Innocence and Guilt as Unrelated Concepts

Elihu justifies his rhetoric with an appropriate reproach to Job's claim to be innocent (33:9). Indeed, Job's insolent tone can seem unwise; after all, in both English and Spanish, *innocent* can mean naïve or foolish.

Nevertheless, denying Job's innocence does not justify Job's unlimited unconscious accountability because innocence and guilt are unrelated concepts. As noted earlier, innocence is a negative concept that lacks substance (innocent of what?), and guilt has different sources and effects, whose origin and measure must be established in each case with its causes and consequences.

Conscience of responsibility and guilt awakens through suffering. Of course, there are unconscious and collective misdeeds with roots at night; even so, Elihu does not justify an unlimited collective liability for someone else's actions and the collective disorder. Elihu exaggerates Job's unconscious and collective guilt. His pompous and contemptuous tone serves a unique purpose: to deny Job's innocence (33:9) and portray him as a divine enemy (33:10–11), compelling him to confess his rebellion. As concluded in the earlier debate with the three friends, a supposed divine inspiration is an incoherent justification for the institution of arbitrary authority and a messianic justification of violence: *Who can oppose him?* (23:13).

c) Elihu's Inspiration Lacks Authenticity

Elihu posits that Job pretends *to have been punished without warning or explanation* (33:10–11), on what he insists in chs. 35–36. As a counterpoint, he invites Job to listen at night (33:12) *since the Lord speaks to us directly, once and twice, and we pay no attention* (33:14). Then *[in the night] he opens the ears of men, and they recognize the root [מסרם] of their misdeeds* (33:16).

Elihu has no doubts about the authenticity of what he supposedly hears at night. He describes three modes of (divine) inspiration: *in dreams, visions at night, and while he is carried away by sleep and lies on his bed* (33:15). Yet Job refers to these same forms—dreams, visions, and sleep—as divine tools of torment (7:14). Elihu presupposes an arbitrary hidden divinity in the night that imputes to men collective guilt, for a supposed misdeed of his parents or authority, in an undeserved redemptive punishment, *to preserve their soul from destruction and prevent their body from falling under the sword* (33:18). *He punishes them with suffering in bed, breaking most of their bones* (33:19).

Elihu's Achilles's heel lies in the lack of authenticity of inspiration at night: man's inability to discern whether divinity talks, his greed and pride, or the grievances of a dramatic past; *if he spoke to me, I wouldn't know who answers me* (9:16). To exaggerate the duty to listen at night (to a concealed divinity) envelops Elihu's inspiration in the duty to submit, threatened by an imminent divine menace and punishment: *He punishes them with suffering in bed. He breaks most of his bones* (33:19). Collective guilt envisions a vengeful divinity who punishes the innocent, condemns a man for some other's misdeeds, and does not value man in his individual and social identity.

16.2 DENIAL OF FREE WILL

a) Confession of Collective Guilt

Elihu pretends to overcome collective disorder and elude divine punishment by confessing unconditional guilt. Elihu affirms that (only) the spirit of the Lord (a confession) builds (32:9) and gives life (33:4). Elihu's indiscriminate confession of collective guilt (as personal guilt) can be praised because it unveils and overcomes the three friends' dogmatic of violent sacrificial rebellion. It must also be applauded because it affirms divine innocence and criticizes Job's pretended innocence.

Of course, Job is not innocent and must assume his delimited (not unconditional) unconscious and collective guilt as an (individual) responsibility that builds the social realm. Overcoming collective disorder begins with personal awareness and responsibility for harm or restitution, and attributing merit and guilt to its (individual) origin (based on personal freedom) prevents imputing evil to divinity and authority. However, Elihu exaggerates man's guilt, and confession of collective guilt does not repair the collective disorder. Shockingly, the book of Job presents confession as divine punishment (33:16–17), to restrain a man and cover his haughtiness (33:17). Elihu overstates Job's guilt (personal liability) and deorbits the exigency of confessing collective guilt.

Only personal merit and freedom can constitute a man's social identity. Only warning and explanation of punishment (identifying and paying personal debts) prevent violence, not the collective confession and renunciation. The most natural content of inspiration (Providence) must be, as the first and second theophany will develop, teaching the authority and the servant, night and day, to build a coherent social order by warning and explaining punishment, which prevents violence and unveils the reasons for the disorder. The prologue criticizes Elihu's confession (patient submission) when rebuking Satan's (second) accusation in heaven (*to take everything from him* [1:11]) as an incitement to vain punishment (2:3).[1]

b) Confession as Falsehood

As a basic principle, confession can refer only to facts, never to guilt, personal or collective. Confession of collective guilt is pertinent as personal debt only when admitting facts after a lawful personal accusation, or by assuming a warrant's duty. As it has been said, collective responsibility can be imputed to Job as a tenant of the earth only for unjust enrichment, damages resulting from negligence, or the failure of a father or authority figure to fulfill the warrant's duty to their innocent descendants or dependents (known as *officium* in Roman law).

To confess collective guilt is a falsehood (false inspiration) deprived of authenticity in identifying the supposed inspiring divinity, the inspirational content, and the collective evil that must be confessed. The confession of collective guilt is false because no one can assume what is nonexistent or unknown. Collective disorder refers to an unjust enrichment or damage that the confessor cannot identify in its origin or measure (and lacks specific content). It is a social fraud because confession of collective guilt imputes guilt to an unknown and nonexistent subject (the collective) with no conscience and will.

The confession of collective guilt, the apotheosis of patient submission, denies the (personal) origin of guilt and accuses the innocents,

---

1. The inspired confession of collective guilt of man (in the night) has no objective or scriptural foundation and cannot be attributed to divinity. It presupposes a divinity who tolerates physical violence, sexual manipulation, and institutional evil without consideration for the defense of the innocent. It undermines man's labor and hospitality as the coherent origin of a social realm.

confronting origins and tradition: parents and lineage. It confuses personal guilt with unconscious guilt (abusing prosperity) and with collective guilt (the [limited] duty to condemn evil and assume intercession).

c) Renunciation as Denial of Social Identity

Elihu presupposes that refraining from bread and food prevents the soul from falling into the abyss and the body from being destroyed by the sword (33:18). The duty to listen at night (to a concealed divinity) envelops Elihu's inspiration in an imminent threat. *He punishes them with suffering in bed. He breaks most of his bones* (33:19).

Bread and delicacies (referring to wealth and sexuality) are considered instruments for testing (temptation) and punishing (servitude). Elihu posits that night inspires man to despise bread and delicacies (33:20) and incites flesh to *be consumed and bones exposed* (33:21). Elihu presupposes that flesh and bones *draw his soul near the abyss* (of a false divinity) *and his life into the hand of the murderous* (king) (33:22). Elihu argues that an intercessory angel (מלאך מליץ), among a thousand, rises at night and shows man *the right path* (33:23).

Elihu interprets renunciation as the *right path* to fulfill the divine mandate (of confession) and rescue man (33:24), stating a misleading argument. Elihu presumes that assuming unconditional guilt means purity of intention, and renouncing prosperity, sexuality, and authority overcomes collective disorder, denying the instruments that build a social identity and overcome servitude.

Elihu does not identify in personal responsibility (free will) a coherent origin for responsibility, guilt, and man's social identity. Renouncing prosperity conceives wealth, sexuality, and the foreign social realm as evil, opposed to divinity, and not testimony of (personal) merit and responsibility (free will). He does not ponder that renunciation incurs guilt and responsibility by omission (for unjust impoverishment or insolvency). It denies the social identity of the confessor, which is grounded in delicacies, flesh, and bones, plausibly referring to authority, organization, property, and marriage.

d) Incitement to Violence

By confessing, Elihu pretends to be chosen by divinity to suffer. Elihu's confession becomes an accusation against the accuser, projecting false charges onto human and divine authority. Elihu's confession builds an animal farm because sexuality and prosperity are seen as a price for violence or submission and not retribution for personal freedom and merit (marriage as free consent). Confession of collective guilt justifies renunciation and intercession and builds a defective ethic of separation and temptation (submissive violence), uprooting the confessor and blaming divinity for a defective creation.

Elihu's renunciation is an autonomous crime of incitement for profit, incurring the crime of sedition. He presupposes that, by renouncing prosperity, he will inherit authority and overcome the collective disorder. The doctrine of renunciation entails constructing an idealistic messianism that aspires to achieve wealth and authority not by improving the social realm and liberating servants but through deceit and temptation. Renunciation to overcome supposed collective guilt undermines human and divine authority, and despises the multitude (the days) and tradition (the old).

Elihu preaches silence in the night and personalizes the anger of a man who condemns authority, sexuality, and property. Elihu's thoughts are exhausted in generalities (praise of good and condemnation of evil) and are mere wordiness to justify servitude.

Rebuking Satan's accusation (*to take everything from him* [1:11]), the prologue criticizes renunciation, which is labeled as an incitement to unjust violence and vain punishment (2:3). Renunciation overcomes personal violence but incites collective violence and does not build a coherent social order. It justifies servility (confession and intercession) as an aggravated accusation of guilt (against humanity and divinity), muddles merit with guilt, punishes the innocent, condones wrongdoing, and presupposes authority and prosperity as evil.

16.3 DEFECTIVE CREATION

a) Intercession as Incitement to Rebellion

Elihu seeks to resolve collective disorder and avert divine punishment through intercession (paying the collective debt). Elihu concludes that intercession restores youth (33:25), appeases divinity, and rewards upright conduct (33:26). *I sinned and perverted what was straight* (33:27). If Job intercedes, divinity promises to restore his youth, pays for his righteousness (33:25–26), and guarantees that he will see the light (33:28).

I have justified that collective guilt does not exist; therefore, it cannot be confessed or interceded for. By renouncing, the confessor cannot intercede because, after renouncing to prosperity, he cannot pay his debts. In the best scenario, the intercessor pays individual debts randomly, not repairing the (imaginary) collective disorder and unjustly enriching the current debtors. He undermines free will and human merit as the origin of property, marriage, and authority, creates (ideally) foreign deities, and imagines corrupted foreign men.

Authority is the debtor of the collective disorder because it must identify (as a warrant) the debts (of life and freedom) to favor the survival of the social realm. The intercessor erodes the social realm, breaching man's warrant duty as a father, author, and authority, as he does not pay debts according to their hierarchy and priority (the only way to improve the social disorder).[2]

b) Supposed Divine Tolerance of Evil

Intercession presupposes a lazy and humdrum divinity who does not know or does not want to impose justice and needs men's sacrifice, suffering, and servitude (confession, renunciation, and intercession) to overcome the personal and collective disorder at night.

Elihu presents a daunting view of Providence, which *two and three times* incites man to repent (to confess guilt, renounce bread and delicacies, and find the right path [33:29]). Elihu posits that divinity resorts to

---

2. In his response to the second theophany (*I know that you can do everything and that no purpose can resist you* [42:2]), Job succumbs to an ideal intercessory separation and renounces his former exigency of a warning and explanation of punishment. The second theophany criticizes intercession as a fraud for profit (*nebelah*) due to anger (40:8). The epilogue depicts and criticizes intercession as Job pretending to inherit the land (double prosperity), praying for his friends (42:7–8), and not praying with preference for the intercessor's debt of guarantee (the duty to fight against evil in defense of the innocent and dependent). The *nebelah* must be considered the punishment for breaking the guarantee's duty in its triple facet of economic, marital, and religious freedom. Intercession often implies stealing prosperity to pay the debts of authority, pretending to supplant authority on the day of the inexorable catastrophe of the foreign social realm. Intercession presupposes temptation as an incitement to violence and is labeled as a false submission fueled by anger (40:8).

collective punishment if a person fails to intercede or does not find an intercessory angel willing to suffer and relieve the sinner from unavoidable punishment.

In Elihu's thought, a violent divinity confronts Job with the burden of repairing a defective creation. Elihu portrays an incoherent macho deity who goes out partying at night to rape the most righteous, boasting his power and, after two or three threats, compels them to confess the collective disorder, repent, intercede, and arrange the collective disorder (someone else's misdeeds). It presupposes an institutionalized evil (concealed and tolerated by divinity) that divine predestination arranges through violence and deceit (temptation), assuming that the end justifies the means.

Yet, as stated earlier in Job's dialogue with the three friends, divinity does not need the help of man (intercessor) to establish justice (9:5–12). Furthermore, divine violence provokes a null confession and renunciation. Evil cannot be created, tolerated, or institutionalized by divinity through temptation (or separation), and it makes no sense to build justice at night and not in broad daylight. Man cannot correct a perfect creation founded on (personal) merit and guilt, and Providence fulfills its purpose with lawful means, not on collective punishment. It is inconsistent that divinity would establish a dictatorship on earth that punishes the just at night, without warning and explanation, for supposed collective (other's) faults.[3]

---

3. Furthermore, Job explains that there cannot be intercession because there is no authenticity of the divine word: *If he spoke to me, I wouldn't know who answered me* (9:16). Reality, not intercession, unveils evil because man cannot correct a perfect creation: *Would you intimidate a leaf that has fallen from a tree?* (13:25). Intercession justifies an arbitrary authority. An arbitrary Creator favors the triumph of evil and gives rise to the nihilistic philosophy of the death of divinity. Nietzsche conceives Job as the personification of the religious morality of eternal submission, destructive of culture. In *The Genealogy of Morality*, he presents the Jewish priests of the Second Temple, promoting Christianity and its morality of slavery (Nietzsche, *Genealogía de la moral*, 37–80). The resentment of the weak explains the concept of original sin, a paradigm of subordination and mental corruption. Through submission (beyond good and evil), the slaves completed their revenge by building the Second Temple. Nietzsche reworks the Hegelian doctrine and poses the death of divinity as an unavoidable consequence of the unworthiness of Job's divinity, which makes man a slave. *Thus Spoke Zarathustra* was written as a critique of the book of Job and as a manifestation of Judeo-Christian culture in crisis, contradicting the Dionysian spirit of tragedy and human merit *Zarathustra*, quotes Job 8:9: "We are of yesterday, we know nothing; for our days are a shadow upon the ground." It is interpreted as an antithesis of Zarathustra. Zarathustra claims for himself the very being of his past and future (Nietzsche, *Así habló Zaratustra*, 79n233). In this same sense, Jung, in *Response to Job*, maintains that Job humiliates divinity with his superior virtue (Miranda, "Priest, Psychiatrist, and Evil," 106–37).

c) Remorse for a Sacrificial Past

The chapter ends with Elihu exhorting the overwhelmed Job to be silent and refrain from speaking (as a serf). Elihu supposes the language (word) to be divine (inspiration) and not a human essence (of social identity). *To rescue man from the abyss and benefit him with light* (33:30), in shocking contradiction, is experienced at night, not in the day (33:30–33).

Throughout the book of Job, all the characters describe Job's past, and it is fair to conclude that *dreams, visions, and sleep* refer to Job's pretended innocence in his three exiles in Canaan, Persia, and Greece. The only plausible coherence of the *dreams, visions, and sleeping in bed* lies in Job's painful emotion after contemplating a violent and tragic story of pretended divine election and the incoherence of the three modes of sacrifice of life, sexuality, and prosperity (the two destroyed temples and the temple's restoration) that personify Job's sacrificial origins. Job's dreams are a rationalization of his past without a coherent conscience of (personal) guilt.

Only the end of divinity can restore the moral balance between man and his Creator; the deity must die to surpass the moral height of Job. Christianity pretends to answer the ethical dilemma presented in the book of Job. Kierkegaard contradicts the Hegelian presuppositions of religion and defines Job as a paradigm of faith (The rule must be to pray for and love one's neighbour not the application of a rule, Mañon Garibay, *Kierkegaard y la mística del silencio*, 338).

XVII.

Providence's Dictatorship

17.1 PUNISHMENT OF THE RIGHTEOUS

a) Insistence on Job's Guilt

The final four chapters of Elihu's discourse (34–37) reiterate similar doctrine as those in chs. 31–34. The narrative underlines repetition to criticize Elihu's crushing.

In a flaunty introduction to his final monologue (34:1–11), Elihu affirms the preeminence of inspiration and reproaches Job, who pretends to be innocent (34:2–3). *I am righteous, and the Lord deprives me of my right* (34:5); *a man obtains no benefit by following the Lord* (34:9). Elihu insists on rebuking Job's unacceptable pretentiousness (34:7). He ardently argues about the impeccable divine justice (34:10–15), contradicts the audacity of Job, who claims to have been punished without warning or explanation, and concludes that claiming innocence and unjust punishment is a rebellion against divine justice (33:8–9; 34:5, 31).

Elihu repeats the same arguments already presented regarding the doctrine of inspiration, confession, renunciation, and intercession. By confronting divine justice and asking for an explanation, Elihu concludes that Job *adds transgression to his sin; he speaks loquaciously among us and multiplies his words against divinity* (34:37).

b) Elihu Asserts Divine Innocence and Justice

Elihu emphasizes heaven's innocence and justice (34:10–30). Divine authority rewards man for his deeds and pays him according to his conduct (34:11). His eyes watch man's ways, attentive to all his steps (34:21).

The nuclear argument states that Job must learn from his misfortune (accept his punishment and servitude) and not protest against the supposedly unjust authority (of his friends), for divinity does not establish a false authority. The intercessory angel (Providence) will punish the corrupt authority without warning or explanation (34:20–25). Following Eliphaz's argument, Elihu asserts that divinity punishes the powerful who fail to protect those at risk of death or social exclusion (34:27) or do not heed the cries of the suffering (34:28).

c) Job's Rebellion

As previously noted, Elihu's insistence on Job's guilt assumes divine tolerance and concealment of unjust authority. *If he keeps silent, who can blame him? If he hides, who might see him?* (34:29). Divinity punishes, hiding his face (34:29). Elihu insists that Job has no sense of justice and behaves like a fool (34:35); to ask for a warning or explanation of punishment and servitude constitutes an act of rebellion (34:33–37) and accusing the divinity of concealing evil (36:13).

In ch. 35, Elihu insists on divine innocence, condemning Job's protests as the greed and pride of a rebel servant. He repeats the argument with which Eliphaz opens the third cycle of dialogues. *What advantages do I have, and what profit if I don't do evil?* (35:3). Elihu refutes Job's statement, as evil does not affect divinity and does not give or take anything from heaven (35:6–8).

Elihu describes Job's supposed rebellion against divine authority as a conflict between servants and masters. The rebellious servant unjustly and ephemerally conquers the earth (the beasts of the land) and institutes authority (the birds of the sky) (35:11). The pride of the wicked deceives him (as an authority), and servants are condemned by their rebellion (against the divinity), for not listening in the night (35:12). Elihu argues that Job's unacceptable innocence pledges that the Lord consents to evil (35:13–16); quite the opposite, Providence oversees the social realm and people's history (33:13–14), and his anger ensures the just punishment of the rebel (33:15).[1]

17.2 ANGER OF VENGEFUL PROVIDENCE

a) Nature and Social Realm as Instruments of Divine Wrath

Elihu focuses his final arguments on exaggerating a supposed confrontation between nature (ch. 36) and the social realm (ch. 37). Elihu praises waiting patiently for Providence amid the friends' greed and the supposed pride of Job's rebellion.

Chapters 36–37 mock Elihu's exaggerated and pompous claims about nature and inspiration as tools of divine Providence and wrath. In a superficial and lofty way, Elihu repeats what he previously said about Job's (collective) guilt. These chapters portray a supposed arbitrary Providence who punishes without warning and explanation (tolerating and concealing evil). Job *should choose poverty, not turn to iniquity* (36:21); Job *should hearken to heaven's inspiration and ponder the divine wonders* (37:14).

Chapters 36–37 mark a shift toward a dramatic turning point, in which suffering is no longer merely a means to restore order, but the very foundation of divine order. The radicalization of Elihu's discourse prepares the reader for the theophanies, which restore personal justice and refute Elihu's silence. It can be said that chs. 34–35 summarize the doctrine of "suffering in the night" to learn and intercede, while chs. 36–37 establish the doctrine of "passively suffering in day and night," assuming the arbitrary and violent divine work of purifying a corrupt man. Elihu separates from nature and the social realm as a being created only to endure the suffering of human rebellion. The last two chapters present

---

1. Elihu claims to repeat Job's words, but he distorts his statements, dramatizes them out of context, and exaggerates them to insist on Job's rebellion. *Job opens his mouth with vanity; he increases words without knowledge* (35:16). The explanation of Job's guilt and responsibility in the theophanies and the conclusion of Job's righteousness in the epilogue (42:7–8) contradict Elihu's doctrine on Job's rebellion. The friends are punished for contradicting Job (42:8), and Elihu must be rebuked for unjustly tempting him and persisting in his unfounded anger over Job's demanding an explanation. The divinity does not heed Job's impertinence, as the book of Job repeatedly recognizes his righteousness. Job imputes to divinity the toleration and hiding of evil, but his intemperate language can be excused, or at least attenuated (amid suffering), by his lack of knowledge or error about the origin of evil. Job's inadmissible protest against divine justice means only an impertinent compliance (excuse of innocence), and it does not presuppose a crime of rebellion (as no one can rebel against divinity).

the alleged submission of nature to the divine will, a systematic recap and critique of Elihu's doctrine denying causality. The divine determination of nature and social order denies merit and personal responsibility.[2]

b) Exclusion of Responsibility by Exaggerating Guilt

In ch. 36, Elihu insists on arguments about human corruption, confession, and intercession. He repeats his doxology of Providence as an apology of servitude, depicting a divinity who builds the social order and directs history by submitting nature (suffering) and with his thundering word (creating a redeemed social identity). In Elihu's thought, nature is an instrument overlapped by Providence to condemn the wicked and reward the righteous (36:6–7).

A jealous and vengeful divinity elects a righteous servant at night to make him suffer the collective disorder and institute authority. *He opens their ears to discipline and commands them to repent of iniquity* (36:10). Elihu presumes that divinity conceals and tempts (induces violence) to shackle men with chains (36:13). Silent suffering, by contrast, educates, promotes attention to the divine word, and seeks redemption (36:15–16). By proclaiming his innocence, Elihu concludes that Job denies Providence and *prefers evil to suffering* (36:21).

Finally, he reiterates his faith in an intercessory Providence (36:26–33). Elihu concludes that men abuse prosperity and authority through greed and pride (36:9); prosperity corrupts the greedy man, who refuses to listen (36:12), and nature rebels against the corrupted man (36:27–33). Elihu excludes individual guilt and responsibility by exaggerating collective guilt and the role of Providence in establishing a social realm.

---

2. The confessor is not the purifying savior but the executor of (unjust) collective punishment. Leviathan "humbly asks for mercy and confesses with bitter words" (40:27). It seems likely that this refers to the exaggerated confession and moral of submission and separation that Elihu formulates and that Job submits to in his response to the first theophany. The first theophany affirms personal guilt (*Who obscures my plans with meaningless words?* [38:2; 42:3]) and criticizes confessing unknown guilt (*I will question you, and you must answer me* [38:3]). Theophanies will explain to Job that confession, renunciation, and intercession are based on anger (violence or submission) and contradict divine justice (40:8).

c) Contempt for Labor and Merit of Man

Chapter 37 insists on the dictatorship and anger of a vengeful Providence. Divinity paralyzes men with the terror of his voice (37:5-6). The thunderous and disturbing divine word directs authority and history (37:9-12).

Elihu does not interpret the word as a tradition (history) that builds the social order but as a divine punishment that establishes the social order (authority) through suffering and servitude. Elihu's approach interprets divine inspiration as a punishment and does not value authority and social order as the merit and labor of man. Elihu demands silence and attention from Job (37:14). His monologue manifests contempt for man, who builds in darkness (37:19), portraying a divinity who remains hidden in the mystery of majesty (37:22).

Elihu repeats the arguments of the three friends, insisting on Eliphaz's denial of warning and explanation of punishment (*corrupt men cannot claim justice* [4:12-21]); on Bildad's determinism (*A mortal cannot be just before the Lord, one born of a woman cannot be innocent* [25:4]); and on Zophar's idealism (*the Lord knows and judges the wicked* [11:11]). The difference lies in that the three friends use the arguments against Job the servant, and Elihu against serfs and lords alike. Elihu concludes that condemning the serf means also convicting authority, dogmatizing the new doctrine of submission to divine Providence.

In conclusion, Elihu has no roots and is sterile. He is presented as a nonexistent mirage or hallucination, Job's exaggerated antihero (alazon). Elihu demonstrates a disdain for property, marriage, and authority, lacking a consistent ethical framework. He also creates a notion of Providence's predestination over nature and social matters. He affirms that the (supposed) divinity does not fear those who feel wise and undervalues human wisdom (37:24). He does not recognize man as a being built in divine resemblance.

THIRD ACT

Job's Moral Riddle

XVIII.

The Apotheosis of Idealism

18.1 DOGMATIC OF AUTHORITY AND ORGANIZATION

a) Debate on Job's Guilt in Jewish Tradition

The Jewish tradition addresses the figure of Satan as part of a discussion aimed at overcoming Persian Manichaeism. Job questions the reasons for his suffering, challenging the unsatisfactory nature of the sacrificial narratives in religious history (in the debate with his three friends).

The formalization of the Jewish canon is attributed to the school of Yabne in the context of a crisis of sacrificial theology. The Talmud discusses whether Job will acquire a part in the future world. Johannan ben Zakkai argues that Job serves divinity out of fear, but Joshua ben Hananiah contradicts him by affirming that Job serves the Lord out of love.

In the Talmud, Raba states that the earth was given to the wicked, that it covers the faces of the judges, and that the Lord consents to it (Baba Batra 16a). Abaye assimilates the vision of a rebellious Satan to Persian Manichaeism, and he presents Satan as a servant of the divinity. Rabbi Akiba, and the later Tannaim and the Amoraim, insists on the righteousness of Job. Job's righteousness of intention is recognized in the consolidated interpretation of the Talmud and the Midrashim (such as the Midrash Rabbah, Zohar, and Pirkei of Rabbi Eliezer), and even compared to Abraham's virtue.

In medieval Jewish doctrine, Maimonides attempts to systematize the rabbinic tradition on Job, especially the Talmud, according to the principles of Greek philosophy's systematic thought.

Maimonides interprets the book of Job as ascension in the personal experience of divinity. The *Guide of the Perplexed* states that divinity has neither created nor consented to evil, concluding: "That is why the following proposition has been established in general terms: All evils are privations" (3.10).[1] He defines evil as a lack of content and assimilates Christian and Muslim dogma into Manichaeism because they conceive Satan as a rebellious or servant angel. In ch. 11, Maimonides justifies the proposition that man is the cause of his misfortunes. In ch. 12, he addresses the problem of evil, which he conceives as something created by man, who engenders his misfortune. Maimonides interprets evil as privation, a perverse inclination, and the result of a disordered imagination, by which, as an alternative, man also achieves his perfection by subduing his depraved inclinations.

Maimonides describes inspiration as the personal ascent in the consciousness of divinity by studying law, showing contempt for the world, and assuming personal guilt. According to Maimonides, Job was not wise, only upright and feared the Lord; before his misfortune, he only knew divinity through his acceptance of authority. Refuting original and collective guilt, he aims to resolve the contradictions posed by the existence of Satan and the tolerance of temptation, the two pillars of the sacrificial dogmatic.

b) Supposed Divine Justification of Authority and Organization

In medieval Christian commentaries, the reality of the incarnation dogmatizes original guilt and conceives Job as the righteous man who experiences the despair of (collective) sin, confesses, and repents. As an individual manifestation of pride, revelation is discarded as irrelevant and admitted exclusively for dogmatic justification.

Gregory the Great systematizes the conclusions of patristic thought. He explains confession as submission to the divine will, not exempt from the dangers of spiritual pride. The church is the new divine covenant with humanity, a testimony of incarnation (divine sacrifice), and he interprets

---

1. Maimónides, *Guía de los perplejos*, 384.

religion founded on divine revelation as Jewish pride. A long historical debate about men's guilt institutionalizes authority and organization as a social reality of the incarnation. The history of man, disordered by sin, justifies an authority that represents the new universal covenant.

Gregory describes the first theophany as a story of the creation and institutionalization of the church, and the second theophany as a struggle against the flesh and Satan, symbolized by Behemoth and Leviathan (an eschatological struggle reproduced in every man). He presents Job as a prophet.

The debate between Job and his friends allegorizes redemption. When the Lord delivers Job into the hands of Satan, it prefigures the sufferings of the Redeemer; the delivery of the world to the wicked symbolizes the crucifixion (*Moralia* 35.13); *I am a stranger in his eyes* (Job 19:15) and Elihu's dogmatic, the rejection of the synagogue. Theophany has an allegorical prophetic allusion to the incarnation but without substantive ethical content, which refers to the (authoritarian) institution of the church. The epilogue (*My servant Job will pray for you* [42:7–8]) explains the intercession of the church and its redemptive mission.

Jewish criticism, especially Maimonides, suggests that patristic dogma on sin may deny personal free will. Thomas Aquinas rebukes Job's immoderate language but insists on original sin corrupting human nature. He describes Job's impotence in his struggle for justice, even strengthened by suffering. He emphasizes that the purpose of the book of Job is to justify free will in an eschatological fight against Satan, which only Providence can guide to personal and collective salvation.[2] The first theophany has an institutional sense describing the wonders of Providence in evil's submission; the second theophany portrays Behemoth and Leviathan as evil's incarnations; and personifies the perversion of Satan, who tempts Job as part of the history of salvation.

Thomas Aquinas blurs the authoritarian sense of the institution of the church that Gregory's *Moralia* hints at. Only free will justifies spiritual judgment, but inspiration and personal revelation have no decisive role in the institutional order that Providence guides. Providence in Aquinas defines the supremacy of the organization over authority, as free will (personal conscience) prevailing over any temporal organization. The divine intervention in the storm reveals the danger of personal pride, as the saint Job is carried away, at times, like Elihu, by intemperance and anger.

---

2. Cabello, "Libro de Job," 42–49.

The epilogue stages the triumph over Satan, personified in Behemoth and Leviathan, and gives meaning to history on a personal and eschatological level.

c) Debate on Legitimacy of Temptation

As I have said, medieval Jewish interpretation, confronting Satan as a servant of divinity, affirms the unjust character of temptation and does not accept that, without guilt, an arbitrary divinity might test man to improve his virtue (Zemah Duran).[3] Satan has no essence and manifests ignorance or error.

The Guide of the Perplexed contradicts the Mutazili trend in medieval Islam, which affirms that divine wisdom tempts the righteous to make him acquire merit. Maimonides states that Satan and temptation are incoherent; divinity does not employ Satan as his servant or tolerate temptation. In ch. 17 on Providence, Maimonides denies that man suffers to increase a future reward, and this is because no evil can come from divinity. Chapter 24 of bk. 3 argues that temptation cannot be understood as caused or tolerated by divinity (as a test) since divinity already knows the future. In ch. 24, Maimonides reasons at length about the lack of legitimacy of temptation, which cannot be understood as consented to by divinity. This is how we should interpret the stories referring to trials and temptations, not imagining that God wants to examine us or test us to find out what he knows in advance. He is far above what ignorant and foolish people imagine in the evil of their thoughts.

Maimonides interprets Isaac's so-called intended sacrifice as an explanation (teaching) to Abraham, not a temptation. It seems that divinity afflicts man to increase his reward, but Maimonides thinks that in Exod 16:4, temptation has the same meaning as Deut 13:4, as a prophecy of a false divinity (*Guide of the Perplexed*, bk. 3, ch. 24).

d) Personal and Collective Responsibility

Calvin pretends to build an ethic based on free will and tries to overcome the contradictions underlined by Maimonides in patristic dogmatic. Through the doctrine of predestination, he pretends to resolve the compatibility of free will with a collective sin that precedes man. Calvin

---

3. Eisen, *Book of Job*, 175.

conceives evil as a servant of divinity and suffering as the instrument of conversion. The prologue, an allegory of the Old Testament, depicts the conflict between divinity and Satan. Before the beginning of human time, incarnation triumphed over Satan; Behemoth and Leviathan are the divine servants that reveal the nature of Satan.

In the first edition of the *Christian Institutes*, Calvin placed the doctrine of predestination as a part of Providence in the treatise on divinity; in later editions, he situated predestination in the doctrine of redemption.[4] Predestination does not mean that a man is born saved or condemned; it explains that divinity plays with time and uses knowledge of the human future to prevent man from sinning. Divinity knows the rebellious man individually, even before creation, punishes and enlightens him (at the opportune time), and uses nature and revelation to favor men's conversion and redemption.

Calvin conceives evil not as a personal character but as a defective inclination of a rebellious man. In the theophanies, Job listens directly to the divinity, who does not institute authority or organization but institutes the church as charity and preaching, testimony of the incarnation; as a triumph over sin, and assistance to man in his struggle against evil. Divine incarnation subdues Satan and human pride, as divinity judges every man according to his responsibility founded on free will. Theophanies refer to themes of creation, redemption, and salvation through the incarnation, rather than focusing on the damnation of mankind.

Elihu listens to the divine word and confesses; he represents the church that realizes the revelation in history as the creative (redemptive) process of man and history. Job discusses divine justice and manifests his sin of pride. After listening to the theophanies, he will be saved by grace, through the confession of guilt, in dust and ashes. Job does not experience the divine presence but hears in the theophanies a reproach and reveals his disordered inclinations; in his responses, he becomes aware of and confesses his sin of rebellion; he repents and manifests faith, the reality of salvation. To confess, however, does not mean justifying sacrifice but trusting in the incarnation as the history of salvation through faith.

---

4. Ong, "John Calvin on Providence."

18.2 EVIL'S LACK OF CONTENT

a) Criticism of Religious Authoritarianism

In the *Short Treatise on God, Man & His Well-Being*, Spinoza argues that Satan, as a being wholly opposed to God, cannot exist because it would lack any perfection, a property essential for an existing thing's duration and essence, making such a being incompatible with Spinoza's concept of an eternal divinity. He also argues that if the devil is a thing that is once for all opposed to God, and has absolutely nothing from God, then he is precisely identical with nothing.[5]

Spinoza's *Theological-Political Treatise* criticizes Maimonides's doctrine for interpreting Scripture through Platonic and Aristotelian perspectives, as he deceives himself with Hellenistic philosophy and culture, expressing an idealist thought.[6] Spinoza thinks that the Aristotelian distinction between matter and form is pure rhetoric and that prophetic knowledge is imaginative and unrealistic. Prophetic revelation grants a subjective moral certainty that justifies the violent authoritarian institution, incompatible with the philosophical truth that must create the laws.

The title of his book summarizes its content: the theological foundation deprives the state of institutional coherence. Authority founded on a religion discriminates against men by their religious beliefs and does not create a stable political order; it provokes internal quarrels and makes the citizen a servant and not a subject. Philosophy itself begins as a reaction to the unjust death of Socrates, which we can interpret, from Plato's dialogues, as the rebellion of thought against an arbitrary divinity who pretends human sacrifice, temptation, and the submission of man.

In the natural life, before a social institution, there is no sin; in the political order, only law defines sin.[7] Individual freedom of thought must prevail over revelation and law because it is impossible to prove the authenticity of a revelation. Religious controversy provokes schism and confrontation, the triumph of fanatics, and the exaltation of flatterers and traitors. In ch. 3 of the *Theological-Political Treatise*, Spinoza conceives a religion founded in wisdom that contradicts the Jewish conception of considering themselves chosen people. Wisdom constitutes the authentic

---

5. "On Devils," in Spinoza, *Short Treatise*, 153.

6. Yaffe, "Providence in Medieval Aristotelianism," 62–64; Parens, "Leaving the Garden."

7. Spinoza, *Tratado teológico-político*, 2.18–19.

reason of the Jewish people, not a supposed subjective divine presence or revelation without a rational explanation.

Due to Satan's shamelessness, Spinoza attributes the book of Job to a gentile.[8] Job distances himself from the world when pursuing purity and wisdom as individual virtues. Adam personalizes the gentile natural world, deceived by the passions of his nature; he cannot be considered guilty but foolish or corrupt.

In Calvinist Holland, at the dawn of religious freedom, Spinoza defines the book of Job as a treatise on Providence.[9] In commenting on Job, Spinoza debates categories later developed in German idealism to criticize religious dogma. He argues that the way Satan and the Lord interact signifies the relationship of the foreign nations to Israel. In the political discussions of his time, Spinoza aims to criticize Hobbes's authoritarian dogma and justify the principles of the Calvinist state of religious freedom, established in Holland and England with the Orange dynasty. The Hobbesian Leviathan restrains the freedom that nature grants to all men. He concludes that no one transfers his natural right to such a degree that he cannot subsequently participate in public affairs.

b) Criticism of Idealism

Spinoza interprets the divine reasoning of the theophanies as a rationalization of a personal experience. The divine accusatory questions do not mean that there was a divinity who melted the earth from nothing and directs history outside of rationality. Spinoza considers that the masses take refuge in authority because they are incapable of rational discourse and fool themselves with desires and inclinations.[10]

Spinoza focuses on the criticism of temptation and conceives the patient submission (that Elihu proposes) as a form of temptation. The criticism of temptation lies in presupposing the supremacy of the organization over the individual (denies free will) and justifies irrational violence.

Spinoza bases his doctrine on considering Job as the natural man. He confronts the essential evil (original or collective sin) of human nature (as Hobbes claims). In the second chapter of the *Theological-Political*

8. Spinoza, *Oeuvres complètes*, 547.
9. Seow, *Job 1–21*, 148.
10. Moreau, "Spinoza et l'autorité."

Treatise, Spinoza explains that only democracy builds a coherent political order.[11]

Law as a revelation denies human merit and justice as the reality of social coherence. The rhetorical questions of the theophanies should not involve submitting to the unfathomable divinity but rather the discovery of rationality as the origin of language and the social realm. Elihu deprives the message of theophanies of rational meaning. It presupposes that history realizes a (Platonic) idea preexisting in itself, which predestines man; Elihu explains man as a perfection of the individual by moral purity and divine illumination, not the coherence of a social being by rationality and justice.

c) Religion and Limits of Reason

Kant develops the dogmatic presuppositions established by Spinoza and Leibniz in the context of overcoming the religious wars in Germany. Kant considers Satan to be inconsistent as a public prosecutor.

Kant portrays Job as an archetype of a religion subjected to the limits of reason. In his essay on theodicy (1791), decisive in the Kantian distinction between pure and practical reason, commenting on the book of Job, Kant affirms the transcendence and inscrutability of divinity and explains religious dogma within the limits of practical reason.[12] To answer Job, Kant concludes that theodicy must explain rationally the prosperity of the wicked and the suffering of the righteous. The fact that a man might not discern between good and evil from an ideal perspective expresses the moral dilemma or contradiction of the book of Job. A rational and universal faith must have its base in social morality beyond a subjective end in happiness or retribution. Satan means a tortured search for the moral law because personalizing Satan loses an objective foundation for coactivity. The endless proliferation of religions shows divine inspiration cannot inspire a coherent moral law.

Practical reason shows that divinity is linked to its creation by a moral nexus that manifests and interprets his will. Theodicy does not seek to discern the unfathomable divine will and interprets nature and social life as human will and creation. Evil has no substance and means a negation. Evil, servitude, and retribution are no longer considered divine

---

11. Spinoza, *Tratado teológico-político*, 2.13–19.
12. Kant, *Fracaso de ensayo filosófico*, 22, 48.

punishment or reward, assumed to be an autonomous moral problem detached from divinity, concerning practical morality in a social realm.

According to Kant, a religion contains within itself the awareness of its contingency, limited in time and space, based on an a priori morality, which seeks to reaffirm itself in a collective society alien to its identity.[13] The critique of pure reason concludes that absolute morality is false and unattainable, given divine transcendence. The presence of evil in history denies the possibility of knowing about the Creator (since evil denies his essence as justice), and a creation determined by evil would be contradictory. Divinity is unintelligible and not essential to build an ethic. Faith founded on revelation has only a particular validity, and to pretend heavenly inspiration is a form of madness: superstition or fanaticism if it departs from rationality, or heresy if it departs from its institutional interpretation. Revelation might not establish universal principles because, as dogmatic, it lacks a practical reason, and only its historical and ethical project can build a religion. The identity between ethics and dogma explains the diversity of churches and religions in its historical context.

Kant does not consider Judaism a religion but rather a political project with a practical methodology. The peculiarity of Judaism lies in the divine donation of the land of Israel, other religions define themselves in the ideal contingency of an unknowable divinity who reveals itself. Kant affirms the immorality of Abraham (which Kant seems to consider the paradigm of the Jew) and his alleged sacrifice that builds the dogmatic of revelation. Christianity pretends the redemption of man and is not statutory but moral, built on the merit of man that redeems Abraham's (unjust) sacrifice.[14]

d) Foundation of Practical Morality

Religion Within the Limits of Reason conceives the churches as a consequence of morality, not founded in revelation (dogmatic).[15]

The *Metaphysics of Morals* deduces that only personal freedom can explain practical laws.[16] Religion is the idea of divinity as a practical reality in ethics and laws. The lack or inconsistency of morality defines

---

13. Kant, *Contienda*, 18.
14. Kant: *Religión en los límites*, 22; *Crítica de la razón práctica*, 148.
15. Kant, *Religión en los límites*.
16. Kant, *Metafísica de las costumbres*, 30.

religion, which generates egoism and irrationality because it does not recognize the supremacy of the rational law.

Divine transcendence deprives Satan of subjective identity. Satan (what is not) is conceived as an a priori character of critical reason to try to explain the problem of evil and to build practical morality from a negative perspective. Evil and its punishment lack substance. Kant develops Leibniz's approach and interprets punishment as the perfection of practical morality; the book of Job questions human innocence, not divine guilt. The book of Job concludes that suffering leads to harmony in creation through the development of moral conscience.

The supremacy of the moral law turns supreme evil into negation, and the empty character of evil is the authentic faith in divinity (thus assuming the idea formulated by Maimonides of Satan as fiction). The supposedly diabolical beings (*ein teuflischer Wesen*) lack freedom of choice and moral responsibility, their actions are predetermined, and they cannot be held accountable.[17] In contrast to the unity of reason, Kant conceives Satan as a logical artifice, a superficial justification of egoism and irrationality.

18.3 REVELATION AS SYSTEMATIC THOUGHT

a) Job as Satan in Disguise

Unlike Kant, who sees Job as the holder of rational and universal practical morality, as opposed to institutional religion (the sacrifice of Abraham), Hegel considers Job (not Abraham, whom he barely mentions) the paradigm of the Jew, who denies personal freedom as consciousness of the absolute; he therefore institutes servitude because he conceives divinity only as a negation of himself (sin and exile).[18]

Elihu and Job embody idealism and build servitude; they personify the essence of accusation as an nonexistent Satan. In the *Lectures on the Philosophy of Religion*, within a dialectical and evolutionary conception of religions, Hegel considers Job's divinity as the contradiction of Judaism as an abstract power of the sublime (*geistigen*) and a determined religion (*bestimmte*).[19] The pure and inert spirit of Job's determined and ideal-

---

17. Kant, *Religión en los límites*, 37–41.
18. Yovel, *Dark Riddle*, 24.
19. Hirsh, "Hegel," s.vv. "Hegel's View of Judaism."

istic religion suppresses individual freedom and the prophetic spirit. It surpasses the Eastern religions—that confuse divinity with nature—but perceives divinity as the other, the revelation as the conscience of sin and exile, which, in its potency, as power, dictates and imposes the law (servitude). To have a meaning, the Jews live accusing the instituted authority.

In the Hegelian philosophy, a lying (contradictory) divinity deceives Job by promising land, prosperity, and family in exchange for submission. Revelation resolves the contradiction of a divinity who exists only as an idea. The redeemed people exist for divine veneration without an understandable end; its idealism condemns them to wander among peoples. The Jewish law is a commandment that creates a people as a collective submission, not the rationality of reality, justification, and search for the collective good. The rigid and unyielding essence of Job's determined and idealistic religion stifles individual freedom and the prophetic spirit.

The Jewish religion, according to Hegel, exists in a concrete determination of the idea (revelation, law) but as a religion and as a people determined to serve the Greek multiplicity (polytheism) and the authoritarian secular discipline (violence) of monotheism (Rome). Hegel interprets the Jewish religion as dogmatic revelation, a sterile morality of individual virtue and divine election (submission), incapable of building a secular and practical law.[20] Revelation (as Elihu underlines) urges only subjective participation in a submissive veneration. It is not a legislator for men, as were Solon and Lycurgus. Its laws are at the service of justice but particular and selfish, to be part of a people and receive prosperity and serfs.

b) Institution of Servitude Through Individual Virtue

Hegel identifies the nuclear problem of the book of Job in the irresolvable conflict between the dogmatic institution of religion and the guarantee of personal merit and responsibility. Hegel interprets Job's response to the theophanies as the meaning of Jewish religion: submission to an abstract divinity without a rational ethic.[21] They are a wandering people, because their divinity determines the stubbornness of selfish subjectivity and the interested greed of the believer.

Hegel criticizes Jewish revealed religion as a religion of the negation of the world (messianism). Individual virtue serves as a counterpoint to

---

20. Barniske, "Negative Sublimity," 442.
21. Rotenstreich, "Hegel's Image on Judaism," 42.

revelation, whose essential content is that man is a sinner and the world condemned (exile). By blindly submitting to divinity, Job betrays rationality, abandons universality, and loses his freedom. The soul of Job that cries for justice ends up conforming and submitting to the divine will through obedience to the commandments and renouncing the rationality of the law. However, his submission defines his faith, conquers the sublimity of revelation, and wins the promise of a future land of wealth, milk, and honey. The divinity (ideal and subjective) chooses Abraham, Isaac, and Jacob and leads the Jews from Egypt to a distant, future, and messianic land. There is no possibility of acting in this way with other people.

Hegel systematizes the book of Job, confronting Job's response to the second theophany, which Hegel calls a return to the faith of Abraham. He concludes that Job (in his final, absolute, and unquestioned submission to divinity) achieves his liberation from hell (Job 33:18) but betrays his initial approach demanding justice. Hegel criticizes Job's idealism for the lack of content of a religion of obedience, which is defined by submission to the commandments, not through rationality and freedom. Divinity exists only for itself, and Job must submit to authority. *I resign myself to dust and ashes* (42:6): "This submission brings Job to inner happiness, closer to the others who wanted to understand and justify the divinity. [It is said]: You have not spoken rightly as my servant Job; offer a sacrifice for yourselves and make my servant Job pray for you, and he gave him double [of what he had possessed, only after humbling himself as a servant]."[22]

c) Denial of Justice Resolves Job's Contradictions

Hegel interprets the book of Job as a critique of the religion founded on sacrifice and servitude. In Judaism, as an individual, Job cannot ask for justice because the fear of the Lord, absolute submission, is instituted as a principle. Nor can he ask for a reward for his virtue because (in Judaism) the law takes precedence over the individual. He concludes that the book of Job is not part of Jewish history, as religion is the essential goal of the Jewish religion. Job represents the universality of rationality and justice.

Job experiences a paradox between his absolute awareness of justice and his destiny. His innocence contradicts his unjust misfortune; he understands that divinity must repay good but submits to divinity in a

---

22. Hegel, *Filosofía de la religión*, 2:42.

superficial and ideal way, with absolute and foolish trust. The believer identifies himself with a participation in divinity whom he conceives as an absolute abandonment of rationality and free will. The fear of God and confessing sin as a separation explains the ritualistic and obstinate individualism of Jewish theocracy. Religion and authority are intertwined, and religious authority suppresses secular thought.

Only by submitting in dust and ashes, after the Lord shows him his power, will Job be reconciled with Judaism as a doctrine (dogmatic religion) and as an organization (ethics), which institutes the authority of divinity. And, by submitting unconditionally, Job will receive twice as much: he will be part of a people and receive the promise of the fruitful land. He contrasts revealed religion with rationality and freedom and argues that a revealed religion institutes servitude.[23]

d) Overcoming Job's Mythical and Irrational Spirit

Hegel develops the Kantian notion of Satan as a lack of content. Hegel conceives the Jewish religion as a paradigm of revealed religions, portraying a jealous and intolerant divinity. Jewish divinity exists in the solitude of eternity and does not require reality to exist, nor are its designs rational;

---

23. Marx does not seem to have paid attention to the book of Job. In *The Jewish Question* (1843), Karl Marx, on strictly Hegelian assumptions, maintains the Christian foundation of the state in Germany. Therefore, the confrontation of the Jews with (German) culture, as Jews represent the only coherent religion: "Emancipation from *huckstering* and *money*, consequently from practical, real Judaism, would be the self-emancipation of our time." (Marx, "On *The Jewish Question*"; emphasis in original). The Jews, like all religions, represent the supremacy of subjective interest over collective responsibility and are accused of selfish corruption, defined by greed, dedicated to usury. They represent the paradigm of religion as the foundation of a classist society. Political emancipation means a denunciation of religion: "Religion has become the spirit of *civil society*, of the sphere of egoism" ("On *The Jewish Question*"; emphasis in original). Religious thought, as a selfish premise of civil society, considers men as servants and enslaves them. The equality of Jews is only possible in a truly secularized state that denounces all religious identity. The Marxist vision of the Jewish question conceives Judaism as the essence of religion, and the authentic emancipation of man results from Jewish emancipation. The liberation of Germany means denouncing its Christian foundation and the Jewish root of Christianity that legitimizes a classist society. The Italian Marxist Antonio Negri denies divine transcendence as an essential prerequisite for achieving the liberation of man. Divinity represents, according to Negri, everything that is oppressive. Job is Adam and the precursor of Christ. Job opposes being a servant of a tyrannical divinity, which he interprets as his antagonist, and he becomes a creator with his rebellion. Theophanies, according to Negri, are the sign of the victory of Job, of man, over capital, which Behemoth and Leviathan (authority and organization) personify (Negri, *Labor of Job*).

it denies images or representations of divinity in the exaltation of the divinity as an idea. The Jewish deity is neither determined nor determinable and manifests itself as an exclusive one, which has no other divinities alongside it. It exists only for itself, consumed in eternity, existent only as a revelation. Its uniqueness contains an abstract unity, concrete in self and manifestation, not in spirit as the reality of unity.

According to Hegel, Jewish religion is built on incomprehensible sublimity, contrary to rationality, which glorifies the divine name as a formal reality. The Greek religion finds the sublime in beauty, without a universal end; Scripture determines the Jewish soul, fundamentally Job, the prophets, and the psalms, which express the sublime in otherness, poetry, and myth, but without coherence, at the service of a supposed individual virtue and purity of submission. Satan manifests the Jewish divinity as an abstract idea, the contradiction of expressing itself as negation.

Satan means the contradiction of creating an imperfection, the apotheosis of irrationality. To exist, the absolute must find its end in the other by perfecting something imperfect, revealing itself to live a meaningful existence. Revelation constitutes the essence of religion, and religion consists of man having an immediate knowledge of morality as divinity creating reality and overcoming Satan. Revelation signifies an ethic that implies the divine intention to manifest itself as meaning and to reveal morality. This could be considered a positive religion because a spirit reaches perfection expressing reality and doctrine. Satan does not exist because reality can only be known with a concrete meaning, not as an accusation, a negation (idea) without content.

Hegel concludes that the Trinitarian consciousness of Christianity, which supposes divinity as otherness and not as submission or accusation, authentically liberates a man from the irrational and mythical spirit of Job's religion. Divinity becomes a real man among men and makes possible freedom, justice, and personal initiative to overcome authority. The incarnated divinity submits to Job's legalism, the particular sublimity of the exaltation of beauty by the Greeks and Roman authoritarianism. It reconciles Jewish revelation, Roman justice, and individual freedom.[24]

Hegel considers Christianity to be the overcoming of Judaism.[25] In contrast to Job's exaltation of individual virtue, Christianity builds an ethical organization that makes individual freedom a reality. The religion

---

24 Hegel, *Filosofía de la religión*, 2:36.
25. Hegel, *Filosofía de la religión*, 2:56.

of beauty (Greece) or the prosaic thought of authority (Rome) subdues sterile Jewish idealism, although at the cost of losing the sense of the divine. Roman authoritarianism loses Jewish idealism or Greek polytheism of beauty. The prosaic world causes infinite pain by losing the divinities and the homeland. The free and responsible man is reborn through divine incarnation, which overcomes the conflict between man and deity. Man is reborn as an individual through the incarnation, which represents the awareness of freedom as the identity of the absolute.

XIX.

Revelation in the Storm

19.1 DEUS EX MACHINA

a) Solving Job's Moral Riddle

The divinity unexpectedly speaks to Job in the storm. The plot employs the technique of deus ex machina, typical of Greek tragedies, e.g., Euripides's *Medea*, solving the moral riddle raised by the three friends and Elihu (Job's guilt and responsibility) as an allegorical portrayal of Israel's dogmatic past.

As noted, early priestly and prophetic literature interprets collective disorder either as an eschatological conflict in heaven or a collective sin on earth. Both theophanies confront a vengeful and Manichaean divinity who tolerates or employs Satan to punish or purify Job. The first theophany contradicts the violent Satan (the dogma of the three friends); the second theophany contradicts the submissive Satan (Elihu's submission).

The theophanies will explain that authority inherits the social order, and the servant holds it; in both roles, Job must assume, in normative terms, the disorder of the land as a duty of guarantee (as civil, not criminal liability) and must accept his individual unconscious and collective responsibility as heir or beneficiary of wealth and deities, with a duty to restore (inherited) unjust enrichment and damage. Job must assume an unconscious (material) responsibility, due to (unjust) use of prosperity, and a collective responsibility (ideally) due to the false judgment of the authority (divinity).[1]

b) The Storm Stages Natural and Social Disorder

Job and Elihu have used the image of the storm to describe an arbitrary and unfathomable Creator (*he destroys me in the storm* [9:17; 30:22]), who demands absolute submission (36:28) and who judges according to collective justice (origins), not personal guilt. Job's reference to the storm as divine injustice receives a response in the storm.

The storm stages the defective origins of social order as a collective disorder (exile) among foreign kings and divinities. A double stormy wind refers to the violent nature and social disaster (that destroys Job's dwelling). The storm describes a man who does not listen on Mount Sinai or in the temple, neither during the day (the authority) nor at night (the servitude). There is no sign to identify the supposed authenticity of the divine intervention. Amid stormy winds, Job does not even clearly understand what he hears; he has to trust in the ethical content of the supposed revelation to guarantee its authenticity.

The two theophanies answer Satan's two accusations (two storms), prevailing over the two temples (sacrifice and submission). The first theophany opposes Job's violent ethic of the First Temple (the violent conquest of the land of Canaan) and, as a counterpoint, teaches hospitality and marriage fidelity on an animal's farm (in a foreign land). The second theophany aims to overcome the polytheism of the Manichaean

---

1. It was widespread, at the end of the nineteenth century and during the first half of the twentieth, to deny the coherence and rationality of the theophanies. Theophanies have been interpreted as an addition to the original body of the book of Job; a poetic, pathetic, irrelevant, and unconvincing intervention worthy of a charlatan. It asserts that an arbitrary and totalitarian divinity, interested only in his confrontation with Satan, concludes his dissertation (in the epilogue) with an immoral apotheosis of submission, and an unjust gift of authority, children, and wealth to the servant Job. The Lord does not answer Job, only humiliates him. The divinity treats Job as an animal, created to suffer and delivered to the slaughterhouse. Feminist assumptions also generally present theophanies as the masculine violence that tortures women in the religious culture. Another attenuated approach to the irrationality of the book of Job affirms that theophanies do not give answers to Job but encourage him to set aside rationalism and seek wisdom in nature and in the divine revelation (that directs the social order and history). It is argued that theophanies insist on the limited knowledge of a man who cannot judge the divine creation.

Persian divinities and the distress of Job's laments (submissive dogma), reflecting the prophetic trend in Judaism.[2]

c) Answer to Job in Due Time

And the Lord answers Job from the whirlwind in due time (38:1). The narrative presents a divinity who does not speak in a threatening tone to Job (as to Satan in the prologue, as to Eliphaz in the epilogue, or as Elihu to Job: ויאמר). The narrator asserts *that the Lord answers* (38:1). There is no formal presentation of divinity; only the message (the answer in due time) is relevant.

The tempest refers to Job's sacrificial past, and "due" time (causality) alludes to the warning and explanation of punishment. Pretending to listen and obey the divine word by sacrifice and submission is the nonsense of the three friends and Elihu. Discerning whether the words Job hears in the tempest come from divinity or a foreign spirit lacks a test of authenticity, as a man might not distinguish between good and evil from an ideal perspective. The narrative praises Job, who refines the terms of his unconscious guilt and responsibility, when confronting the three friends, still failing to oppose Elihu's doctrine.

He would not crush me with a tempest (9:17). Job overcomes abusing prosperity (his unconscious guilt) in the dialogue with the three friends but fails to challenge Elihu's doctrine of collective guilt. The tempest refers to the supposed collective condemnation. The answer emphasizes Job's foolishness of pretending to be innocent and looking for someone (authority or deity) to blame for the collective disorder as an alibi for his (personal) unconscious and collective responsibility. The theophanies emphasize the necessity of rebuilding a coherent social order based on free will and (individual) responsibility, paying attention to the warning and explanation (*due time*) of punishment and servitude on earth.

Confronting Elihu's doctrine, theophanies develop a coherent theory of limited unconscious and collective guilt (as personal guilt), giving coherence to a religious system (the canon) and teaching Job to build a

---

2. The storm is described as the destruction of the house of the firstborn by the desert wind (1:18) in *due time* (reality in history). The storm refers to what Job pretends to hear in the day or at night. It criticizes the three friends' dogmatic ontological violence and Elihu's submission, representing Job's doctrinal past. It is fair to underline that the divinity does not reproach Job and Eliphaz (the three friends) at night or in the storm but in broad daylight (42:7–8).

coherent social realm on individual merit, guilt, and responsibility. The first theophany rebukes sacrifice (against the established power) as an abuse of the earth (it unroots his lineage), and the second contradicts patient submission as an abuse of the heavens (that destroys his farm). The first theophany warns in the night (the punishment of Job), and the second explains in the day (a punishment to Eliphaz). The warning reveals unconscious responsibility (abuse of the land), and the explanation rationalizes collective responsibility (abuse of the divinities, the *nebelah*). The epilogue struggles to identify the personal origin of merit, guilt, and responsibility and explains the contradictions of a social order founded on violence or submission to (pretended) divine will (42:7–8).

The exigency to assume social responsibility answers Job's complaint about divinity tolerating evil. The theophanies explain that authority is established by building a house and receiving the foreigners (hospitality), submitting the (original and unjust) violence, building matrimonial and economic (religious) freedom, and unleashing the bondage of serfs (by justly redistributing prosperity and paying the debts of the land).[3]

---

3. Elihu exaggerates Job's collective guilt, and his arguments must be considered an anticlimax to the theophanies, which explain the incoherence of a social order justified in violence or submission to (pretended) divine's will, and not on man's labor and responsibility. Elihu presupposes the institutionalization of evil by divine concealment and accuses the heavens of a defective creation that Job must suffer. Elihu does not engage in dialogue, nor teaches or pretends a response. He only dogmatizes and dramatizes by affirming *collective* guilt, denying the right to warning and explanation of punishment, and the legitimacy of Job's protest. Theophanies contradict Elihu's doctrine and justify the personal origin of merit, guilt, and responsibility. The first theophany challenges the violent conquest of the land of Canaan, and the second theophany aims to overcome the submission dogma of Esther's sexual sacrifice. The first theophany reproaches Job for not assuming his (personal) responsibility, and the second theophany, praising Job for his right speech (42:7–8), confronts the exaggeration of guilt and improperly tempting or separating from the social realm. Theophanies will answer Job and base ethics on individual guilt and responsibility. Leviathan *humbly asks for mercy and confesses with bitter words* (40:27). Elihu preaches an exaggerated confession of guilt and a moral of submission and separation that the second theophany portrays as Leviathan. The theophanies will teach Job to cease blaming himself (confession) without knowing why, as accusing himself without fault means accusing divinity of concealing evil.

19.2 UNCONSCIOUS GUILT AND COLLECTIVE RESPONSIBILITY

a) Individuality of Guilt and Responsibility

Who is this who obscures my plans with meaningless words? (38:2; 42:3). In both theophanies, this first accusatory question formulates the personality of guilt and responsibility as the nuclear doctrine of the book of Job. It accuses Job of disguising himself as Satan (employing sacrifice and submission), obscuring divine plans by affirming a supposed collective guilt, and hiding his (individual) responsibility.

Obscuring divine intentions must be interpreted in light of the many texts, especially in the prologue and epilogue, which affirm Job's righteousness, concluding that Job obscures but does not deny divine intentions. *Meaningless words* refer to Job's untimely and unfounded protests (sacrifice) and silences (submission). *Meaningless words* contradict confession as a collective accusation of authority and servants that deprive words of meaning, claiming to be chosen by the divinity for violence (the three friends) or submission (Elihu and Job) and not assuming responsibility in the construction and reparation of the social realm.

Squeeze your kidneys like a man (38:3) emphasizes that Job is not guilty (criminal liability) but responsible (civil liability) of collective disorder. The reference to "man" hints at the warrant duty of a father, authority, author, and tenant; as an *officium* presupposing a limited collective responsibility.

The defective earth persists as part of a just creation because reality means that violence and servitude do not institutionalize but subsist only as a (personal) responsibility for an unfair distribution of wealth (civil liability for damage or unjust enrichment) or as an ideal abuse of divinity (servitude). Until violence is overcome and the false divinity unveiled, defective origins establish a temporal and defective authority and organization. *Like a man* personifies individual responsibility. It underlines that a collective accusation conceals individual responsibility and accuses Job of an incorrect assumption of debts as proprietor or tenant (father or husband).[4]

---

4. The epilogue will explain that the social realm is not conceived as the divine institution of authority in history (as the friends claim) or as the revelation to the prophet or mystic at night (as Elihu claims); only personal freedom and individual responsibility (Job will pray for you [42:7–8]) institute a coherent social realm. Merit is not an ideal concept (authority) but a real one (the construction of the social order),

b) Warning and Explanation of Punishment and Servitude

The narrative presents Providence as an accusatory question (a legal dialogue). *I will question you, and you must answer me* (38:3). Question and answer illustrate the nature of Providence (as a warrant of justice) through teaching (warning, *I will ask you*) and man's accountability and duty of reparation (explanation, *you must answer me*). It recognizes Job's right to a pertinent warning and explanation that prevents evil and reveals the reasons and measures for personal punishment (of the social disorder) and restitution. It also criticizes confession of unknown guilt because confession is pertinent only as a duty of reparation or compensation, admitting facts after assuming a lawful accusation.

The warning is (on earth as) the duty to assume the rightful protest; the three friends attend to Job's protest but do not restore the damage or enrichment (42:7–8), and Elihu does not attend and sacralizes the injustice. Warning and explanation are essential elements of the divine's warrant of his creation, written and published on earth. The previous warning (a protest that identifies guilt) and its explanation (that delimits the damage and unjust enrichment by its publicity) define the legitimacy and limits of the punishment. The intention (warning), act, and result (publicity) are three elements of guilt and responsibility in their ideal origin, material reality, and causal imputation (for restitution or compensation).

c) Accusatory Question

The accusatory question reveals the individual origin of collective disorder that persists in the land, left unresolved as unjust enrichment or damage of the heirs and tenants. The question unveils evil as individual abuse of prosperity and servitude (by violence or submission) in a disordered land submitted to imaginary vengeful divinities who tolerate or conceal the catastrophe of the unjust origins (until men compensate the damage or restore the unjust enrichment).

The accusatory question is an answer, as an accusatory mirror, revealing Job's false accusation against a deity as a mirage of himself. Twice, Satan will be rebuked in heaven, for he accuses in heaven and confuses

---

and evil (servitude, guilt) is not a real threat, just a mere appearance (damage or lack of authority or social order). Evil exists only as a testimony of the defective earth (due to damage or restitution).

guilt and responsibility on earth. The accusatory questions mock his accusatory protests against heavens and earth, treating evil as a collective disaster and not rescuing man and the social order. The theophanies resolve Job's moral dilemma, teaching him to confront collective disorder by assuming (personal) responsibility for the land (and its divinities or servants); without sacrifice or submission but by paying debts in their normative range. Divinity does not speak at night, as Elihu dogmatizes, but in the tempest; the answer explains the rightful intervention of Providence, questioning and accusing (warning and explaining), not by divine omnipotence or predestination but showing the unjust distribution of wealth and servitude on earth.

The accusatory questions solve Elihu's riddle, start a dialogue, and contradict Elihu's dogmatic monologue. The temptation (sacrificial) is the crime of authority (unconscious responsibility), and incitement (ideal) is the sin of the servant (collective responsibility). The accusatory questions criticize Elihu's doctrine. Elihu thinks that violence and servitude destroy themselves as part of a just creation; still, violence and servitude subsist in reality as a testimony of a just creation (38:2), denouncing an individual man who profits from the unjust distribution of wealth and the abuse of divinity (servitude) until violence is repaired and the false divinity unveiled on earth.

d) Two Nuclear Accusatory Questions

The two theophanies display two nuclear accusatory questions about the material and spiritual exile (the two storms).

The narrative portrays a double accusation against Job: unjust prosperity and tolerance of evil. *Where were you?* (This serves as a warning referring to the indetermination of a collective being.) The earth's foundation refers to personal merit and guilt (the institutionalization and protection of man's labor). *Where were you when I laid earth's foundations?* (38:4). This describes the earth as the origin of Job and opposes his wrongful protest against authority and the social realm (by violence or submission). It teaches Job to overcome the collective disorder by building a house through labor and hospitality, affirming personal merit and guilt.

The second theophany describes sacred submission to social disorder (the abuse of servitude). *Will your anger contest my justice? Will you condemn my justice to justify yourself?* (40:8). This refers to Job's submission as accusing divinity of tolerating or concealing evil. The text discusses the divine warrant of justice as a response to material or spiritual rebellion represented by Behemoth and Leviathan.

The earth becomes an allegory for exile, and the two allegories of the first theophany symbolize the former sacrificial history of Israel and respond to the accusatory questions: the desert staging the abuse of the land (dogmatic of sacrifice), and the animal farm the abuse of the foreign divinities (dogmatic of submission). In a foreign land, Job understands the violence and falsehood of the foreign kings and servants (their disordered origins) and foresees their unavoidable destruction in due time. Job contemplates his past in Canaan (the lion) and Persia (the eagle); he critically examines the authority (the kings) and the foreign social order (the foreign woman and serf), ruled by violent or patient divinities (blind, deaf, and mute). The struggle against an inert nature allegorizes the violent entry into the land of Canaan (the First Temple). The Second Temple, the exile in Persia, is compared to life on an animal farm. After punishment, Job rationalizes his past and identifies the foreign land as a desert or animal farm (founded in the dogmatic of temptation or separation).

XX.

Allegories of Exile

20.1 INSTITUTION OF AUTHORITY IN THE DESERT

a) Earth (Reality) as Formalization of the Past

Earth (reality) represents the formalization of the past. *Let me know, if you know* (38:4) criticizes the confession of collective guilt as a false confession of unknown facts. The accusatory reiteration affirms the meaninglessness of violence and servitude, a mirror of Job's falsehood (unconscious and collective responsibility).

Job is encouraged to rationalize the incoherence of his former prosperity and social order, which led him to exile rather than battling himself by projecting blame onto foreign kings and deities. The allegories of the first theophany answer Job's riddle and explain that Job must search in his individual and social past for the warning and explanation of his punishment and serfdom.

b) Desert with No Man

The first allegory of the first theophany incites Job to cultivate the desert land, employing an analogy with the creation narrative in the book of Genesis, encouraging Job to trust in personal merit and responsibility for creative means.

In a social order founded on violence (in a foreign desert *where there is no man*), working the land builds a house, providing food and shelter for the innocent, and welcomes the lion cubs and the young ravens. Earth (reality as testimony of justice [38:4]) is based on personal labor and hospitality. *Who placed its measures?* (38:5). Only personal merit defines the measures; only personal responsibility lays its cornerstone (38:6). It sings (38:7), shuts the sea (38:8), fixes the limits (38:8–11), and unveils evil (38:12–20).

In the desert (exile), Providence watches over life and social identity, rooting man's labor. As I have mentioned, constructing a house (as an alternative to rebellion or submission) describes a personal struggle where no man exists, referring to the sacrificial dogmatic. The construction of a house allegorizes the defense of Job's life, his family, and prosperity in an exile of fierce nature and arbitrary social realm. The house signifies the earth as a testimony of (personal) justice, where the individual merit prevails over the collective disorder. Building a dwelling in the desert means creating a social realm that awakens personal responsibility and overcomes collective disorder.

Building a house poses an analogy for Israel's journey to the promised land. Job sits on the limits of the (Red) sea (38:8). The sea symbolizes the unconscious and collective guilt and responsibility for the social disorder (the incoherence of sacrifice and submission). The sea is accused of pride, an allegory of foreign kingdoms, surrounded by clouds and enveloped in darkness (38:9), enclosed with doors and bolts (38:10). Job builds barriers and defenses, puts light to defend the house, and identifies the vermin from the onslaught of the sea (the apparent disorder of nature and social order). *He says [to the sea], this far you have come, no further; here the pride of your waves will stop* (38:11), underlining the lack of identity of a collective being. *To say* means the arrangement of nature and the unveiling of the false divinity in its due time (building a house).

Rain on the desert in which there is no man (38:26) refers to a social realm founded in violence or submission as an institution of servitude that Job must labor and drain. The narrative of the first theophany allegorizes the creation of a social realm in exile, a light that shakes the wicked (38:12–15), searches into the deep, unveils the shadows of death (38:16–18), and builds a tradition (38:19–21).[1]

---

1. The material and spiritual realms are two faces of the same coin in a man created in the divine image. The material realm is the conscience of (personal) evil that develops simultaneously with the coherent formation of a social realm as a product

c) House on the Edge of the Abyss

A house on the edge of the abyss (38:16) protects life and freedom (the innocent) amid chaos. Violence is contested by justice, not by violence or submission. Justice gives orders to the morning to expel the wicked (38:12–15), dominates the depths of the abyss, closes the doors of death and subdues evil (38:16–21), irrigates the uncultivated lands that man has not trodden (38:22–30), directs the symphony of the stars that govern time (38:31–36), and feeds the children of the violent and the impious (38:37–41).

In contrast to the dogmatic of rebellion or submission, the allegory emphasizes the gradual construction of the social order (tradition) through labor and study (teaches to make proper use of wealth and to reveal the order of the stars). The house discloses the gates of death (38:17), the inexorable destruction of the social order founded on violence or submission.

It emphasizes that Job cannot judge the foreign collective order (founded on sacrifice and submission) because he does not know its origins; he was not born on the day of its foundation and cannot count the number of its days (38:21). The social order founded in justice, as the building of a house (supremacy of the individual over the collective responsibility), will reveal in its due time the bloodthirsty and false divinities (the foolishness of idealism).

d) The Lion and the Raven

The house sets down roots in exile through food and shelter (hospitality) for the stranger (Job's wife), fleeing tyranny and wickedness. It institutionalizes Job's labor (in the desert of violent authority and patient serf).

When Job triumphs over material chaos and earns food and shelter, he watches the arrival of the servant and the maid at his house; he earns the submission of the social order founded on violence and emotional manipulation. He hunts the prey for the old lion, fills the appetite of the young lions (38:39), and prepares for the raven his prey (38:41). Then, he confronts the temptation of economic prosperity, complicity, or concealment of evil, and the delicacies of serfdom.

---

of (individual) merit. By building a house (instituting a just authority), not employing violence or submission, the social realm overcomes evil (the incoherent origins), shaping the identity between the consciousness of evil and man's merit.

The lion and the raven allegorize the submission of the (supposed) foreign deities. A lion placed in its den, lying in wait for prey in its tents (38:40), could represent the violence of the entry into the land of Israel as the allegory of the triumph over the lion. Working the land means not taking unfair advantage of prosperity and not being deceived by the delicacies of false divinities (abuse of the land and servitude by the sacrifice of Esther).

As an alternative to violence, the raven seeks food in waste and carrion (38:41) and feeds Elijah, which could refer to the collective order of submission founded on religious idealism and the sacrifice of sexuality (the condemnation of Jezebel and the delivery of Esther to foreign kings). In the desert, the lion and the raven institute authority (while Job's house feeds the lion cubs and the raven chicks).

20.2 INSTITUTION OF SOCIAL ORDER IN AN ANIMAL FARM

a) Wakefulness of Bloodthirsty Divinities

By sacrificing sexuality and prosperity, Elihu's confession builds an *animal farm* because sexuality and prosperity are seen as a price for submission and not conceived as retribution of personal merit. The departure from Egypt initiates reckoning time as the wakefulness of the bloodthirsty divinities. The entry into the (foreign) land (of Canaan) means establishing an animal farm (an imperfect social order) of lords and servants, based on a marriage ethic of authority, lineages, and strains, and governed by patient divinities who personify servitude (who incarnate in those who believe in them).

Job recognizes the foolishness of his past acts of violence and sacrifice but persists in accusing divinity and distorts his social identity. *Do you know the time when the goat gives birth on the mountain? (39:1). Have you learned to count the moons? Do you know the time of birth? (39:2).* Conception and birth (of an animal) are used as allegories of a social being with a foundational defect (the idealism of submission) and a defective social life (the woman without a proper husband, the goat and the stork).

A hidden, sanguinary, and mysterious (imaginary) deity (defective origins of submission) defines the social life of wild and domesticated animals founded in violence or submission. The house in the desert evolves into an animal farm that manages food and shelter, welcomes the servants who flee from the foreign sacrificial divinities (domesticates them), and receives the coin and the ring stolen from the foreign divinities. The coin symbolizes the work of the wild bull, subjected to the yoke (39:10), and the ring, the horse's submission that leads the warriors by the sound of the trumpet (39:24).

On Job's farm, animals work the land and make life possible in a hostile environment (39:2-12), institute and protect development (39:13-25), while the eagle and the falcon in the skies clean up the social order (when their time comes) and remove the inert corpses (39:26-30). The emphasis lies on hospitality to the foreigner (Job) as the wakefulness of evil (the goat that gives birth in the mountains) and the incoherent foundation of a (defective) social order in submission (the stork that lays its eggs in the sand).

b) Due Time (Historicity) of Justice

The goat on the mountain (allegory of a supposed subjective revelation) loses its offspring in the desert and the salt plain (defective origins). The animals that descend from the mountain illustrate a doctrinal past (of sacrifice) as the allegory of a wild animal. The transition from boar, wild ass, and buffalo allegorizes the domestication of the animals in their descent from the mountain (Sinai). It shows a gradual evolution of social life from the high rock to the fertile valley (the conquest of the land), the gradual formation of an ethical and political order, increasingly complex and perfect, overcoming sacrifice.

The female characters rationalize the social history of Israel. The goat (foreigner), who conceives on the mountain (the law), perhaps allegorizes the (ideal) formulation of social order (by divine revelation at night). The stork (servant), who lays her eggs in the sand, perhaps allegorizes a social order of submission (Esther's sacrifice). The goat and the stork might represent allegories of Israel building the First and Second Temples. The dance of its wings, the beauty of its feathers, and the majesty of the stork, as it rises in the air, symbolize the progressive perfection of religious ritualism (patient submission) that challenges violence and aristocracy, horses, and knights (39:18).

The stork (Esther), which lays its eggs on the earth, has neither wisdom nor intelligence (39:17). In a foreign land, horseback and knights (servants and lords) establish marriage and social order on authority, not on personal freedom. The dance of its wings, the beauty of its feathers, and its majesty as it rises to perform might represent the defective submission of a religious rite that overcomes violent sacrifice. If the first allegory stages the conquest of the desert, the second allegory illustrates the conquest of the foreign social order (the goat and the stork submit horses and knights). Nobility and servitude give way to a popular conception of social order.

c) Twilight of Tyrants and Perverts

The allegory concludes that animal violence (the violent and the wicked) submits to food and shelter (social order). Judging guilt should not be focused on punishment at night, as Elihu proposes, but on recognizing the foundation and consolidation of the social order as the unveiling of evil and hospitality with the innocent and dependent. The horse (a domesticated animal) adorns its neck and decorates its mane as an allegory of the foundation of the social order by religious rite; the knight, an allegory of the political order, subdues by force the unjust violence of the origins.

A daylight environment, presided over by hospitable female characters, overcomes the dark, masculine, and distressing atmosphere of submission at night. It allegorizes the triumph of the goat in the mountain and the stork in the plain over sacrificial and submissive violence.

Who assigns the barren plains to the wild animal (39:5–8), *who organizes his work* (39:9–12), *who gives strength to the horse and intelligence to the falcon and the eagle?* (39:19–30). I think these refer to the mystery of a social order whose principle is hidden in the defective origins of the foreign land and shored in the work of justice.

The eagle that removes the corpses (39:30) illustrates that Job should not condemn man (the foreign king) by sacrifice or submission because dead animals (the violent and the servant) are eaten or buried by an earth that testimonies justice. By building a house, Job commands nature and the social order (descends from the mountain) and removes the corpses of men who submit to bloodthirsty and servile divinities. By building a social identity, Job testimonies the unveiling of the defective origins (evil). Dead animals depict the unavoidable death of violent warriors or patient servants due to their lack of essence. Job rescues the social order only when he correctly assumes his (personal) guilt and responsibility for the collective disorder by building a house and overcoming sacrifice (the desert) and submission (the animal farm).

d) Allegory of Violent Past

The mineral or animal imagery of the first theophany reveals the feet of clay of foreign kings and deities (servants), ferocious in appearance but inert, blinded in the desert, mute to reality in the animal farm, whose corpses the eagle removes. Job recognizes in foreign kings and deities the reality of himself in the past (David and Mordecai). Animals are allegories of the foreign kings and serfs that have their place and purpose, and Job must care for and respect them. Social beings defectively established by violence fall by violence, and those founded on emotional or economic submission are buried underground by their sterility and lack of roots. The tyrant authority and the wicked serf (created by violence and submission) create a defective social realm.

The fables of the house in the desert and animal farm illustrate Job's exiles: Israel in the desert, Canaan, and Persia. In exile, Job must recognize the merit of the foreign man (authority and serf). Fierce and domestic animals portray Canaan and Persia as an allegory of social order that protects the innocents (the lion cubs and the young ravens). Job's labor prevents the inexorable final of violent sacrifice and promotes the liberation of the servants (affective and economic hospitality); it averts the dissolution of foreign societies. Job must shore up and correct a defective social realm to defend life and liberty amid the violent desert and a deceitful animal farm.[2]

---

2. This summarizes servility as an effect of a renewed and aggravated imputation of collective guilt (against men and divinity). To insist on an accusatory question (*let me know, if you know*) reiterates (aggravates) Job's reproach for an abuse of heaven (separation, as an origin of unconscious responsibility) and earth (temptation and separation, as an origin of collective responsibility). After the violent conquest of Canaan and the fall of Persia, the allegory mocks the submissive Job for an attenuated accusatory ethic of separation, still accusing foreign kings of (nonexistent) collective guilt.

XXI.

Job's Answer to the First Theophany

21.1 JOB'S INTERPELLATION

a) Face-to-Face Questioning

Following the first theophany, divinity addresses Job directly: *And the Lord stands [ויען] before Job and says to him* (40:1). Job listens without intermediaries or veils, not on Elihu's abyssal night nor in the tempest. The divine interpellation, framed by accusatory questions, functions as an allegory of Providence: in the heavens, there is no difference between a word and the reality it signifies.

The first theophany provides Job with a coherent ethic to overcome the collective disorder of a foreign kingdom and address Elihu's aggressive submission. *To say* means a reproach to Job (for his abuse of divinity) and a disclosure of the personal origin of unconscious and collective responsibility.

b) Two Accusatory Questions

As a conclusion to the first theophany, two censures are formulated against Job. Following his debate with his three friends, the conclusive questions aim to summarize the first theophany, provide insight into the meaning of its two allegories, and overcome the individualism of Job's monologue.

Will you continue a rebellion against the Almighty to become a master...? (40:2). The first accusatory challenge to Job highlights the flawed wisdom in Job's reasoning with the three friends. Job correctly contradicts the friends' doctrine of sacrifice as a rebellion against divine justice; however, the accusatory question reproaches Job's messianism, justifying the destruction of his present social realm (supposed foreign kingdom) to the idealism of winning a supposed future kingdom. The accusatory question is also a rebuke to Job's monologue, which justifies separation and temptation, not confronting Elihu's doctrine of collective guilt and accusing divinity of tolerating evil (1:22).

Will you continue to argue against the Almighty and have the final say? (40:2). The second interpellation specifically rebukes the idealistic messianism of separation (submission without sacrifice) and anticipates Job's replies. It reproaches Job's persistent submission, which refers to abusing servitude, inciting sedition, denying its designs (38:2; 42:3). Job accepts an evil that presumes comes from divinity, promoting patience as elected for suffering and contesting human freedom of will. The interpellation refutes Elihu's doctrine of intercession, which charges divinity with concealing evil.

c) Rationalization of His Doctrinal Past

In the past, Job unlawfully intended to destroy or submit foreign kingdoms and peoples (in Canaan, Persia, and Greece) as the reality of their damned kings and deities (idealism). The divine interpolations incite Job to overcome a theocratic vision of history as an epic dispute between the foreign divinities and Job's divinity (the approach of Jeremiah and the second Isaiah), staged as a (false) sexual submission in the book of Esther and as an economic submission in the school of Shammai (Phariseeism).

In exile, Job foresees the fall of foreign kings that abuse prosperity and foreign divinities who institute serfdom. The face-to-face questioning requires Job to engage in creating a coherent social order and to fulfill his responsibilities as a father and tenant in this foreign land. He is summoned to protect the weak and vulnerable, and not to wait for the destruction of foreign kingdoms to inherit their prosperity and serfs. The accusatory question aims to protect the innocents and dependents from their inexorable doom, instead of promoting (by temptation) or waiting (by separation) for the destruction of foreign kingdoms (imagining a messianic future).

Following the first theophany, the divine rebuke (*Will you continue to rebel and argue against the Almighty?*) foreshadows Job's responses, which will accuse divinity of employing (tolerating) and concealing evil. Nevertheless, once again, Job's submission will be praised as the overcoming of sacrificial dogmatic, and his righteousness will be recognized rather than his submission condemned.[1]

21.2 JOB'S RESPONSES TO THE FIRST THEOPHANY

a) Job Persists in Avoiding His (Individual) Responsibility

I am of small account, what shall I answer? My hand shuts my mouth (40:4). In his answer to the interpellation of the first theophany, Job does not know how to respond to the divine face-to-face questioning and repeats an attenuated doctrine of patient submission. Now, he condemns men and himself by a collective accusation (without identifying the origin and measure of damage or enrichment). He pretends to exonerate divinity for the collective disorder but avoids his (personal) responsibility, pretending to be of small account in a defective creation that condemns justice.

Defining himself as a man of *small account*, Job repeats an argument that he has already hinted at the three friends (7:20). He persists in imputing to himself guilt only as a part of collective corruption. *What shall I answer?* This question manifests an attenuated patient submission, insisting on his innocence. Job presumes that divinity turns him into a worm, buried in the mud by the generic sin of the parents and authority. He presumes that the evil (of the parents and foreign kings) persists on earth for some time, concealed by divinity, to purify Job through patient and silent suffering.

His answer must be interpreted as an undue confession of collective guilt, presuming a lazy divinity who tolerates and conceals evil, and who

---

1. The divinity stands and speaks. The narrative underlines that divinity speaks when Job stands; divinity speaks when Job overcomes the violence of war and submission of sexuality, the two sanguinary accusations of Satan. There is an analogy between divine rebuke to Satan (*Where do you come from?*) and the accusatory question to Job (*Will you continue to rebel?*), referring to the use of violence in the conquest of prosperity. Job pretends to circle the earth and walk through it (in exile). And the divinity questions him: *Have you seen Job, my servant?* This is equivalent to *Will you continue to argue [as a servant]?* In both instances, as authority or servant, Job accuses the foreign divinities and kings and fails to acknowledge his unconscious responsibility (taking unfair advantage of the earth) and his collective responsibility (his patient silence). He does not reveal evil and does not redeem servitude.

does not respond to the two fundamental demands of the first theophany. However, his answers reveal a gradual rationalization of submission, partially diminishing the accusation against divinity and assuming some responsibility. This shows a progressive rationalization of submission, partially exonerating divinity for causing or tolerating collective disorder (assuming separation and accusing divinity only of concealing evil).[2]

b) He Preaches Patient Silence

I have spoken once, I will not argue again; twice, I will not insist again (40:5). He promises not to speak again (not to tempt), not to continue claiming his innocence (he separates), and intends to suffer patiently. *I will not argue again* plausibly refers to renouncing temptation. He has understood that the two allegories of the first theophany (the desert and the animal farm) are a criticism of the bloody sacrifice of life and sexuality. Likewise, he presupposes that he has spoken twice (the conquest of Canaan and Persia); from now on, he pretends to remain silent (separating in Greece) by assuming submission without knowing how to answer Elihu.

His silence avoids open rebellion, as it overcomes sacrifice and lacks the requirement of the uprising (proper to rebellion); however, it is labeled as sedition since it condemns foreign kings and deities by his separation. Job embraces the doctrine of an unjust divinity, accusing divinity of tolerating and concealing evil to purify Job.

It is possible to interpret Job's silence (separation) both as merit and guilt: merit for not taking unjust advantage of prosperity; guilt from the collective accusation of silence as incitement to violence, condemning foreign authority, and failing to protect the innocent and fulfill legal duties as father or authority. Job's silence (not speaking again) is behavior typical of an animal soul, submitted to the incoherence of unjust violence and the sterility of submission.

---

2. Job *shuts his mouth with his hand*. He has not fully understood the first theophany as an explanation of personal responsibility and pretends that divinity does not offer a reasonable explanation for his punishment. He ceases to accuse the divinity of creating evil (and demanding the sacrifice of life, sexuality, or prosperity); nevertheless, shutting his mouth and remaining silent (not protesting), he insists on his innocence and hints at his exile as a divine injustice.

c) Job Fails to Establish a Coherent Social Order

I have spoken once; twice, I will not speak again. This refers to Job overcoming the sacrifice of life, sexuality, and wealth, renouncing the three modes of sacrifice (once, twice, and not again). Yet the narrator seems to accuse Job of being deceived by Elihu. *The Lord talks to us directly, once and twice, and we pay no attention* (33:14). Job continues to look for evil in a disproportionate collective imputation (collective guilt, serfdom) without assuming his collective responsibility in the limited terms of his warrant duty to protect the innocents as father or authority.

After the destruction of Persia, Job sees himself as elected for suffering, in a renewed exile (Greece). Dreaming of a future land of milk and honey, he considers foreign divinities and kings as man's inventions to justify violence, greed, and pride. Separation is another mode of collective accusation, but he distinguishes himself from Elihu, asking for an explanation that attenuates Job's submission and credits his right intention (42:7–8). *Not speaking* means not building a coherent social order with words.

Job conceives foreign divinities as his doomed past, a kingdom of tyrant kings and wicked deities he must overcome by separating (purification); he does not assume that foreign deities do not and cannot exist. Submission means temptation as incitement to violence: *You incite me to punish him in vain* (2:3). In the answers to the theophanies, Job still interprets exile as the progressive decline of violent deities who demand sacrifices of life, sexuality, or prosperity without realizing that his exterior is an image of his soul, and what he sees as foreign divinities mirrors the measure of his (own) responsibility.[3]

---

3. By promoting separation, even renouncing temptation, Job still conceives a vengeful divinity who exiles and persecutes him at night to promote his purification. Job has criticized the sacrificial dogma and submits to divinity because he is overwhelmed by Elihu's submissive violence, without understanding individual guilt and responsibility and accusing divinity of concealing evil in a defective creation that condemns justice.

XXII.

Second Theophany in the Storm

22.1 PERSONAL RESPONSIBILITY

a) Introduction to Second Theophany

Following Job's response to the divine interpellation, the narrator introduces the second theophany in reply (ויען) to Job and reiterates the headline of the first theophany: *And the Lord answers Job in the storm and says* (40:6). The repetition reveals (ideally) the inconsistency of Job's answer to the first theophany, as he reiterates a collective accusation and persists in his submissive dogma.

The narrator repeats another command of the first theophany (38:3): *Tighten your belt like a man, for I will question you, and you will answer me* (40:7). The insistence signals blame; the repetition underlines that Job has not listened carefully to the rebuke of the first theophany; he has not assumed his responsibility as authority or tenant. Instead of projecting collective blame onto foreign rulers and deities, Job is invited to denounce and repair collective harm, fulfilling his civic duty "as a man," and to denounce and repair the collective damage. He must assume his civil responsibility for the collective disorder (*tighten the belt*) in the limits of his warrant duty as father and authority or holder of the land (as a man).

I will question you, and you will answer me underscores the accusatory sense of the second theophany meant to criticize Job for persisting in a collective accusation. The patient submission of Job's responses to the first theophany (separation) represents a diminished form of sacrifice.

b) Veiled Anger Toward Divinity

Will your anger denigrate my justice? Will you condemn me to justify yourself? (40:8). A nuclear accusation of anger denounces the irrationality of all kinds of collective accusations and infers a theory of personal responsibility. Job's response to the first theophany reveals a less rigid approach to sacrificial dogma, yet actual anger remains in Job's responses to the first theophany, and his denial of divine justice reflects a mitigated, though still irrational, form of sacrificial thinking.

Wrath is the common rebuke of Elihu's sedition (32:2), Job's servility (40:8), and the violent three friends' rebellion (42:7). Rage summarizes the essence of the dogmatic sacrifice (of the three friends), the submissive protest (of Job), and the radical patient submission (of Elihu). All three characters reject the concept of divine justice by accusing divinity of punishing a supposed collective guilt, failing to hold each individual accountable for his actions.

Job's separation and temptation presuppose divine concealment of evil to purify men. Job credits his righteous intention by protesting and demanding an explanation for punishment and servitude, which softens the reproach and distinguishes him from Elihu (and the three friends). *Will your anger denigrate my justice?* (40:8) praises Job for not accusing the divinity (or the woman) of causing evil. Furthermore, the reproach is formulated conditionally (*Will you condemn me with your anger to justify yourself?*).

In the first theophany, an accusatory question reproaches Job for not assuming his civil liability. In the second theophany, he is not accused of *obscuring divine intentions with meaningless words* (sacrifice) and is supposed to speak rightly (42:7–8). The second theophany accuses Job's silence of exaggerating his guilt and postponing his responsibility. Accepting collective disorder, he does not correctly assume the hierarchy of debts: his family, social, and public burdens of guarantee. Still, the nuanced reproach of Job's rage (40:8) does not exclude his final blessing (42:12).

c) Duty to Master Anger

If your arm [behaves] like that of the Lord, go and raise your voice (40:9). As a lesser form of sacrifice, the second theophany rebukes silence and servility as masked forms of anger, criticizing the doctrine of sacrifice held by the three friends and Elihu's absolute submission.

The arm refers to personal merit and is the voice that overcomes wrath, an alternative to aggressive violence or patient submission. The hand that covers his mouth (40:4) and represses the speech submits to the social disorder (violence of the origins). Job's arm (40:9) should raise (the voice that the arm symbolizes) to defend justice. *Go* symbolizes a duty to overcome servility (exile and servitude).

Job, like Satan in the prologue, will leave the divine presence (*go away*) after his answers to the first theophany labeled as a collective accusation to foreign divinities and kings. *Raise your voice like him* (40:9). Job is not encouraged to remain silent or resign, as Elihu preaches. Instead, he is summoned to unveil the underlying (personal) causes of social disorder and rectify the unjust use of authority and prosperity, thereby liberating the serfs. To overcome servitude, he must unweave his fawning confession and learn to manage prosperity. The narrative emphasizes the individual identity of merit and guilt, rebuking Job for incessantly repeating laments and his intemperate outcry against divine unfairness, as his protest against injustice reflects an unresolved inner anger.

22.2 ALTERNATIVE TO INSPIRATION

a) Gradual Patch of Collective Disorder

Bear witness, please, with wisdom [גאון], *and with glory* [וגובה]; *and clothe yourself with splendor* [והוד] *and with majesty* [והדר] (40:10). Four testimonies contradict Job's pretended small account. This exigency to bear witness through majesty, dignity, splendor, and glory counters Job's claim of insignificance and invites him to repair—gradually and ethically—the chaotic social order grounded in sacrifice, submission, and exile.

Wisdom, glory, splendor, and *majesty* refer to overcoming the three modalities of sacrifice (of life, sexuality, and prosperity) and separation. They challenge the initial depiction of Job in the prologue: honest, upright, fearful of divinity, and fleeing from evil. Reality (earth) testifies to justice, not sacrifice or submission; and only assuming personal debts regularly (building a house in the desert) repairs the collective, gradually and peacefully. The construction of a social realm corrects a chaotic collective organization founded on sacrifice and submission, unveiling violence and submission as defective origins.

Bear witness explains that wisdom and glory are a testimony of life and social identity, rebuking the sacrifice of life and sexuality. And *clothe yourself* refers to decisive social virtue (splendor and majesty), confronting temptation or separation from the foreign kings and deities as a rebel or serf, teaching to assume social responsibility, and rescuing yourself, your family, your house, your social order, and the land. The theophany encourages Job to take the terms of the duty of guarantee (respect for the hierarchy of debts).

b) Despising the Greedy, the Proud, and the Serf

The second theophany aims to unveil the man who abuses authority, servility, or prosperity, as such violence destroys the social realm. *Turn your anger, look at every proud person, and despise them* (40:11).

As noted earlier, the narrative denounces wrath in the rebellion of the three friends (42:7), Elihu's sedition (32:2), and Job's servility (40:8); portraying Eliphaz's violent greed, Elihu's pride, and Job's serfdom. The narrative encourages Job to despise the greedy, the proud, and the serf without rage. The theophany does not advocate blaming tyrants for their tyranny; instead, it condemns specific abusive actions, imputing individual guilt and responsibility in the abuse of prosperity (the three friends), serfdom (Job), and divinity (Elihu). This emphasizes the absurdity of asserting that one is elected by a deity to either rebel against authority or submit.

Look at every proud person, rescue the servant, and destroy the violence under them (40:12). Submission refers specifically to Elihu (the proud) and Job (the servant). *Look at every proud person* proclaims the personal principle of guilt and responsibility. *To look* refers to reveal and to correct, and praises despising the servant (who takes advantage of authority) and the proud (who takes advantage of divinity). *Destroy the violence* under their feet refers to contradicting and unveiling the authority that steals wealth and the serf who waits to inherit from his master.

c) Importance of Rules of Etiquette

Then I will praise you, and your right hand will save you (40:14). In my opinion, triumphing by the right hand means eluding unjust violence or submission (collective imputations) and not being tempted (as serf) by the delicacies of men who take unfair advantage of violence or servitude (authority and servility). Triumph by the right hand praises respect for personal work and merit (condemns temptation and separation as collective accusations). It applauds building a house with hospitality (first theophany) and not being carried away by the unjust and temporary benefits of sacrifice or submission (second theophany).

The second theophany underscores the role of etiquette and ritual in affirming personal guilt over collective blame and pondering speech over silence. It extols the "yielding of right," the respect for social order and institutions, as a foundation for justice.

The theophanies rationalize religious history, and it seems plausible that this second theophany intends to criticize Job's answer to the first theophany and the persistence of sacrificial submission that took root during the Greek exile, pretending to rebuild an attenuated sacrifice of prosperity through the dogma of temptation or separation. It emphasizes that foreign deities do not exist, and ethical behavior in exile must overcome servility to the imaginary heavens (temptation) and also ideal condemnation of worldly authority (by separation).

22.3 INTERPRETATIONS OF BEHEMOTH AND LEVIATHAN

a) Rabbinic Tradition

The second theophany presents Behemoth and Leviathan as mythical or figurative beasts. The animals described in the first theophany, the raven, the lion, the goat, the ostrich, and the eagle, are perfectly recognizable; still, those of the second theophany, even though they resemble the hippopotamus and the whale (or crocodile), do not seem real beings but rather allegories of spiritual or social entities, aggressive and deprived of freedom.

Under the influence of monotheism, Irving Jacobs explains the rabbinic tradition that considers Behemoth and Leviathan personifications of a social realm, the divinities of the peoples over whom Israel triumphs, destined to be submitted in the eschatological era.[1] This confronts the interpretation that sees them as characters opposed to divinity. He highlights the dual nature of Leviathan: the Lord condemns Leviathan but plays with him (teaches and encourages).[2] There are two Leviathans, one destroyed at the beginning of time (Ps 74) and another that will be extinguished at the end of history (Isa 27).

The submission of mythological animals to Israel is part of the banquet of the righteous in the eschatological future. Baba Batra 74b points out that Leviathan was conceived as both male and female; the male was castrated, and the female was preserved in salt for the future banquet of the righteous. The divinity plays with Leviathan for the last three hours of the day (Avodah Zarah 3b). In the future, the Lord will invite the righteous to a party to eat his flesh and make a tent with his skin (Baba Batra 75a). Until the day of that messianic celebration, the animal image represents a companion with whom the Lord rejoices and subdues the idolatrous peoples.

b) Evolution of Medieval Dogmatic

To identify Leviathan with Satan and Behemoth as a devil is common in Christian dogmatic that considers them an objective reality of sin or as a perverse spiritual inclination.

In bk. 31, in the sixth part of *Moralia*, Gregory comments on the figures of Behemoth and Leviathan as related to preaching the gospel, the conversion of sinners, and the efficacy of divine grace. The rhinoceros refers to the secular powers that serve the church (proposition 2). In bks. 32–33, Leviathan alludes to Satan (proposition 17), caught with a hook. Leviathan is the evil spirit of reprobate men (proposition 55). In proposition 18, the Lord chains Leviathan with the rope of the incarnation, unveiling his false doctrines. The terror between his teeth refers to the same false doctrines (proposition 46). Leviathan presents to the wicked the nefarious things they intend and dresses himself in the appearance of Holiness (proposition 44). Leviathan has eyes to see a wicked proposal (proposition 57). Leviathan has fire in his lies (proposition 61) and hidden suggestions (proposition 67).[3]

---

1. Jacobs, "Book of Job," 301.
2. Jacobs, "Book of Job," 20, 34n4.
3. Schreiner, *Where Shall Wisdom Be Found?*, 47–80.

In an Aristotelian vision of evil as irrationality and impurity, Maimonides considers Leviathan and Behemoth a manifestation of a defective understanding of creation; a man must struggle against his perverse inclinations and false representations, not against foreign divinities. In the commentary on the Sanhedrin treatise, he considers the banquet of the righteous an intellectual pleasure that submits the animal soul.

Calvin specifically opposes Gregory. He states that theophanies speak of creation and not conflict. Calvin interprets the animal representation of Behemoth and Leviathan as the admirable order with which the Lord masters the world. Domestic animals became wild after the original sin, but the Lord contains their fury and puts them at his service. Calvin confronts the view of Behemoth and Leviathan as devils or rebellious carnal nature and considers them executors of a divine will, referring to the admirable order of creation. Behemoth and Leviathan cease to be allegorical figures and become the manifestation of divine glory fighting against evil.[4]

c) Animal Representation of Political Theory

The secular realm, faced with the chaos of religious struggles, confronts the eschatological context of Behemoth and Leviathan, and it refers to them as the denial of authority or rebellion against the social order.

In the *Six Books of the Republic*, Bodin, a thinker of absolutism in France, interprets Behemoth and Leviathan as an opposition to the sovereign will of the Christian prince by those powers or interests that oppose nature and rationality. He affirms that an absolute state epitomizes the Christian faith, and rational or natural thought cannot replace it.[5]

In the context of the religious wars in England, Hobbes, champion of Episcopalianism, opposes the Calvinist vision of the English church as a continuity of the divine election of the Jewish people and the only path to salvation. He pretends to overcome the personalist version of the Jewish kingdom and replace it with the sovereign king. The social pact makes the Christian kingdom a reality, not instituted by divinity but representative of the people who overcome the chaos of the state of nature through divine incarnation and redemption.[6]

---

4. Schreiner, *Where Shall Wisdom Be Found?*, 141.
5. Bodin, *Coloquio de los siete sabios*, 91.
6. Hobbes, *Leviatán*, 102.

Carl Schmitt, professor of political law at the University of Berlin during the time of National Socialism, reinterprets Behemoth and Leviathan as the reality of opposition to the National Socialist state, and a personification of Jewish hypocrisy that undermines the foundations of a sovereign state.[7]

d) Other Modern Interpretations

Many modern authors interpret Behemoth and Leviathan as manifestations of the divine immoral, irrational, tremendous, and fascinating essence.[8] In a similar sense, psychoanalysis conceives them as metaphors of the tortured human body and images of the loss of a root and human gestures of disorientation, monsters that evoke sinister magic and violence.[9] They fulfill the function that psychoanalysis attributes to totem, image, or figure of the emotional content of a collective identity, protective and benevolent, revered and feared. The myths and taboos justify marital morality (exogamy).

Job is also considered a depressive and compulsive patient, obsessed with perfectionism. The book explains the healing progress of his divine paranoia in group therapy (with the three friends and Elihu). Elihu will rescue Job from his obsessions, and the theophanies will enlighten him about reality and invite him to abandon his pretension of dominating the indeterminate; he will rationalize his paranoia (Behemoth and Leviathan) and enable him to assume a social integration.[10]

22.4 ANIMAL REPRESENTATION OF THE SECOND THEOPHANY

a) Toleration and Concealment of the Tyrant and the Wicked

The first theophany criticized the dogmatic of sacrifice. The second theophany, in turn, rebukes Job's responses to the first theophany, interpreting his submission as an institutionalization of violence. The *animal representation* of the second theophany presents a dreamlike

---

7. Schmitt, *Leviathan*, 6.
8. Habel, *Book of Job*, 533.
9. Sungjin, "Identity of the Spirit," 198–201.
10. JiSeong, "Psychosomatic Approach."

reinterpretation of the two allegories of the first theophany. Behemoth refers to the doctrine of the conquest of the desert by the virtuous man, and Leviathan to the organization of a social order by the faithful woman. Job, in his answers to the first theophany, persists in pretending to conquer the land by unjust methods (the sacrificial temptation of Behemoth or the false separation of Leviathan), instead of seeking the personal origin of evil and correcting a defective earth. As a defective identity of a social realm, Behemoth refers to authority, and Leviathan alludes to organization.

The narrator presents Behemoth and Leviathan as the sterile and ephemeral conquest of prosperity by sacrifice (temptation) and submission (separation), which creates authority and organization. In the second theophany, mythical animals characterize the doctrine of temptation (Behemoth) and separation (Leviathan) as a bloodless repetition of Israel's sacerdotal and prophetic dogma. The second theophany reveals the violent origins of the animal farm (Behemoth) that an organization based on submission perpetuates (Leviathan), institutionalizing a flawed social realm. Behemoth and Leviathan are the managers and employees (authorities and divinities) of the animal farm referred to in the first theophany.

See any haughty man and subdue him, and crush the wicked in their place. Their divinity does not exist; Behemoth and Leviathan have their origin in the defective social organization, the dust: *Hide them together in the dust* (40:12).

b) Legitimate but Unjust Institution of Behemoth

The term Behemoth should be interpreted as the singularity and identity of the animal tale of the second theophany. Behemoth represents the authority that arises from a legitimate rebellion against tyranny; however, unjust rebellion does not confront the acts of a tyrant, but rather the collective responsibility of tyrannies. *Behold Behemoth, whom I have made at your side* (40:15).

A violent rebellion for collective causes presupposes a fight against divinity, an accusation to heaven of tolerating and concealing evil. Violent rebellion (through the servility of renunciation and temptation) is a false and temporal remedy to the (unconscious and collective) abuse of prosperity: *Scatter your raging anger.* Behemoth *feeds on grass like the ox*

(40:15). This means praise and reproach. It applauds the rebel (as an individual) because he does not abuse prosperity and fights for justice; and it means a stain, like an ox (castrated), because the rebel institutionalizes servitude by a collective accusation and does not fight properly (individually) unveiling and submitting (personal) evil (enrichment or damage). Rightful confrontation must be proportional and against individual crimes or abuses.

The narrator refers to Behemoth as a well-intentioned rebellion that prevails through unjust means (violence). *Have you not given to him?* (1:10). Behemoth establishes a collective order supported by righteous violence and momentarily subdues a defective social order. *The Lord gives him a sword* (40:19) and (temporarily) blesses his effort in the fight for justice. Nevertheless, the triumph of violent rebellion is fleeting because it does not free the servant.

c) Behemoth's Inconsistency

Behemoth and his violence (the righteous sword of discipline and temptation) establish a social order on authority. He is called the *first fruits of the works of the Lord* (40:19).

In all this, Job did not sin because he did not attribute evil to divinity (1:23). Plausibly, this refers to Behemoth's violence against a collective disorder, not rescuing a social order of servitude and only conquering authority. The narrative highlights the violence of rebellion (through discipline and temptation) as a collective failure.

The mountains feed him with their fodder (40:20). The mountain refers to the violent ethic of the conquest of Canaan. *No one can pierce his nose when his eyes are open*; his power is in the iron and copper: he triumphs in a legitimate and violent rebellion, which does not subdue Leviathan (41:19). He sleeps among the lotus flowers; this explains that a just rebellion is only a dream of justice, because he becomes aware of and overcomes evil only in the day (material evil, the abuse of prosperity), not at night (the abuse of the servant). He does not illuminate the personal origins of evil. Leviathan deceives him at his very origin at night, as nothing can destroy him while awake. His triumph corrupts Behemoth when he takes shelter under the lotuses, referring to the pleasures of the servants, as he has not revealed evil (the economic origin of servitude).

The narrative criticizes his idealism; *he trusts that he will draw the Jordan into his mouth* (40:23).

d) Institutionalization of Behemoth

After Job's awakening from his violent sacrificial past, Leviathan personifies the second answer to the first theophany: *I have spoken once, I will not argue again; twice, I will not insist again* (40:5). Submission to the Persian king means an exaggerated conscience of personal guilt that assumes collective guilt and names the foreign divinities. It ideally imagines a spiritual organization without considering that foreign deities are fictional and cannot exist.

The second part of ch. 40 explains the institutionalization of violence (Behemoth) and the downfall of foreign and imaginary divinities in their origin (Leviathan). *Can you pull the Leviathan with a harpoon or press down his tongue with a rope?* (40:25). *Can you insert a fishhook into his nose or pierce his jaw with a barb?* (40:26).

This likely refers to the exaggerated confession and moral of submission and separation that Job formulates in his second response to the first theophany. Leviathan is described as *humbly asking for mercy and confessing with bitter words* (40:27). He is defined as a lifelong slave (40:28), an incarnation of Elihu's doctrine. Leviathan (Job in disguise), as a patient serf, submits to Behemoth, an animal spirit of the rebellion who triumphs ephemerally through violence (temptation), pretending to represent divinity and condemned to an unavoidable failure.

And Job concludes that he has submitted sexually to the Persian kings (the messianism of a violent authority) and awakened in servitude. *You will take him as a slave for all time* (40:28). Through the sacrifice of Esther, he exaggerated the power of the doomed Persian divinities, which exist only ideally and ephemerally as a defective organization of authority (violence) and servitude (submission to violence). Job instituted the Persian Empire by his submission and fell with it.

Following his nightmare, Leviathan makes a pact of eternal servitude and becomes a pet of the reborn (nonexistent) foreign (Greek) divinities. The dogmatic of renunciation (temptation) and separation condemns foreign idealism and kings (an act of collective violence). Job intends to build a messianic future over the ruins of the (Greek) foreign kingdom by building a tent with his skin (40:31)—symbolizing the sacrificial messianism of prosperity, the supposed Third Temple. The end of the chapter describes Leviathan's cage (40:30–32) in a supposed divine reconstruction of a social order.

22.5 DOGMATIC OF COLLECTIVE GUILT

a) Dual Essence of Leviathan

Leviathan is an ideal and imaginary being who presents a dual and Manichaean nature. He embodies both the tortured social identity of Job in exile, who feels persecuted by the (nonexistent) foreign divinities (ch. 40), and also the very (nonexistent) foreign divinities in exile from whom Job intends to flee (ch. 41) and whom he names (identifies, condemns, and creates ideally). Job is the reality of what he imagines.

The confession provokes silent exile and condemns Job (by separation). Job (Leviathan in disguise) attempts to purify (with separation) and fights against divinities as personifications of corrupt foreign peoples—rather than recognizing them as the defective institutionalization of merit and punishment. Submission (confession) favors the downfall of men into a closed and sectarian organization that Leviathan portrays (separation).

No foreign deities can stand before divinity: *Who can stand before Me?* (41:2). *I will not be silent* (41:4). Confession submits to authority and the yoke of servitude, progressively and incessantly, the hook (individual irrationality), the rope on the tongue (he does not triumph by the word), the pierced nose (the anger of the servant), hanging from a hook (the accusation of the foreign divinities).

b) Formalization of Foreign Divinities

Behemoth personifies violent rebellion, imposing justice by submission; and Leviathan separation, experiencing the lack of reality and essence of foreign divinities. The narrative seems to mock the foolishness of attributing guilt to foreign kingdoms and kings a priori or of exaggerating their collective guilt.

The sea monster (Leviathan), created by the abuse of divinity (violent injustice of sacrifice and submission), is described as the king of proud beasts (41:26) and serves as an institutional counterpoint to the beast of the earth (the legitimate but unjust rebellion of Behemoth): *Behold, it is impossible to overcome him, his very appearance imposes* (41:1). *Who will dare to awaken him, before me who can stand?* (41:2). Job has fought a challenging battle against foreign deities and authorities. Upon realizing the absurdity of his idealism, he intensifies this struggle internally by assuming collective guilt indiscriminately. Leviathan was created from the dust and will dominate it: over the dust, *no one rules him, as he is not made to feel dismayed* (41:25).

c) Personification of Collective Guilt

In exile, Leviathan's appearance causes awe and admiration. *I will not hide his appearance, the greatness of his works, and the perfection of his structure* (41:4). His mystery makes him sacred; his majesty roots in an authoritarian submissive organization (the institutionalization of Behemoth), which validates authority as a defective source to social identity (authority and organization). He disguises his human nature with the violence and reproach of his despair. *Who has lifted the hem of his garment and has penetrated the double order of his teeth?* (41:5).

Divinity claims to be the author of Behemoth (40:7); on the contrary, he does not claim to have made Leviathan. Leviathan is self-made (as the institutionalization of Behemoth). Leviathan, the strong and solitary dragon, both fish and bird, lacks identity because it is not rooted in a tradition; it personifies, like Satan, the illusion of idealism, submission to violence (of Behemoth), conceived as a serpent or dragon that lives in the sea (the exile of idealism), and that will be destroyed when its day comes (Isa 27:1).

Leviathan must be considered the dummy servant who dethrones or inherits from his master (Prov 30:23) and perishes in his contradictions (collective guilt). The narrator identifies Leviathan with the man who tries to dominate by confessing guilt; he is subject (in his origin and by omission) to the same divinities he imagines and abuses (by exaggerating his collective responsibility).

d) Strength and Fire Without Uttering a Single Word

Leviathan is part of the animal kingdom and does not possess the ability to speak. He represents the supremacy of the organization over the individual, which expresses the meaning of renunciation and separation. *His breath kindles coals, and the flame goes forth from his mouth* (Job 41:13).

The narrator introduces a second round of accusatory questions. He repeatedly emphasizes the majesty and mystery of his appearance, אל מרא'ו 'טל. His social identity is a mere appearance of *wisdom, glory, splendor,* and *majesty* because Leviathan is not a real being. His internal fire expresses his mystery; it shows that he lives prostrate and feels shame and guilt. His strength is in his neck (41:14), which may represent his yoke (Deut 28:48). If one overtakes him with a sword, he will not endure (Job 41:18).

He has strength in his teeth and fire in his mouth and nostrils, but he does not utter any coherent word and does not build justice. The contradiction lies in the fact that, by his submission, Leviathan corrupts Behemoth. Leviathan is a defensive character, a hidden structure turned inward and unfathomable. *Under him are rays of the sun, where he lies is gold upon the mire* (40:22); Leviathan displays the majesty and rite of a temple, the violent conquest of authority by unconditional confession of guilt. No one can reveal the hem of his garment (פני לבושו), and his beauty is not incompatible with the terror (אימה) caused by contemplating his teeth (animal and spiritual submission as violence). Suffering will reveal to him the foolishness of a collective condemnation of foreign divinities and kings by rebellion or submission (authority and organization). The allegory hints that there cannot be collective redemption with a violent or submissive disguise. *He looks at all high things; he is king over all proud beasts* (41:26), referring to the submission of Leviathan to Behemoth's unjust violence.

XXIII.

Job's Answer to the Second Theophany

23.1 JOB REITERATES HIS PROTESTS AGAINST DIVINE JUSTICE

a) He Persists in Considering Himself Innocent

In the second theophany, Job intervenes (responds) without being prompted by heaven: *Job answers the Lord and says* (42:1). He reiterates his innocence, protests against divine justice, and contradicts (or does not understand) the doctrine of the second theophany. He persists in a dogmatic of confessing collective guilt as personal guilt and assuming unlimited responsibility.

The divinity will address Eliphaz directly (42:7) and seems to disregard Job's arguments, which do not differ from his response to the first theophany. In his answer to the second theophany, Job still imagines a deity covering up an evil that he is supposed to suffer without guilt. His protest is characterized as a confrontation with both divine and secular justice through separation. In this second reply, Job's pigheadedness again envisions a deity who conceals evil, which does not prevent a final blessing (42:10).

b) Job Assumes Divine Predestination

Job declares: *I know that you can do everything and that no purpose can resist you* (42:2). *I know*; Job proclaims the apotheosis of a priori ethics. *You can do everything* suggests that divinity conceals evil (collective guilt) to cleanse Job through suffering, plausibly meaning that (only) divinity can overcome evil.

In his answer, Job does not acknowledge man's freedom and merit in establishing the social order and shaping history, and he presupposes the existence of evil. He assumes that man creates evil (masked by divinity) and that he has to overcome institutionalized evil (only) through pain. While praying for his friends (42:7–8) and not fighting against evil, Job waits patiently for the destruction of a foreign social order, pretending to inherit authority.

Job's response to the second theophany organizes an animal farm by separation and persists in a collective accusation, concealing and inciting divine violence to destroy the innocents: *You incite me to punish him in vain* (2:3). In doing so, he undermines his social identity.

c) Historicity of Messianism

You can do everything, and nothing can resist you. He conceives a divinity who founds the world on revelation and predestination. This text highlights a historical vision of messianism, where Job imagines his divinity battling foreign deities. *You can do everything* refers to the establishment of Israel, while *nothing can resist you* alludes to revealing and dismantling foreign social structures.

Job persists in a catastrophic vision of creation, one grounded in the punishment and submission of evil (foreign divinities) and not in the respect of the social realm, as the work and merit of a free man. He gives foreign divinities a name (he does not understand that they do not exist), and he tries to overcome them (their authority) by separation, awaiting a divine outburst of wrath. He yearns for the destruction of foreign authority (who supposedly the foreign divinities institute) and hopes to inherit a future social order without concern for the innocents.

23.2 JOB ELUDES PERSONAL RESPONSIBILITY

a) Job's Pretended Innocence Exaggerates Personal Guilt

Job asks himself: *Who is this who senselessly blots out [מעל'ם] my plan?* (42:3). In his answer to the second theophany, Job exaggerates the accusatory question of the first theophany (*Who is this who obscures [מחשיך] my plans?* [40:2]), referring to words that lack meaning (40:2), underlining individual responsibility (*who obscures*). He sees himself as part of a human rebellion against divine justice (an impossible crime). He attempts to address divinity by magnifying an accusatory question directed at him.

I spoke without knowledge, I did not understand (42:3) suggests that he repents from employing temptation as incitement to crime. He was accused of protesting against divine justice, concealing the divine plan (מחשיך) by words, not of denying it (מעל'ם) by facts. Job now thinks that divine plans will restore divine justice (in the future) by his separation. Now, he reiterates that divine justice will be restored in the future without his participation; and redemption will be achieved only through submission and suffering, denying free will and personal responsibility.

Hearken now and I will speak; I will ask you and (you) inform me (42:4). The divine accusatory question has become Job's stupid question in the night and with no content to his imaginary deity, accusing himself and demanding an explanation. In his answer to the first theophany, he accused himself of speaking too much, once and twice (the two bloody sacrifices of life and sexuality), and decided to remain in silence (40:5). Now, he pretends a lack of understanding of his supposed guilt at night, presupposing a defective creation where he is born with collective guilt. The specificity of the question concludes the foolishness of sacrifice (of life, sexuality, and prosperity), assuming patient submission (separation) as divine predestination (due to his lack of understanding).

Marvels that I did not understand, affirming the perfection of creation that man corrupts, he hints at predestination, longing for a future divine purification of creation only by human suffering. He imagines an avenging divinity who saves rebel humanity by submission, assuming that divinity concealed evil and chose him to overcome the collective damnation through servitude. As in Elihu's final words, Job sees providence overlapping nature and the social realm.

b) Job's Vision

The second theophany requested Job to master his anger and stop accusing the divinity of tolerating evil (40:8). Job nevertheless persists in justifying patient suffering with a moral certainty derived from a vision. *I listened to what you told me, but now my eyes have seen you* (42:5). In a logical contradiction, he pretends to hear but claims to see. What does Job claim to have seen? Without a doubt, camaraderie with the divinity has allowed him to see (understand) the supposed foundations of ethics in collective guilt. The vision is akin to that of Eliphaz (4:12–17) and Balaam (Num 22). He has seen (understood) the (exaggerated) awareness of guilt (that he imputes to himself). *To see* is employed symbolically, meaning inspiration, as he still pretends to be chosen by divine election.

You cannot see my face; for no one can see me and live (Exod 33:20). Job has not seen divinity. He has seen the allegories of the second theophany, which supposedly ratify the collective damnation. He likely saw (suffered) the radical punishments of Behemoth and Leviathan (behold [40:15; 41:1]), an allegory of the destruction of the First and Second Temples, and he is terrified by a supposedly just but arbitrary divinity who punishes him for a hypothetical collective guilt without personal fault. *Seeing* might refer to praying for friends and building an ethic a priori (from revelation), separating from the constituted (sacrificial) authority of the three friends, and putting his trust in his supposed ethical supremacy (separation without temptation). Job experiences, like Leviathan, the punishment of his exile, go (40:9) (לך).

The book of Job opposes vision to speech and individual certitude to social identity. Words represent a social identity, and vision means subjective confidence, justifying arbitrary power. Elihu's intercessory angel sees: *My life will see the light* (33:27–28). Job has seen the wonders of creation (42:3). He now formulates a doctrine of non-sacrificial submission (without temptation), letting creation express itself as perfect, exaggerating his collective responsibility that exceeds the terms of his duty of guarantee, supposing the unjust domination of foreign kings and deities. Job submits to a marvelous creation (a foreign land that welcomes and purifies him through patient suffering). He still does not understand that foreign divinities do not exist and accuses divinity of covering them up.[1]

---

1. The Greek tragedy is an allegorical criticism of the Greek divinities accused of promoting incest (the sexual corruption of greed). The book of Job criticizes the former Jewish dogmatic of sacrifice and submission that builds an aristocratic sexual ethic. Job

c) Job Reinterprets Exile

I protest [אמאס] and despair [נחמתי] on dust and ashes (42:6). The nuanced confession after the second theophany names the foreign kings and divinities (greed and pride) and creates them ideally. He ceases eating the delicacies of the foreign kings (dust) and divinities (ashes) (in exchange for his sacrifice or submission). He commits to work the land so that the earth (testimony of justice) spits out and buries the tyrant and the wicked (as he purifies himself by work and silence).

The *protest* (אמאס) and *despair* (נחמתי) hint at tolerating and concealing evil, as will be unveiled by the brothers, sisters, and friends who accompany Job (וינדו לו) and console him (ינחמו אתו), for *all the evil that the Lord has brought upon him* (42:11). He does not retract his previous illusory confession of collective guilt and continues to uphold a similar doctrine as in his responses to the first theophany.

Dust is a recurring image that refers to exile (separation from foreign kings) and ashes to the despair of damnation (separation from foreign deities). Dust and ashes refer to Behemoth and Leviathan, the dogmatic of temptation (sacrifice) and separation (submission). The epilogue shows Job renouncing sacrifice and initiating the reckoning of time: from the dust of the earth and the ashes of the divinities, a man is born (in exile). Job gives names to the deities and kings as incarnations of collective responsibility without assuming their nonexistence and his (personal) responsibility.[2]

---

sees four generations (he accuses foreign sexual corruption) (42:16).

2. In conclusion, the response to the second theophany reiterates the doctrine of his answers to the first theophany. He mitigates submission, as Job renounces employing sanguinary and economic temptation to fight evil but is far from building a coherent social realm. Nevertheless, divine anger is not kindled against Job after responding to the second theophany (42:7-8) because he overcomes the sacrificial dogma and assumes separation without temptation. The narrative presents anger as the counterpoint of sacrifice and justifies submission in Job's right intention and hospitality (praying for his friends). Job incurs responsibility for omission (the abuse of divinities and servants). He does not assume the principle of individual responsibility for the collective disorder in defined terms. Accusing a foreign divinity of evil violates the accusatory principle that requires accrediting imputable damage (causality) and assumes that divinity employs evil (tolerates or hides foreign deities) to redeem man. Job persists in a comfortable servitude (separation), yet accusing innocents, and unheeding and careless of the anger reproach of the second theophany.

FOURTH ACT

Guilt and Responsibility

XXIV.

Job's Righteousness

24.1 FINAL REPROACH TO ELIPHAZ

a) Abuse of Authority

And it came to pass [ויהי], after the Lord had spoken these words to Job, that the Lord reproached Eliphaz of Teman (42:7). It came to pass denotes Providence warning Eliphaz and explaining guilt and responsibility to Job. *It came to pass* (ויהי) warns Eliphaz about the violence (guilt) of (supposed) inspiration; *after* explaining to Job the historicity of creation as a conflict between personal identity and social integration, relating the individual origin of a social realm and the causes of its eventual disintegration.

And it came to pass (ויהי) sums up the meaning of the epilogue in a final reproach to Eliphaz and Job, as the two faces of Satan (accusing authority in the name of divinity). Eliphaz personifies Job before the punishment (sacrifice). The epilogue shows Job gradually becoming aware, after punishment, of the guilt and responsibility of submission.

And it came to pass (ויהי) underscores the misguided inspiration behind both sacrifice and submission. It is coherent to conclude that the epilogue explains that both the violence of the lords (Eliphaz) and the violence of the servants (Job) provoke servitude and exile. None of them establishes a coherent social identity, both damned by the flawed origins of the social realm. The prologue summarizes the doctrine of sacrifice, while the epilogue outlines the doctrine of submission.[1]

b) Job's Separation

After saying these words to Job hints at a reproach for the abuse of the earth (sacrifice of Eliphaz) or the abuse of the heavens (Job's submission). Job does not listen carefully, and although he overcomes sacrificial dogmatics in his response to the theophanies, he persists in an aggressive dogmatic of separation (patient submission), inciting divine punishment of foreign countries and kings and pretending to inherit the doomed foreign kingdoms in exile.

Speaking to Job and Eliphaz, Providence protects life and institutes authority. *After*, as an adverb, portrays an allegory for Job's history. It suggests that Job's submission, akin to Esther's sacrifice, did not save the Persian Empire because it complies with violence. The reproach to Eliphaz of Teman after speaking with Job hints that Job's submission represents a mitigated violence, which collaborates with Eliphaz's violence.

The epilogue also explains Israel's (Job) relationship with the foreign peoples (Eliphaz and his cronies). Israel listens to the first theophany and renounces the institutional violence of sacrifice, which persists in foreign peoples (subjected to their violent and bloodthirsty origins, which allegorize divine wrath). After listening to the second theophany (exile), Job gradually renounces the dogmatic of temptation (though he still assumes a defective stance of separation). Merit, therefore, lies not in submission or sacrifice but in surpassing past doctrines—namely, the violence of Behemoth and the resignation of Leviathan—and to restore the defective origins.

---

1. The divine anger toward Eliphaz manifests reproach and teaching. It supposes a great privilege (praise) to hear a reproach and suffer a justified punishment. Since evil (collective disorder) preceded him, the anger against Eliphaz, even though it rebukes sacrificial dogma, praises a right intention (*and now* [42:8]) in fighting against evil (the previous collective disorder) to protect the innocent (exaggerating his duty of guarantee). The authenticity of Job (*go to the servant Job*), who speaks with righteousness (but not necessarily acts with righteousness), refers to ceasing bloody sacrifice (response to the first theophany) and, by separation, renouncing the bloodless sacrifice of prosperity (response to the second theophany). Now that you have acknowledged that Job, the servant, is not primarily responsible for the collective disorder (32:1), Eliphaz and the three friends should recognize their warrant duty as authority. Their responsibility (sacrifice as rebellion) and their duty to liberate the serfs culminate in the divine interpellation: *Go to my servant Job*.

c) Anger Against Eliphaz's Companions

My anger kindles *against you and your two companions*. The text shows a contemptuous tone. It treats Eliphaz and his two accomplices as a criminal association and does not call the two companions by their names, as they *did not speak of me with justice as my servant Job* (42:7).

Eliphaz embodies violent authority; he appropriates the wealth of the land and institutes servitude (subjugates the dependent, woman, servant, and foreigner). With defective means, Eliphaz conquers or inherits a disordered social structure and bears the duty to repair it (as a duty of guarantee). He is the architect or heir of a sacrificial system, Bildad and Zophar are his accomplices, who benefit from violence and sustain it.

To maintain power, Eliphaz must share and distribute the benefits and delicacies of prosperity and servitude. How does Eliphaz institutionalize his rebellion? He gives Bildad an exclusive wife (the aristocracy) and shares prosperity with Zophar (in exchange for obedience). He establishes a matrimonial and economic morality. Violence represents the rebellious warrior (Eliphaz), sexual submission refers to emotional manipulation, the sacrifice of Esther (Bildad), and the sacrifice of prosperity alludes to the economic temptation in Greece (Zophar).

The abuse of power and failure to fulfill the warrant duty of a father and authority (personal responsibility for omission) explains the extension of the three friends' reproof. They institute or inherit (Eliphaz), collaborate (Bildad), or not reveal (Zophar) the false authority of a pretended divinity (the false origin) that institutes the social order (by sacrifice and submission). The three friends personify the three pillars of the former history of Israel as three successive modes of sacrificial violence (physical, emotional, and economic). The defective origins doom the social realm established by the violent Eliphaz. His two companions personify the socialization of sexual anger and the unjust distribution of prosperity.

d) Admonishment of Submission

Take [for yourselves] seven bulls and seven goats and go to my servant Job (42:8). Is not a private sacrifice like an abomination? The text does not promote or incite but reproaches sacrifice. Eliphaz and his friends are instructed to renounce sacrifices, the violence of authority, and the falseness of submission. Authority should not be based on coercion.

The reproach reveals the (ontological) selfish nature of sacrifice. Sacrifice treats a man like an animal and denies his divine resemblance (as a father, authority, and author). Does a holocaust benefit divinity? A sacrifice is not proper conduct for human beings, as social identity determines the retribution of merit and the scope of the individual duty to assume the collective disorder.

Seven bulls and seven goats refers to the aggravated responsibility of Eliphaz and the three friends (the sacrificial responsibility for violence and the sacrificial responsibility for sexual or economic submission). As it has been repeated, history is the formalization of the past, and the three friends personify Job's sacrificial past. In turn, the responsibility for submission refers to sexual submission (Bildad) and economic submission (Zophar). The friends do not blame Job but exploit his offerings and intercession, consuming the temple vessels and benefiting from the prayers of the submissive servant.[2]

24.2 DEBATE ON JOB'S VIRTUE

a) Contradictory Texts About Job's Righteousness

The double praises of Job in his presentation as a righteous man in the prologue (1:8; 2:3), in his positive approval after the accusations of Satan (1:22; 2:10), and his related righteous speech (42:7–8) seem to contradict the theophanies. The first theophany accuses him of *speaking nonsense* (38:2), and the second theophany affirms that Job condemns divinity *to justify himself* (40:8).

The reiteration of Job's double praise (42:7–8) seems at least surprising and lends itself to contradictory interpretations. Many consider the incoherence a result of the juxtaposition of texts from different epochs, a remnant of multiple versions of the original fable of the book of Job. Others resolve the paradox by appealing to a disorder of verses; they argue that his righteousness matches the resolution of the dialogue with his friends, not the final epilogue. Some claim that they are irreconcilable texts.

---

2. The servant's submission presupposes a defective creation (collective accusation). The sacrifices of animals and prosperity are not praised, nor are the three friends punished with sacrifices. The violent person who makes sacrifices becomes the victim of sacrifice and faces contempt and ruin, and the submissive person will also be destroyed by violence. Sacrifice and submission are the instincts of animals that do not speak. Submission by separation is also an abuse of authority, and Job is responsible, at least as a lucrative participle, for the violence that instituted the social order.

The entire debate between Satan and divinity, the discussion of Job with his friends, and Elihu's long monologue affirm Job's guilt. Theophanies reiterate the reproach, and Job recognizes guilt in his answers to the two theophanies. Is it contradictory to affirm Job's rightfulness? Of course, there is no such contradiction. The nuclear question of the epilogue is to overcome the Manichaean confrontation that collective guilt presupposes.

b) Jewish Tradition

Jewish religion seems to have argued for centuries about Job's guilt. As I have mentioned when discussing the nature of Satan, classical Jewish texts evolve from considering Job's guilt to, at times, comparing his virtue to Abraham's.

In traditional Jewish thought, Job's virtue cannot be compared to Abraham's faith. Job is not representative of Jewish identity but an extravagant and stubborn character who does not want to assume his guilt or fully assume his family and social responsibility. Abraham loves the Lord, and Job fears the Lord. Abraham is hospitable to strangers, while Job receives only family and friends (42:11). Abraham speaks with sense, Job with bitterness (Bereshit Rabbah 49). Job does not control his anger (Pesiqta Rabbati 49:20). Abraham affirms that divinity does not condemn the righteous or the wicked alike, even though he cannot find a grave for Sarah (Baba Batra 16a); Job, instead, disputes divine justice (Job 9:22).

The Talmud systematizes a doctrinal tradition on Job's guilt (Sanhedrin 106a). The Gemara (Sotah.11a.12–13) reports that Rabbi Ḥiyya bar Abba says that Rabbi Simai says that three offered advice to Pharaoh: Balaam, Job, and Yitro. Job is found guilty of remaining in silence and condemned to suffering. Balaam died for his advice to drown newborns. Yitro fled and endured persecution from Pharaoh but deserved to have his descendants seated in the Sanhedrin.

In this allegory, in my opinion, Balaam represents the theology of sacrificial violence of the First Temple, Yitro personifies the theology of patient submission of the Second Temple (the sacrifice of sexuality), and Job illustrates the dogmatics of exile simplified in his answer to the second theophany: falling silent in dust and ashes to the Pharaoh (the foreign power in exile). The allegory invites us to search for the meaning of the book of Job in the epilogue, which concludes a coherent theory of (individual) guilt and responsibility as a nuclear clue for the systematic religious thought that builds the Jewish canon.

Rabbi Akiba and the later Tannaim and Amoraim affirm Job's righteousness despite his incorrect language, which his suffering justifies. A doctrinal trend articulated in the Talmud and Midrashim, such as Midrash Rabbah and Zohar, is decisive in the formalization of the Jewish canon. A consolidated rabbinical Judaism affirms Job's righteousness.

c) Idealistic Interpretations

A dogmatic of an alleged original sin blesses Job for keeping his faith and accepting the divine designs. Job is justified in retracting from the accusation against divine justice despite not being the perpetrator of any crime. Job is righteous because he denies retributive ethics; he tells the truth by denying the relationship between suffering and guilt and affirming the redemptive suffering of the innocent. His friends could not accuse Job of sin for his misfortune since sin is original and collective.

Another idealistic perspective emphasizes inspiration and not suffering. Job's restoration credits his innocence; the divinity intended to incite his devotion with his disproportionate punishment. His true virtue is his willingness to address the divinity directly; friends talk about the divinity, but Job addresses the Lord. His protests and despair show his overflowing love; his faith is praised, not his words or acts. Divinity values those who confront authority by showing their faith, not those who submit indiscriminately (such as Elihu and the three friends).

The debate on guilt is related to the coherence and meaning of his final prosperity. In idealism, the doubled prosperity of the epilogue is a commitment to orthodoxy (an affirmation of predestination), as recognition of Job's collective guilt and personal innocence, and an exaltation of the (temporal) suffering of the righteous. Additionally, the book of Job does not deny the connection between human actions and personal guilt; it underlines that divinity inspires men within a polyphonic thought in terms that might appear inconsistent to a rational mind. Faith credits that Job will enjoy prosperity (at least) in another world and that value behavior cannot be accurately assessed by humans.

d) Confrontation of Idealism

Many oppose Job's final response as unconditional submission to the divine. He does not repent and expressly opposes the divine will. The uncertainty of the translation allows many commentators to interpret Job's final words as an admission of divine power and sovereignty but not to suppose that Job acknowledges any guilt or resigns himself to suffering.

Many conclude that Job gives an evasive answer and continues his rebellious defiance before an arbitrary divinity. Others interpret his response to the theophanies as ironic or rhetorical. Job does not justify the supposed divine justice that makes him suffer without fault but confronts a proud and overbearing divinity in the storm. Job definitively rejects or denies a divinity whom he considers arbitrary and unjust. Since Job does not admit to having received a reasonable explanation, he abandons his quarrel with divine justice but turns his back on the content of the theophanies.

24.3 DOUBLE PRAISE OF THE SERVANT JOB

a) Nuanced Praise and Reproof of Job

In a context of reproach, because *Job speaks nonsense* (38:2) and *condemns divine justice to justify himself* (40:8), Job's nuanced praise in the epilogue (42:7-8) must refer to his two responses to the two theophanies, in which he renounces the dogmatic of sacrifice and the dogmatic of temptation (submission and intercession).

Nevertheless, the repetition of praise is an implicit critique, a reproach for persisting in separation as an attenuated submission. Job is applauded for his separation without temptation as the lesser evil because submission accuses the constituted authority (*speaks nonsense*) and undermines (by a collective reproach) his warrant duty of the social realm (*condemns divine justice*). The narrative opposes separation as an incitement to violence, a diminished form of sacrifice.[3]

---

3. *Raising the face* (42:9) might refer to instituting a separated social identity in exile. In a foreign land, Job roots through his family and social ethic (at least temporarily). Nevertheless, Job pretends to inherit the land (in a messianic future) as a serf, praying for his friends (42:7-8), accentuating their contradictions. He does not fight against evil in defense of the innocent and to repair the defective origins of the social realm but to inherit authority.

b) Job's Personal and Social Ethics

The epilogue of the book of Job concludes by affirming Job's righteousness, which overcomes Satan's temptations (twice) (42:7–8).

My servant Job will pray for you, for I will lift his face, and he will avoid your nebelah (42:8). To pray means to overcome sacrifice, and avoid the *nebelah* preaches not assuming indiscriminately undue debts. Preventing and overcoming *nebelah* refers to mastering the temptation of submission (and ceasing to condemn foreign deities that do not exist). Job's prayer for his three friends is twice exalted because it signifies his triumph over the temptations both of prosperity and of servility (to avoid *nebelah* refers to liberating the serfs). Overcoming *nebelah* means building a social ethic on labor, marital ethics, and religious freedom (praying for the three friends without submission).

To pray for his friends (authority) overcomes any form of sacrifice or collective accusation against secular or religious institutions (offering Esther, economic temptation, and intercession). To praise Job for overcoming *nebelah* (נבלה) views Job's servitude as an abuse of divinity, a submission to evil waiting for divinity to intervene and restore justice, which accuses the heavens of tolerating and concealing evil. *Nebelah* refers to the *mabul* (מבול), Noah's flood, illustrating the idea that unconditional submission to divinity is an abuse of divinity, the construction of (מהדל בבל) the tower of Babel.

An authority must be based on the duty of guarantee, not on divine inspiration. A servant must assume responsibility for the social realm to the extent of its use of social prosperity. As authority or serf, the conclusion of the epilogue will applaud (bless) Job for assuming the collective responsibility as proprietor or tenant (42:12). To *avoid your misfortune* and *lifting the face* refer to warning and explanation, as a social commitment to repair the foreign social realm.

c) Job Institutes Marriage in Exile

Marriage is a personal sign of individual liberty and a cornerstone of religious freedom and the servant's social commitment. It means valuing personal responsibility (denouncing collective guilt). Monotheism institutes monogamy; however, overcoming sacrificial dogma demands recognizing marital freedom (which criticizes the sacrifice of Esther and prosperity as immoral).

Raising the face means renouncing intercession and temptation (spiritual condemnation), a first step toward correct collective disorder. Job's lifting of his face is repeated twice (42:8; 42:9), correlative to the two praises of Job. Why is *I will lift his face* repeated twice? Job builds a house by the sea and receives the goat on the mountain and the stork on the plain, an allegory of the two institutionalizations of marriage in exile. Job institutes marriage after the response to the first theophany, as he renounces the sacrifice of Esther and prosperity (he renounces subjugating the woman and the foreigner by violence). Job establishes a second marital institution when he ceases accusing foreign divinities (who do not exist), rescues the firstborn, and elaborates a dogmatic of the marital and religious freedom of the servant (submission without temptation).

Job's institution of marriage in marital freedom is particularly praised and lays the coherent reconstruction of the social order; and even though he accuses the woman of *nebelah*, as the abuse of prosperity (temptation) and witchcraft (separation), Job dialogues with her, a sign of his respect for authority (marriage as a sign of restored social order).

24.4 MEANING OF THE EPILOGUE

a) Divine Anger Kindles Against the Three Friends

My anger [חרה אפי] kindles against you and your two companions [for] not speaking properly as Job does (42:7). It seems contradictory to praise Job with a double rebuke of the three friends. A plausible interpretation concludes that the negative narrative (*not speaking properly like the servant Job*) also formulates the criticism of Job's servility: the three friends did not speak of me with justice as my servant Job, who does not act with complete justice. His praise lies not in establishing justice but in resisting the friends' violence.

The book of Job criticizes both the friends' unjustified anger (as violence) and Job's submission (as distorted anger [40:8]). The three friends *considering Job righteous* (32:1) admit Job's innocence and attribute evil to divinity (as Job does). Collective guilt attributes divinity tolerance and concealment of evil. In contrast, a coherent social order must rest on individual freedom, merit, and responsibility.

b) Reproach of Job's Improper Language

The repetition of Job's righteousness implies doubt about the perfection of his righteousness. After the reproach of the three friends (sacrifice), the narrator rebukes Job by inference (*not speaking properly*) for protesting against divine justice with improper language (protesting without causal reason), rage that abuses divinity (40:8).

The narrative presents a scenic context. Confronting Eliphaz, divine anger threatens violence; in contrast, Job merits double praise (and double retribution) for intention and labor. The threat to Eliphaz refers to (the punishment of) sacrifice as a rebellion; the praise and banquet of Job (he receives double prosperity) teaches respect for man's labor and hospitality, and the sterility of submission and temptation (which enriches unjustly and ephemerally the damned tyrant and his nonexistent divinities).

Job prays for the authority, but by separating, he does not rescue (his) servitude. The narrative explains exile as the violence of the lords (the three friends) and the submissive violence of the servants (Job). Job does not understand that foreign deities do not exist and that unjust authority and submissive servitude harm the social realm.

The warning (reproach) to the violent and the explanation (praise and interpellation) to the servant explain the work of Providence. They expose the foolishness of violence, governed by anger, which inexorably leads to exile and servitude; and they illustrate the sterility of servitude, which does not subdue evil but perishes under it. Neither Eliphaz nor Job speaks rightly of divinity, as both implicitly accuse heaven of a flawed creation; only a correct word in due time (warning and explanation) subdue evil.[4]

---

4. The prologue (the beginning) summarizes the ethics of authority (sacrificial dogmatic), and the epilogue (posterity) the ethics of the servant Job (in dust and ashes). Job gradually rationalizes as incoherent the ethics of suffering (patient submission) for accusing divinity and causing the *nebelah* (not fighting evil). The right intentions of Eliphaz and Job only prevent (for some time) the *nebelah*. It is plausible that the narrative intends to criticize the reiteration of an attenuated messianism (dogmatic of a supposed Third Temple, a new submission to the authority in Greece). Job lights the lamps and is instituted ephemerally on foreign land, assuming the dogmatic of intercession (temptation) and separation. The struggle against evil is achieved through words, by warning the violent and explaining to the servant the defective conditions of the social order and the individual (not collective) origin of evil, which is remedied by preventing unjust profit and repairing guilty or negligent damage.

c) Job Does Not Pray for Elihu

The limited praise and rebuke of Eliphaz and Job suggest a disregard for Elihu, omitting the most severe warnings and forgetting someone during the shipwreck rescue. Elihu's anger faces a terrible silence (sterility), confronting a frightful divine indifference as the only character without a role in the redemptive epilogue (because Elihu assumes servitude as a divine damnation).

Elihu's anger is not reproached in the epilogue; the narrative criticizes only the anger of the three friends (42:7–8) and of Job (40:8). Elihu's righteous intention, which seeks to exonerate divinity, does not receive a direct rebuke from heaven. However, the reproaches in the epilogue (of the three friends and Job) do not mention Elihu because his silence is not considered a language and does not arouse divine praise, only contempt for abusing serfdom. Silence (at night) lacks meaning and punishes itself into nonexistence (sterility). Elihu does not speak, only Eliphaz and Job deserve a personal rebuke for confronting evil.

It seems unlikely that divinity would forget to ask Job to pray for Elihu, and we must assume that praying for Elihu is expressly excluded. Does this make any sense? The only reasonable explanation is that Job and the three friends must overcome Elihu's pretended divine inspiration. Job must pray for the authority and social realm (the three friends) and despise spirits (which do not exist). Not praying for Elihu teaches not to favor him who fails to fulfill his duty of guarantee (as a father and authority), tempts the world with renunciation, and pretends intercession (accusing divinity of a defective creation). The epilogue concludes that Elihu, like Satan, should be treated as a nonexistent character. To confront them means to create them (ideally) when they do not exist. Divinity does not rebuke Elihu because religious freedom is a part of men's social identity, and men must build their social identity (even being defective) in freedom.

XXV.

Establishing a Social Realm

25.1 INCOHERENT PROSPERITY OF JOB

a) Thoughtful Reproach of the Three Friends

And Eliphaz of Teman, Bildad of Shuah, and Zophar of Naamah went and did [ויעשו] as the Lord had told them (42:9). The three friends went to the servant Job refers to exile and reveals that the ultimate fate of sacrificial authority is to become dependent on those servants who intercede for it. The lords become servants to their faithful servants, not the reverse.

The three friends explain the former history of Job. Job flees the foolish sacrificial dogma, as (unjust) violence only generates violence. He works the land (and builds a house), respects the servant (his life and property), and stops blaming servants for the defects of the ship (respects the economic and marital freedom of the servants); however, he does not rescue his servitude (the three friends do not repair the defective origins). Likewise, they only temporarily prevent the *nebelah* because they abuse divinity by allowing themselves the wealth and prosperity offered by foreign deities (the servants).

b) Benefit of Praying for the Friends

And the Lord restored to Job all that he once had because he prayed for his friends (42:10). The final prosperity of Job scandalizes the dogmatic of sacrifice, as it makes the debate on suffering meaningless in light of its reward.

When Job stops blaming the authority for the collective disorder and overcomes the sacrificial doctrine, he prays for authority, assumes his submission, and takes root in the land (builds a house beside the sea). When he recognizes marital freedom, Job builds an estate (an animal farm). He takes deeper root because he receives a wife; as, without a woman, the estate is desolate (Prov 31:10–21).

Foreign kingdoms, founded on false divinities (defective sacrificial origins), must establish and sustain retributive justice (patrimonial) and matrimonial justice (religious freedom) to survive. They are doomed by their abuse of authority and endure for a short time, eating the lentils that the servant Job provides them (praying for authority). *My servant Job* expresses the element of limitation of Job's righteousness. It denounces the falsehood and pride of unjustified submission and separation.[1]

c) Paradox of Double Prosperity

And the Lord adds double to all that Job had (42:10). In the book of Job, the management of merit and success is more problematic than rationalizing misfortune. Double refers to the doubled prosperity of the epilogue, compared to Job's ephemeral welfare presented in the prologue.

The epilogue depicts the unjust enrichment of the submission to violence, which means inheriting from the violent man (who soon ruins). Job *the servant*, as a thief, must pay back double. If Job eludes corruption of prosperity, he has to overcome the temptation of foreign servant's submission (deities). In my opinion, double praise must be considered a double warning. If Job works the land and prays for his three friends (hospitality), he overcomes the unconscious sin of abusing the land (sacrificial dogmatic). He then confronts the collective sin of abusing the servants (the *nebelah*), the delicacies of foreign peoples

---

1. Praying for his friends refers to the exile in the foreign kingdom of sacrifice, which fights to conquer the earth, that is, to establish justice (he uses unjust means to institute authority); receiving double refers to the doctrine of patient submission, which reconquers the earth through submission. Job's submission, imagining a false divinity, builds ephemeral justice because what is conquered with servitude is destroyed by its sterility. Job prays for his friends (he consolidates the social order), respects authority (monotheism), and asks for an explanation (he is faithful to his wife), for which he will be blessed (42:12). Job builds an ethical tradition (matrimonial and social) that will prevent, for a time, *nebelah* (despite the defective origins of the social order).

and divinities (defective origins), and the spiritual temptation of foreign deities (servitude). Avoiding *nebelah* refers to avoiding the double and triple temptation of the Second and Third Temples, the temptation of Esther and Leah. Overcoming the *nebelah* alludes to preventing a collective accusation against men, the temptation of condemning sexuality, or assuming undue debts as a divine warrior (renouncing prosperity).

The prologue explains that sacrifice brought Job seven sons and three daughters, a livestock farm, and the establishment of authority (being the greatest from the beginning) with many servants. The epilogue presents the dogmatic patient submission (avoiding *nebelah*, the second temptation of Satan) that brought Job a new livestock farm (with a double number of heads), the return of seven sons and three daughters, the joy of his beautiful daughters, and a long life. In both fables, overcoming sacrifice and patient submission did not guarantee him a coherent social order but only a fleeting conquest of the land.

And it happened (ויהי) that all prosperity achieved by triumphing over the divinities is transitory, as foreign deities do not exist. Job receives a double wealth corrupted by its defective origins, which must return to its rightful owner. As in the Greek fable of the donkey carrying a statue of divinity, Job (the donkey) receives a double beating from the muleteer (servitude and exile) for assuming that the believers prostrate themselves before the donkey and for refusing to carry the weight of the statue.

25.2 JOB'S SOCIAL DEVELOPMENT

a) Arrival of Brothers, Sisters, and Friends

Job's answers to the second theophany overcome the dogmatic of sacrifice; however, he persists in an attenuated submissive dogmatic of separation. The epilogue narrates Job's social reconstruction in exile, where he builds a separate social order based on labor, marital ethics, and religious freedom (symbolized by praying for his three friends). Job overcomes the sacrificial presuppositions of the three friends (Eliphaz, Bildad, and Zophar) and assumes the historicism of a social order of separation based on marriage, personal dependence on food and shelter (an attenuated intercession), but without establishing a coherent social realm founded on (personal) merit and guilt.

In the debate with the three friends (the exile), Job gradually learns to institute a personal ethic (respect for life) and welcomes his brothers;

he institutes a sexual morality (respect for marital freedom) and receives his sisters; and he institutes a social (economic) justice (religious freedom) and welcomes his friends of old. Personal ethics overcome rebellion against authority (brothers), marriage ethics prevail over incest (sisters), and religious freedom bridles temptation (the institution of servitude).

In the epilogue, *all his brothers, sisters, and friends of old came to him* (42:11). This stages Job's roots in a (doomed) land established in violent sacrifice and submission (of sexuality and prosperity). The innumerable servants of the prologue are now friends in Job's house, treated equally, with fair compensation for their work and respect for their marital freedom and religious identity (without discrimination). The brothers, sisters, and servants flee from doomed sacrificial kings and foreign divinities, and Job offers them food and shelter (the animal farm) in his secluded social realm.[2]

b) Overcoming of Sacrifice

All the brothers represent Job's triumph over the sin of the brothers: the murder of Abel by Cain (Gen 4). No brother is missing because Job surmounts sacrificial violence to build social order.

All the sisters point to Job's overcoming of the bloody sin of Egypt and the Philistines, who do not respect the sexual freedom of women (to choose): *Say that you are my sister, since there is no fear of the Lord on earth* (Gen 12:13; 29:2). All the sisters arrive because Job no longer

---

2. As explained, the reference to brothers, sisters, and friends symbolizes Job fully triumphing over the three types of sacrifices (of life, sexuality, and wealth). Brothers signify the triumph over the sacrifice of life, sisters the triumph over incest, and friends the construction of social order on retributive ethics, not abusing the earth. Welcoming one's brothers means not condemning the gods of the (foreign) earth, because condemning foreign gods is a form of violence against people through temptation and separation. The friends of old symbolize the foreign deities because they are the reality of Job's past. *Bread in his house* (separation) envisages a mitigated alternative to the bread of the divinities (sacrifice); with submissive and quiet work, hospitality, and care for the dependent and alien. In contrast to the Job of the prologue who sacrifices and lives worried about the sin of his sons and daughters, in the epilogue [the exile], we are presented with Job who rejoices in the beauty of his daughters, a sign of his prosperity and the blessing of his posterity in a foreign land. Schifferdecker, *Out of the Whirlwind*, 208. Job views the foreign kings and divinities as a bloodthirsty and artificial superstructure, doomed to collapse under the weight of their inherent contradictions (collective guilt); and naming the nonexistent foreign divinities, Job brings them into being, condemning himself to exile in a foreign kingdom. In exile, Job does not liberate the foreign servant or reveal the falsehood (and nonexistence) of foreign divinities.

tempts foreign kings by sexuality to obtain prosperity (no longer submits Esther to the Persian king).

The arrival of *all the old friends* signifies Job's triumph over the lack of hospitality to the foreigner. The friend of old represents tolerance and concealment to those who escape from bloodthirsty divinities and authoritarian kings. Job overcomes temptation and the denial of religious freedom.

The counterpoint to the brothers and sisters (and servants) of the prologue who organize parties, banquets, and bacchanals, and destroy their house (1:14) (in the realm of sacrificial dogmatic) is the account of the epilogue, where *all* the brothers, sisters (and friends) come to eat bread in Job's house (in the social realm of patient submission). Nevertheless, separation is an attenuated sacrifice, also reproached for abusing prosperity. In both scenarios of sacrifice and submission, Job separates himself from the foreign social order and does not redeem the land (he corrupts his roots).

c) Sheltering Those Fleeing from Violence

Eating the bread of the earth overcomes sacrifice (the bread of heaven) and establishes religious freedom. Nevertheless, Job's isolation from foreign powers does not resolve the collective chaos. *All* the brothers, *all* the sisters, and *all* the friends refer to an impersonal relationship of Job with innumerable brothers, sisters, and friends who come to his house and are not recognized (counted) individually as the seven sons are, have no name, as the three daughters have a name; and whose origin is unknown, as the three friends who come from a determined land (Eliphaz of Teman, etc.).

All refers to the dogmatic of separation. *All* alludes to a collective identity that excludes weighing personal merit and guilt; *all* signifies breaking the personal ties of paternity, authority, and social identity (assuming indiscriminate collective debts). Job's idealism receives *all* his brothers, sisters, and friends, but not *his* brothers, sisters, and friends (all is an element of limitation), because his submissive separation defies his tradition.

The brothers, sisters, and old friends *eat bread with him in his house* (42:11). *Eating bread at home* refers to building justice in a personal, family, and social (economic) sphere (his home). It praises Job because condemning foreign deities and rulers does not establish justice; on the contrary, it provides shelter to those who flee violence and falsehood.[3]

25.3 RATIONALIZATION OF EXILE

a) Company, Consolation, and Condemnation

In exile, the brothers, sisters, and friends accompany Job (eating his bread) and console him (sharing the shelter of his house). They *all* experience the violence of the foreign land and *all the evil the Lord has brought upon Job* (implying divine tolerance of evil). To accompany refers to food (brother's labor), comfort alludes to the warmth of a home (sister's hospitality), and not condemning the foreigner means establishing an autonomous social order based on religious separation.

All the evil divinity has brought upon him attributes evil to divinity, a cunning assumption that supposes that the divinity uses evil (conceals foreign divinities and kings) to achieve redemption (to purify Job and help him rebuild the earth). Brothers, sisters, and friends presuppose a collective evil (insolvency) and attribute it to (an ideal) foreign divinity tolerated and concealed by divinity (42:11).

In his new exile of submission (segregation), Job does not keep silent for seven days and seven nights (description of the desert of temptation in sacrificial dogmatic) but offers bread to family and strangers. Nevertheless, he takes advantage of the foreign servants (lucrative responsibility) and does not assume that foreign divinities do not exist. Job neither unmasks false divinities nor rectifies earthly injustice.[4]

b) The Coin and the Ring

The brothers, sisters, and friends of old came to him and *gave each man a silver coin and each man a golden ring* (42:11). In a foreign country,

---

[3]. A man allegorizes individuality, and a woman represents the family. The coin and the ring symbolize the new submissive dogmatic of marriage without employing the temptation to assume authority. Job's wife no longer criticizes him for keeping his (excentric) integrity, highlighting a flaw in the failed sacrificial ethic. Job is now presented as the sterile idealist who overcomes sterility (like Hannah and Rachel) by praying for the three friends after his wife awakens him from sacrifice and submission (42:7-8).

[4]. Job confronts the sophistry of exile (rebuilding the temple) but does not build a coherent authority and organization. He flees from evil and does not confront it. He only receives those who submit to his new ethic of patient submission.

after overcoming the dogmatic of temptation, Job bases his community on laboring the desert (food) and constructing an animal farm (shelter). The coin and the ring realize the unjust enrichment of submission.

The narrative emphasizes *each man*, underlining the masculine origin of social disorder (of violence or submission). *Each man a coin and each man a ring* refers to the prosperity of temptation and separation, as an incoherent ethic of masculine guilt and defective (submissive) marriage doctrine, accusing foreign authority and women of collective disorder and not assuming a warrant responsibility as a tenant of the land. *Shall we receive benefit from the Lord and not accept evil?* (2:10). Two men symbolize the violent and the proud, concealing a reference to Eliphaz and Job, who separate from the (supposed false) foreign divinities. The coin depicts Eliphaz's violent flight into exile, while the ring illustrates Job's idealistic separation, naming falsely nonexistent foreign deities. Job receives the coin and the ring, with which he builds limited economic prosperity (religious food) and marriage fidelity (religious shelter), personal authority without rescuing the defective foreign social realm.

The rake and the ashes in the prologue symbolize the fate of the bloody sacrificial dogmatic; violence does not redeem the land (rake), and sexual submission degenerates into a damned servitude (ash). The coin and the ring in the epilogue symbolize the dogmatic of temptation and separation, which achieve (ephemeral) success through submission. They signify an authority and organization determined by their origins (coin and ring). Temptation does not conquer the land because it steals wealth (authority, coin) and names the nonexistent foreign divinities (justifies a separate organization, ring). The coin symbolizes Eliphaz (authority), and Job represents the ring (the praying servant as the origin of an organization). These explain the foundation of a religion based on separation (ring) and a secular organization founded in a retributive ethic of temptation (coin).

c) Lucrative Benefit of Submission

Job receives the coin for triumphing over responsibility through action (the abuse of the earth), and the ring after overcoming the responsibility of omission (the sexual or economic temptation of the servants [deities]). Job receives a coin and a ring for sheltering the servant and the maid who flee from the tyrant and perverse. He unjustly enriches by a share of the foreign temple. Job enjoys stolen wealth with his attenuated sacrifice of sexuality and prosperity, and the earth will treat and punish him as a lucrative beneficiary of sacrifice and submission.[5]

The coin and the ring are tokens of Job's lucrative responsibility toward foreign kings and deities, as Job is enriched from the foreign land where the supposedly exiled stole their share. Nevertheless, the paradox of double prosperity makes him a lucrative beneficiary of the submission to foreign kings (authority) and deities (servants).

Job has no guilt (as the cause) in the defective institution of the defective foreign social order (in exile) because the servant Job has not participated in the violent social foundation and prays for his friends (he works the land and respects the established authority); but as long as he does not redeem his servitude (pays the price of the land, rebuilds the social order, and frees the servants), Job takes advantage (by the coin and ring) of the merit of the kings and the sacrifice of the divinities who have founded the foreign social order (the three friends as a violent criminal association from which Job takes advantage). In conclusion, Job participates in unjust enrichment as a lucrative beneficiary of a crime and incurs responsibility (as a landlord or tenant who violates his duty of guarantee).[6]

---

5. The coin and the ring testify to a persistent defective authority and organization (servitude). He gives food in exchange for the coin and stages the triumph over Satan's first accusation of greed (*Have you not given him?*). Job can now answer that he receives the coin in exchange for bread, not from heaven (the violence of the conquest of Canaan). The ring (which can also refer to a key) signifies Job's triumph over Satan's second accusation (*hit him*) by giving shelter to the stranger. Job can now answer that he has received the woman (the stranger) freely (although not as equal) and that he has not subjugated her (the servant) either by violence or by deceit (Esther's submission). This explains the submission of religion and secular organization to individual labor and merit (building a house and sheltering the foreigner). The coin is a symbol of authority (providing food), and the ring represents submission to an organization (shelter in exile) (Gen 41:42; Esth 3:10). Job keeps the coin after he escapes from the First Temple (in Canaan), and the ring is the key (organization or house) that he establishes over the ruins of the temple of incest (in Persia).

6. The animal farm provides food and shelter to the wild animals that flee from the foreign kings, and gains in exile a stolen coin and a ring. The coin symbolizes the work of the wild bull, subjected to the yoke (39:10), and the ring, the horse's submission that leads the warriors by the sound of the trumpet (39:24).

XXVI.

Job's New Prosperity

26.1 JOB'S BLESSING

a) Blessing from the Beginning

The Lord blessed Job's posterity from the beginning (42:12). This defines systematic thought as a determined origin, which establishes a defective organization. *The beginning* refers to the violent and defective origins (sacrifice and submission) because systematic thought counts, weighs, and measures from its beginning. *From the beginning* there is a limitation because only from the onset (right intention of the violent or submissive Job) was the posterity blessed, not in its (personal) identity. Instituting an organization puts inspiration and authority over justice, rejecting tradition. This criticizes systematic thought because it explains and justifies prevailing by sacrifice and submission (over individual merit and guilt), thereby instituting serfdom.

A warning precedes Job's bonanzas, ויהי, announcing a catastrophe (the *nebelah*) for the defective origins (abusing prosperity and perpetuating servitude). Job's submissive labor and hospitality tolerate or conceal arbitrary authority founded in nonexistent foreign violent deities (coin and ring).

The cattle, the daughter's name, and a long life symbolize the gradual development of a social identity. Job is blessed in his posterity because he gradually surpasses the sacrificial (violent or submissive) dogmatic of the beginning. The upright intention of sacrifice, temptation, and separation blesses posterity and stages of a torturous development (the historicity) of prosperity (family and social ethics) built by a divine blessing *from the beginning* (despite its defective origins).

b) Doubled Restoration of Cattle

There is an analogy between sacrifice and submission, as both give rise to a systematic thought and an arbitrary organization (based on collective accusation). In this context, the doubled restoration of Job's prosperity refers to sacrifice and submission as violent ethics that institute servitude and steal and plunder the land.

He had fourteen thousand sheep, six thousand camels, a thousand pairs of oxen, and a thousand donkeys (42:12). This displays Job's prosperous life in exile, praying for the three friends as manager of an animal farm, established over the dogmatic of submission to a doomed violent authority that subsists (ephemerally) paying Job the coin and the ring (tolerating the fleeing servant).

The sheep, camels, oxen, and donkeys double those of the prologue, mocking the double prosperity obtained by submission (to the sacrificial dogmatic). The cattle that Job receives double testify to the restoration and expansion of his animal farm (referred to in the prologue and the first theophany). Doubled prosperity unveils the profit motivation of Job's messianism and shows the contradiction of his pretended (false) submission. The text suggests that submission reveals disdain for established authority and the desire to overthrow and usurp the foreign ruler. The mention of oxen and donkeys refers to sterility (since they are sterile animals), signifying the violence of the submissive doctrine as an attenuated sacrifice.

In the doctrine of submission, as the (passive) flip side of sacrifice, Job acquires or cohabits with domestic animals (servants), subject to the fierce animals (foreign divinities), supposedly perverse (kings and deities, dust and ashes, Behemoth and Leviathan), and Job witnesses the faulty foundation of the foreign social order in his communal farm.

c) Restoration of Sons and Daughters

And he had [ויהי] seven sons and three daughters (42:13). What a happy coincidence! In the epilogue, as in the prologue, Job has seven sons and three daughters. But this symmetrical restoration seems incoherent. Seven sons and three daughters makes no sense, presumably with the same woman; besides, Job's restoration and blessing would not be authentic with other children because he would never overcome the pain of losing his first family.

It is plausible to consider the death of his children in the prologue as unreal and fictitious as their replacement in the epilogue, depicting the fictitious death of the children (in the prologue) and a virtual exile (in the epilogue). The fabled stories of the prologue and epilogue show that the children, sheltered in a blessing from the beginning (his right intention), never died. After the terrible experience, would Job have the strength to start his married life again? It is coherent to conclude that the misfortune announced by the messengers in the prologue is not the effective death of the children but their uprooting and exile, the desperation of divine abandonment.

It seems plausible to conclude that, in the epilogue, he recovers all his children from the beginning (from uprooting). Job's posterity survives the defective collective realm of exile, even if he betrays justice by submitting his social identity and does not construct a coherent social order. The cattle placed before the sons and daughters in the epilogue must hint at a reproach, intending an analogy between sons and cattle. The cattle in the epilogue, referred to before the children, hints at Job's deceptive prosperity. Seven sons correspond to the seven thousand sheep and three daughters to the three thousand camels, with the peculiarity that the epilogue does not duplicate sons and daughters, only cattle.

26.2 DAUGHTER'S NAME

a) Overcoming of Foreign Deities

The act of naming praises and criticizes the idealism of separation and applauds fleeing violence, yet reproaches persisting in servitude.

Naming (the divinities) identifies the defective origins and assumes their existence or representation (idealism). This is a fallacy because foreign deities do not exist or have (social) identity and lack a name (his name is false). The name of a foreign deity is nothing but a deceptive excuse of the man who created it to elude his responsibility for the collective disorder. Naming means the fallacy of judging authority by an idea (a name), a supposed representation of a more authentic divinity who overcomes the current deity of the land without rectifying the chaos of its defective origins (servitude). The fable insists on Job's foolishness, who gives a name and despises the foreign divinities (separates himself) without assuming responsibility for fixing the collective disorder.

Naming implies assuming (partially) social responsibility. Job assigns a name to his daughters as a sign of his social integration, receiving brothers, sisters, and friends, overcoming violent sacrifice, and building a social realm on matrimonial freedom. Still, assigning names to each daughter parallels the creation's tale, where Adam names the animals (Gen 2:20). Naming foreign divinities means separation from the (supposedly violent) foreign collective realm, condemning it. Three daughters might refer to the (three) kingdoms whose sacrificial divinities (of life, sexuality, and wealth) Job unveils in exile and to whom he gives a name (the three orders of unconscious responsibility, personified in Canaan, Persia, and Greece). Job names the divinities when he reveals their disordered origins without assuming responsibility for repairing the earth.

b) Historicity of the Name

He named his three daughters. The daughters represent the three friends, the three orders of unconscious responsibility for abusing prosperity. To name reflects Job's idealism, establishing a social order based on submission rather than justice. To name means a collective accusation.

The name refers to the gradual development of ethics in monotheism, unveiling the three orders of sacrificial idealism (the sacrifice of life, sexuality, and property). It also shows Job's false and disproportionate assumption of collective guilt (by submission).

And he called [ו׳קרא] the first ימימה, *and he called the second* קציעה, *and the name of the third was* קרן הפון (42:14). This plausibly refers to the historical formation of the canon (Law, Prophets, and Wisdom). To name the daughter stages Job's arduous journey, encompassing his departure from Egypt, the revelation in the desert, and the conquest of the land of Israel. ימימה takes the reference from יָם (sea), crossing the Red Sea; קציעה seems to refer to the root קץ, the boundary, the desert as the boundary of the land of Israel; קרן הפון refers to the rooted vineyard, an image of the land of Israel (Gen 9:20; Num 20:5; 22:24, Deut 8:8; Josh 24:13; 1 Kgs 21:1; 2 Kgs 18:31; Job 24:6; Ps 80:8).

c) Beauty as a Sign of the Name

It is impossible to find more beautiful girls in all the land (42:15). Beauty points out the narcissism of idealism and interprets the world according to a personal imagination (inspiration). *To find* suggests the analogy of the daughters' beauty with a treasure of which no one knows to whom it belongs: the hidden treasure of wisdom, minerals in the center of the earth (28:39, the uncertainty of idealism). Maybe the treasure belongs to divinities; perhaps it should be attributed to Job, who builds a house; or peradventure it enriches the lucky guy who finds it. Beauty may reveal a thief's virtue who uncovers hidden treasure. Beauty is an allegory of religion.

Job's daughters are beautiful because they have a name (economic, marital, and religious autonomy after overcoming sacrificial dogma). The name also defines an element of limitation; they are beautiful because of the wealth, hospitality, and magnificence of Job's table. The intellectual, familial, and social virtue that unveils the sacrificial foreign divinities, ponders the beauty of Job's daughters. Their beauty praises an individual virtue in exile (his days) but not his servitude (the disproportionate assumption of collective guilt that announces the end of his prosperity). Job separates and does not conquer the land, subject to the greed, servitude, and pride of exile as an a priori submission to foreign violent dogma.

The beautiful girls critiques with irony and insinuates the future ruin in exile (it does not mention Job's wife, and without a wife, the house is in ruins). *All the land* is a limitation; it refers to an organization that prevails over the individual, and it means contempt for the daughters of the rulers. *The beautiful girls* symbolize the construction of a house founded on selfish divinities, a prosperity defectively rooted in exile (food, shelter, and name). Their (artificial) attractiveness is especially valued after receiving a name (to condemn foreign divinities), and it seems that beauty is a consequence of the name. The beauty alludes to a more coherent ethic; in Job's context, it plausibly refers to overcoming the dogmatic of sacrifice.

26.3 INHERITANCE OF THE DAUGHTERS

a) Aesthetics, Expression of an Ethic

The beauty of his daughters dazzles the land with limited praise, analogous to the doubled rectitude of Job in speaking better than his friends

(42:7-8). Beauty is a relative compliment: it overcomes sacrifice but not servitude.

The beauty of his daughters allegorizes Job's ethical life in exile among supposedly violent kings and impious divinities. Job builds a house in the (foreign) land in the name of divinity (the name of the daughters), but Job does not establish an order of freedom, equality, and justice. He finds himself in what Hegel would refer to as a religion of nature, a narcissistic exaltation of beauty (know yourself) that is rooted in sweet words (individual beauty) rather than justice.

The beauty of his daughters suggests wealth and inheritance (coin and ring), which stirs up feelings of envy and resentment. His daughters' beauty uses Elihu's doctrine to seduce others by embodying the humility of confession, practicing patient waiting, and engaging in nightly intercession. The daughters live separately as servants (divinities) in a realm dominated by violent men.

b) Distribution of Inheritance

Their father gives them a portion of the inheritance among their brothers (42:15). The (defective) inheritance is the property acquired by submission (without temptation) in a foreign land (messianism). The inheritance refers to the marriage law instituted by separation in exile (primogeniture), which uproots Job's siblings in a foreign land and institutes religious freedom as due respect for the foreign deities (overcomes temptation).

To what profitable inheritance is the narrative referring? Inheritance identifies the land and prosperity received without violence and alludes to the promise to the lineage of Abraham (Gen 15:4; Exod 8:8; 32:9), linked to Job's messianism. Mosaic law establishes the son's preference (the divinity blesses men with prosperity); giving a portion to daughters means a (limited) criticism of the Mosaic law (Num 27:8) and a partial payment of an undetermined promise.

Marriage justifies inheritance in a separated social order of religious freedom that guarantees the continuity of man's labor and merit. The inheritance of the daughters refers to the marital freedom of the servant. To share signifies the reality of the social order that Job builds in exile through submission when he renounces the violence of temptation and intercession. Marriage freedom is a sign of limited religious freedom.

Inheritance signifies the foundation of property and tradition (lineage), which defines the social order as the work of parents and authority, overcoming the accusation of sin to ancestors.

c) Share Among Brothers

The sons inherit because foreign peoples base their social order on the ritual sacrifice of life (sacrificial violence against their sons). A part is missing because divinities promise to men the land they stole from women. The upright Job, who overcomes the sacrifice of his son, redeems half of the collective disaster and gradually becomes aware of the social disorder caused by the indiscriminate assumption of debts.

The epilogue subtly criticizes Job because the inheritance is the earth, not meant for Job's sons or daughters (nor for foreigners) but blessing the social order of freedom and responsibility (which marriage signifies as an order of personal liberty). Success in a foreign land will confront Job with the resentment of foreign kings, princes, and peoples when his prosperity compromises their authority.

XXVII.

Job's Death

27.1 JOB'S LIFE

a) Separation Dogma

And [ויהי] Job lived, after this, 140 years (42:16). This seems to be an expression of relentless catastrophe (ויהי) referring to the rest of his life. The narrator praises Job's submission (*Job lived*), but 140 years is a limitation; it reproaches him for not building a coherent social order (because he does not assume his collective responsibility).

The verse celebrates Job's victory over sacrificial dogmatism. Traditionally, seventy years mark a complete human life (Ps 90:10). Job, now in a new exile marked by submission and conditional prosperity, is granted a second life of seventy years, symbolically doubling the conventional lifespan. This doubling echoes the fourteen thousand sheep he receives: he lives longer but still as one of the flock.

He lived *after this*, which hints at a limitation to his life, plausibly criticizing his incorrect answers to the second theophany: separation does not build a coherent social order. Nevertheless, *he lived after this* should not be interpreted as the announcement of Job's death but as the overcoming, after 140 years, of the dogmatics of sacrifice and submission. The narrator explains that the dogmatic of patient submission supports and prolongs the sacrificial kingdom only for some time, unless Job rescues the defective origins of the social order.

b) Four Generations

What happened after this? *He saw his sons and sons' sons, until the fourth generation* (42:16) refers to praise and reproach, as he institutes a family and social ethic in a foreign land (four generations). Job establishes a family ethic in a foreign land. Four generations signify continuity but not transformation. He sees his descendants, but he neither reveals nor restores the broken foundations of the social order. He knows his children but does not know his wife, and the epilogue does not mention her (the stranger), nor does he know the land (the foundation of justice).

Four generations allegorically mark Job's triumph over the three friends (who represent the active sacrificial dogma), yet also his submission to Elihu's passive theology. The narrative explains that Job's separation (as opposed to the aggressive submission of temptation) does not rescue the defective origins of a collective realm; it only builds a separate community on an ethic of marriage (authority and separation). His days are counted and measured unless he listens carefully to the second theophany and overcomes sacrifice (old) and submission (*full of days*).

c) Allegory of Exile

Four generations may also allegorize Job's own four life stages: childhood, youth, maturity, and old age, perhaps as an allegory of marital fidelity. A young and rebellious Job (ch. 3) faces the unjust social order, which he identifies with divinity, and uproots himself. In his maturity, he evolves (the three friends) and considers the principles of justice (he institutes marriage). In his old age, he assumes, although he exaggerates, the blame for his imperfect past (Elihu, the essence of idealism). Nevertheless, he receives a woman and roots in a social realm, although he accuses her of good and evil.

Four generations could also be an allegory of the people who share or can share the same roof, food, warmth, and dreams. Four generations symbolize the community of chair, table, fire, and bed, reflecting authoritarian marital fidelity and extended responsibility for the tenure of the land, where the sins of the fathers fall into the children through the third and fourth generations (Exod 20:5; 34:15; Num 14:18; Deut 5:9).

The four generations may serve as an allegory for the four times Job is referred to as a servant in the reproach to Eliphaz (42:8). These four generations represent what Hegel would identify as a religion of nature, as a social order deeply rooted in family and aesthetics. It acknowledges and appreciates the beauty of daughters, but it does not offer redemption from servitude in economic, social, or religious servitude.

27.2 VIRTUAL DIMENSION OF JOB'S DEATH

a) Job's Old Age and Countless Days

And Job died, old and full of days (42:17). Does the book of Job contradict itself? Did Job live (42:16), or did he die (42:17)? It seems fair to interpret Job's death as the same fictitious account of the deaths of his children— more a critique of the defective social foundation than a literal ending.

Old and full of days praises Job's overcoming of sacrificial doctrine, describing him as violent (young) and submissive (old, sterility). The narrator describes Abraham and Job as old and full of days, referring to a similar character in two specific individual and historical dimensions, praising their work (old) and hospitality (lineage, days). *Old* is likely to signify Abraham's sacrifice, and to be *full of days* alludes to the historicity of Job overcoming submission.

Old refers to Job's initial complicity with violent sacrificial order (Canaan); *full of days* symbolizes survival in exile (Persia, Greece). *Old* signifies Job's house in the desert, and *full of days* refers to the animal farm as a representation of the successive empires of his sons. Serving as a counterpoint to the doctrine of sacrifice or submission as collective damnation, *old* and *full of days* ponder personal merit, as they were *not born on the day of its foundation and cannot count the number of its days* (38:21). They will unveil in due time the bloodthirsty and false divinities (the foolishness of idealism), building an ethic (38:19–21).

Yet, the narrative also hints at the defective origins of a collective realm, criticizing Job, as Elihu, for waiting to speak after men older than him and full of days (32:4). Referring to the limited time of prosperity founded in an idealistic doctrine, it criticizes the doctrine of sacrifice and submission as not to speak (42:7–8). The narrative emphasizes the irresponsibility of impertinent waiting (old and full of days) and the significance of ensuring justice in due course (safeguarding the innocent and upholding individual responsibility and authority). The narrative conceals a veiled reproach that hints at untimely silence and rage as an uncovering of servility and violence. Job's unjust delay is an abuse of Providence, accused of hiding evil and redeeming humankind by defective means; the narrative highlights that responding in due course builds justice.

Silence, without a word, refers to the animal soul of sacrifice and submission. The seven days are each of the empires among which Job survives, in the seven nights of the virtual death of a social order founded on sacrifice and patient submission. The days of the banquets (*thus, Job did all his days* [1:5]) describe a religious cult and its tempting divinities (meant to be unveiled). *Full of days* alludes to the seven days of silence (exile) between Job and his friends. Job experienced pain, anguish, and despair over the destruction of the social order founded on sacrifice and submission.

b) Meaning of Job's Blessing

In exile, *Job* learned how to manage prosperity, ויהי. Job did not die, but rather Job's past (the attribution of defective origins as guilt). Job's death refers to the *servant* Job of the laments and the monologue; his blessing allegorizes overcoming Elihu's falseness. Job ceases to be subject to the bloodthirsty divinities when he overcomes violence, and he ceases to be subject to the patient divinities when he prevails against submission (by warning authority and explaining serfdom). Still, he rescues the social order only when he correctly assumes his (personal and limited) guilt and responsibility for the collective disorder.

Job's final blessing stands in contrast to his earlier sterile lamentations. The epilogue portrays Job's life mastering exile and assuming his (individual) responsibility according to the hierarchy of debts. His wife tells him to *bless the Lord and die* (2:9), not as a curse or to announce misfortune but as a spur to overcome his individualistic pride and greed (sacrifice and submission) and build a coherent social order. She encourages him to worry about his family and the social order rather than submit to imaginary divinities demanding human sacrifices or sacrificing their son. Deities do not bless submission with prosperity and power but bless labor (praying for friends) and hospitality (avoiding *nebelah*) with the construction of a coherent social order (which the woman and children represent).

c) Death as Inconsistency of Social Order

Job's death (old and full of days) intends to criticize Elihu, who supposedly confesses guilt for the collective disorder without revealing the cause of the supposed collective punishment. The fable of Job, by contrast, affirms the personal character of guilt and responsibility.

Job (the old man) dies because he destroys his social roots, abusing wisdom (for his benefit) and accusing divinity of the collective disorder, not assuming his (personal) responsibility. Death reproaches the days of Elihu's impertinent waiting (32:4; 32:6) and rebukes abusing a delay in the restitution of unjust enrichment and damage (long days).

The Lord blesses Job (42:12), but Job dies (42:17). A reference to Job was implicit, yet he is expressly named, which means an element of limitation to his death. The past Job dies but blesses his merit (old) and lineage (full of days) as a path to building justice (he values man above the system). It is coherent to conclude that the past Job, who practices sacrifices and abuses prosperity, dies. He does not reveal the secret of his nights, the flaws in the foreign social order. In contrast, Job lives when he confronts the idealism of sacrifice and submission.

The book portrays Job as a hero because, as an old man, he will overcome unjust violence (rage) and live long days building a family, earning an identity for his daughters (a name), and correctly distributing his assets among his heirs. He will learn the art of speaking at the proper time, measuring guilt (harm) in his (personal) origin, and merit (enrichment) in respecting the social identity of men.

Bibliography

Alter, Robert. *The Hebrew Bible: A Translation with Commentary*. 3 vols. New York: Norton & Co., 2019.
Álvarez Caperochipi, José A. *El libro de Job: Proceso a la idolatría*. Madrid: Opera Prima, 2017.
Andersen, Ragnar. "The Elihu Speeches." *Tyndale Bulletin* 66 (2015) 75–94.
Aquinas, Thomas. *Commentary on the Book of Job*. Edited by Joseph Kenny. Translated by Brian Mulladay. Lander, WY: Aquinas Institute for the Study of Sacred Doctrine, 2016. https://isidore.co/aquinas/english/SSJob.htm.
———. *The Literal Exposition on Job: A Scriptural Commentary Concerning Providence*. Edited by Martin D. Yaffe. Translated by Anthony Damico. AAR Classics in Religious Studies Series. Atlanta: Oxford University Press, 1989.
Barniske, Friedmann. "Negative Sublimity: Hegel's Description of Jewish Religion." In *The Being of Negation in Post-Kantian Philosophy*, edited by Gregory S. Moss, 439–52. Cham, Switz.: Springer, 2023.
Baskin, Judith R. *Pharaoh's Counsellors: Job, Jethro, and Balaam in Rabbinic and Patristic Tradition*. Brown Judaic Studies 47. Chico, CA: Scholars, 1983.
Bishop, Paul. *Yung's Answer to Job: A Commentary*. East Sussex: Routledge, 2002.
Bodin, Jean. *Coloquio de los siete sabios sobre arcanos relativos a cuestiones últimas (Colloquiuum heptaplomeres)*. Translated by Primitivo Mariño. Clásicos Políticos. Madrid: Centro de Estudios Políticos y Constitucionales, 1998.
Cabello Llano, Ignacio. "El libro de Job y su recepción en el cristianismo medieval." MA thesis, Universidad Complutense de Madrid, 2019. https://hdl.handle.net/20.500.14352/14377.
Calvin, John. *Commentary on the Book of Psalms*. Translated by James Anderson. Vol. 1. Edinburgh: Calvin Translation Society, 1745. https://calvin.edu/sites/default/files/migrated/centers-institutes-meeter-center-files-john-calvins-works-in-english-Commentary-20008---Psalms-Vol.-1.pdf.
———. *Institutes of the Christian Religion*. Translated by Henry Beveridge. Peabody, MA: Hendrickson, 2008.
Calvin, John. *See also* Calvino, Juan.
Calvino, Juan. *Calvino sermones sobre Job*. Archive, 1991. https://archive.org/details/calvino-sermones-sobre-job/page/n13/mode/1up.
Calvino, Juan. *See also* Calvin, John.
Clines, David J. A. *Job*. 3 vols. Word Biblical Commentary 17, 18A, 18B. Dallas: Word, 1989–2015.

———. "Job and the Spirituality of the Reformation." In *The Bible, the Reformation and the Church: Essays in Honour of James Atkinson*, edited by W. P. Stephens, 49–76. Library of New Testament Studies. Sheffield: Journal for the Study of the Old Testament, 1995.

Eisen, Robert. *The Book of Job in Medieval Jewish Philosophy*. Oxford: Oxford University Press, 2004.

Glatzer, Nahum. *The Dimensions of Job: A Study and Selected Readings*. New York: Knopf Doubleday, 1969.

Gordis, Robert. *The Book of Job: Commentary, New Translation, Special Studies*. New York: Jewish Theological Seminary Press, 1978.

———. *The Book of Job and Man: A Study of Job*. Chicago: University of Chicago Press, 1965.

Gregorio Magno [Gregory the Great]. *Moralia I–V*. Translated by José Roco Paves. Vol. 1 of *Libros Morales*. Madrid: Ciudad Nueva, 1998.

———. *Moralia VI–X*. Translated by José Roco Paves. Vol. 2 of *Libros Morales*. Madrid: Ciudad Nueva, 2004.

Habel, Norman C. *The Book of Job: A Commentary*. Westminster: Philadelphia, 1985.

Hall, C. A. M. *With the Spirit's Sword: The Drama of Spiritual Warfare in the Theology of John Calvin*. Zurich: Keller, 1963.

Harvey, W. "Maimonides and Spinoza on the Knowledge of Good and Evil." In *Binah: Studies in Jewish Thought*, translated by Yoel Lerner, 2:131–46. Westport, CT: Prager, 1989.

Hawley, Helen. "The Composition of the Elihu Speeches." *American Journal of Semitic Languages and Literatures* 27 (1911) 97–186.

Hegel, G. W. F. *Escritos sobre religión*. Translated by G. Amengual. Salamanca: Sígeme, 2013.

———. *Lecciones sobre filosofía de la religión*. Translated by Ricardo Ferrara. 3 vols. Madrid: Alianza, 1984–85.

Hirsh, Emil G. "Hegel, Georg Wilhelm Friedrich." *Jewish Encyclopedia*, 1906. https://www.jewishencyclopedia.com/articles/7477-hegel-georg-wilhelm-friedrich.

Ho, Edward. "A Quest for Coherence: A Study of Internal Quotations in the Book of Job." PhD diss., McMaster Divinity College, 2012.

Hobbes, Thomas. *Leviatán o la materia, forma y poder de una república eclesiástica y civil*. Mexico City: Fondo de Cultura Económica, 2017.

Jacobs, Irving. "The Book of Job in Rabbinic Thought." PhD diss., University of London, 1971. https://discovery.ucl.ac.uk/id/eprint/1381932/.

Jauss, Hans-Robert, and Sharon Larisch. "Job's Questions and Their Distant Reply: Goethe, Nietzsche, Heidegger." *Comparative Literature* 34 (1982) 193–207.

JiSeong, James Kwon. "Psychosomatic Approach to Job's Body and Mind: Based on Somatic Symptom Disorder." *Journal of Religion and Health* 59 (2020) 2032–44.

Jung, Carl G. *Antwort auf Hiob*. Munich: Deutsches Taschenbuch, 2006.

Kafka, Franza. *El proceso*. Translated by Miguel Sáenz Sagaseta. Madrid: Alianza, 1978.

Kalman, Jason. "With Friends Like These: Turning Points in the Jewish Exegesis of the Biblical Book of Job." PhD diss., McGill University, 2005.

Kant, Immanuel. *La contienda entre las facultades de Filosofía y Teología*. Translated by Roberto Rodríguez Aramayo. Madrid: Debate/CSIC, 1992.

———. *Crítica de la razón práctica*. Translated by Granja Castro. Mexico City: Fondo de Cultura Económica, 2005.

Bibliography

———. *Fundamentación de la metafísica de las costumbres*. Philosophia, 1785. https://www.philosophia.cl/biblioteca/Kant/fundamentacion%20de%20la%20metafisica%20de%20las%20costumbres.pdf.

———. *La religión en los límites de la mera razón*. Translated by Martines Marzoa. Madrid: Alianza, 1961.

———. *Sobre el fracaso de todo ensayo filosófico en la teodicea* [On the failure of all philosophical attempts at theodicy]. Translated by Rogelio Rovira. Madrid: Encuentro, 2011.

Keynes, Will. "The Trials of Job: Relitigating Job's 'Good Case' in Christian Interpretation." *Scottish Journal of Theology* 66 (2013) 174–91.

Kierkegaard, Søren. *La repetición*. Libros Tauro, 1997. https://web.seducoahuila.gob.mx/biblioweb/upload/Kierkegaard,%20Soren%20-%20La%20Repeticion.pdf.

Leibniz, Gottfried. W. *Teodicea: Ensayos sobre la bondad de Dios, la libertad del hombre y el origen del mal*. Philosophia, 1710. https://www.philosophia.cl/biblioteca/leibniz/Teodicea.pdf.

Luther, Martin. "Preface to the Book of Job." Translated by C. M. Jacobs. In *Works of Martin Luther*, 6:275–77. Albany, OR: Ages, 1997. Ebook.

Mañon Garibay, G. J. "Kierkegaard y la mística: El silencio." *Revista Jurídica de la Universidad Autónoma de México* 338 (2017). https://revistas.juridicas.unam.mx/index.php/hechos-y-derechos/article/view/11132/13144.

Maimónides, M. *Guía de los perplejos*. Translated by David Gonzalo Maeso. Madrid: Nacional, 1984.

Marx, Karl. *La cuestión judía*. Translated by Fernando Groni from the 1843 ed. Buenos Aires: N.p., n.d.

———. "On *The Jewish Question*." Marxists, 1843. Edited by Andy Blunden et al. https://www.marxists.org/archive/marx/works/1844/jewish-question/.

Miranda, Punita. "The Priest, the Psychiatrist and the Problem of Evil." *Phanês: Journal for Jung History* 2 (2019) 104–43. https://phanes.live/wp-content/uploads/2019/12/Punita-Miranda-Article-Phanes-2-2019.pdf.

Moreau, Pierre-François. "Spinoza et l'autorité d'un modèle: L'état des Hébreux." In *Spinoza: État et religion*, 21–34. Lyon: ENS, 2005. https://books.openedition.org/enseditions/6252.

Negri, Antonio. *The Labor of Job*. Translated by Mateo Mandarini. Durham: Duke University Press, 2009.

Newsom, Carol. *The Book of Job: A Contest of Moral Imaginations*. New York: Oxford University Press, 2003.

Nietzsche, Friedrich. *Así habló Zaratustra*. Edited and translated by Andrés Sánchez Pascual. Madrid: Alianza, 1983.

———. *La genealogía de la moral: Un escrito polémico*. Translated by Andrés Sánchez Pascual. Madrid: Alianza, 2011.

Nutt, Roger W. "Providence, Wisdom, and the Justice of Job's Afflictions: Considerations from Aquinas' Literal Exposition on Job." *Heythrop Journal* 56 (2011) 1–23.

Ong, Meng-Chai. "John Calvin on Providence: The Locus Classicus in Context." PhD diss., King's College London, 2003.

Paolo de Petris. *Calvin's Theodicy and the Hiddenness of God: Calvin's Sermons on the Book of Job*. Peter Lang AG, Bern, 2012.

Parens, Joshua. "Leaving the Garden: Maimonides and Spinoza on the Imagination and the Practical Intellect Revisited." *Philosophy & Theology* 18 (2006) 219–46.

Bibliography

Rosner, David J. "Self-Deception and Cosmic Disorder in the Book of Job." *Cosmos and History: The Journal of Natural and Social Philosophy* 11 (2015) 285–98.

Rotenstreich, Nathan. "Hegel's Image on Judaism." *Jewish Social Studies* 15 (1953) 33–52.

Schere, María Jimena. "El alazón en la comedia aristofánica." *Classica: Revista Brasileira de Estudos Clásicos* 32 (2019) 11–22.

Schifferdecker, Kathryn M. "Out of the Whirlwind: Creation Theology in the Book of Job." PhD diss., Harvard Divinity School, 2008.

Schmitt, Carl. *El Leviathan en la teoría del estado de Thomas Hobbes*. Translated by Francisco Javier Conde. Granada: Comares, 2004.

Schreiner, Susan E. "Exegesis and Double Justice in Calvin's Sermons on Job." *Church History* 58 (1989) 332–38.

———. *Where Shall Wisdom Be Found? Calvin's Exegesis of Job from Medieval and Modern Perspectives*. Chicago: University of Chicago Press, 1994.

Seow, C. L. *Job 1–21: Interpretation and Commentary*. Illuminations. Grand Rapids: Eerdmans, 2013.

Spinoza, Baruch. *Oeuvres complètes*. Translated by Émile Saisset et al. N.p.: Arvensa, 2014. Ebook.

———. *Spinoza's Short Treatise on God, Man & His Well-Being*. Translated by A. Wolf. London: Black, 1910.

———. *Tratado teológico-político*. Translated by Atiliano Domínguez. Madrid: Alianza, 1986.

Sungjin, Kim. "The Identity of the Spirit (*rûᵃh*) in Eliphaz's Vision (Job 4:12–21) and its Significance for Understanding the Book of Job." PhD diss., Southern Baptist Theological Seminary, 2017. https://hdl.handle.net/10392/5987.

Thomas, Derek W. H. *Calvin's Teaching on Job: Proclaiming the Incomprehensible God*. Ross-shire, UK: Christian Focus, 2004.

Uzanne, Octave. "Conversations and Opinions of Victor Hugo: Unpublished Papers Found at Guernsey." *Scribners Magazine* 12 (1892) 558–76.

Yaffe, Martin D. "Providence in Medieval Aristotelianism: Moses Maimonides and Thomas Aquinas on the Book of Job." *Hebrew Studies* 20–21 (1979–80) 62–74.

Yovel, Yirmiyahu. *Dark Riddle: Hegel, Nietzsche, and the Jews*. University Park: Pennsylvania State University Press, 1998.

Zöckler, Otto. *The Book of Job*. Translated by L. J. Evans. New York: Scribner & Armstrong, 1872.

Subject Index

Alter, Robert, 108n9
Andersen, Regnar, 104n6
Aquinas, Thomas, 15, 16, 50, 60, 104, 106, 134, 135, 173, 174
Averroes, 16, 30n1, 31

Barniske, Friedmann, 143n20
Bodin, Jean, 174

Calvin, Jean, 16, 17, 60, 61, 106, 107, 136, 137, 174
Canon, 5, 102n1, 133, 150, 194, 211
Collective guilt, 1, 3, 7, 11, 12, 13, 17, 18, 19, 20n11, 25, 35, 36, 38, 41, 44, 46, 50, 57, 59, 63, 65, 66n6, 69, 71, 73, 75, 76, 77, 79, 82, 83, 87, 90, 92n3, 94, 99, 101, 102, 104, 113n2, 115, 117, 118, 119, 120, 121, 122, 123, 128, 129, 134, 150, 151 n3, 152, 156, 157, 162n2, 164, 165, 167, 169, 178, 179, 180, 182, 183, 184, 185, 186, 193, 194, 196, 197, 203n2, 211, 212

Cabello Llano, Ignacio, 59n3, 60n4, 104n4, 135n2
Clines, David, 73n2, 104n5

Eisen, Robert, 105n7, 136n3

Glatzer, Nahum, 104n3
Gordis, Robert, 102n1
Gregory the Great, 14, 50, 59, 103n3, 104, 106, 135, 173, 174

Habel, Norman, 108n9, 175n8
Harvey, W., 17n7, 18n8
Hawley, Helen, 108n9
Hegel, G. W. F., 106, 108, 109, 142, 143, 144, 145, 146, 213, 216.
Hirsh, E. G., 142n19
Hobbes, Thomas, 139, 174

Jacobs, Irving, 102, 172, 173n1, 173n2
Jiseong, James, 175n10
Job's rebellion, 17, 19, 26, 27, 29, 30 n1, 41n2, 42, 44, 49, 58, 61, 71, 82, 84, 85, 86, 88, 92, 104, 111, 118, 126, 127, 128, 137, 145n23, 155, 157, 158, 164, 166, 169, 171, 203
Job's sedition, 19, 20, 26, 27, 30n1, 44, 164, 166
Jung, Carl, 123n3

Kant, Emmanuel, 18, 58, 89, 106, 140, 141, 142
Kierkegaard, Soren, 106, 109, 125n3
Keynes, W., 104n4

Leibniz, G. W., 18, 140, 142
Luther, Martin, 104, 107

Maimonides, Moshe, 17, 18 n8, 30 n1, 31, 57, 58, 60n4, 76n1, 105, 106, 107, 134, 135, 136, 142, 174
Manichaeism, 1, 15, 73, 75, 105, 133, 134
Mañon Garibay, G.J., 125n3
Marx, Karl, 145n23
Moreau P. F., 139n10
Miranda, Punita, 124n3

Nebelah, 24, 53, 54, 83, 97, 123n2, 151, 196, 197, 198n4, 200, 201, 202, 208, 218
Negri, Antonio, 145n3
Nietzsche, Friedrich, 124n3

Ong, Meng Chai, 137n4

Parens, Joshua, 138n6
Plato, 1, 3, 5

Rabbi Akiba, 102, 133, 194
Rabbi Yohanan ben Zakkai, 102
Rotenstreich, Natan, 143n21

Satan, 2, 4, 5, 6, 9, 13, 14, 15, 16, 17, 18, 19, 20, 21, 22, 23, 24, 25, 26, 28, 29, 30, 31, 32, 33, 34, 35, 40, 41, 42, 43, 44, 45, 46, 47, 48, 49, 50, 51, 52, 53, 57, 58, 59, 60, 61, 63, 65, 70, 73, 80, 89, 97, 102, 103, 109, 110, 133, 134, 135, 136, 137, 138, 140, 142, 146, 148, 152, 153, 170, 173, 180, 189, 192, 193, 199, 202
Schifferdecker, Kathryn, 203n2
Schmitt, Carl, 175
Schreiner, Susan, 16n4, 17n6, 59n3, 60n4, 106n8, 173n3, 174n4
Seow, 139n9
Sócrates, 1, 3, 138
Sons of Elohim, 18, 22, 40, 62, 65, 73n2

Spinoza, 18, 138, 139, 140
Sungjin, Kim, 175n9

Temptation [legitimacy of], 16, 17, 18, 21, 29, 30n1, 31, 32, 39, 41n2, 42n3, 44, 45, 46, 47, 48, 51, 54, 58, 59, 61, 71n1, 73, 79, 89, 91, 95, 97, 109, 121, 122, 123n2, 124, 134, 136, 138, 154, 155, 158, 162n2, 164, 166, 167, 169, 171, 172, 176, 177, 178, 184, 185, 186, 190, 191, 195, 196, 197, 198, 201, 202, 203, 204, 205, 206, 209, 213, 216, 230
Thomas, Derek, 16n3

Unconscious Guilt, 11, 12, 21, 25, 26, 54, 69, 71n1, 75, 76, 87, 90, 101, 113n2, 115, 116, 118, 121. 148, 150, 157
Unconscious Responsibility, 11, 12, 24, 25, 26, 34, 35, 37, 45n4, 47, 55, 65n6, 66n6, 71n1, 75, 76, 83, 90, 93n3, 113n2, 115, 118, 119, 148, 150, 154, 156, 157, 162n2, 163, 165n1, 176, 201, 211

Yaffe, Martin, 60n4, 138n6
Yovel, Yirmiyahu, 142n18

Uzanne, Octave, 110n12

www.ingramcontent.com/pod-product-compliance
Lightning Source LLC
Chambersburg PA
CBHW060602230426
43670CB00011B/1933